SKIING AND BOARDING

D1308914

SKIING AND BOARDING

PETER OLIVER

Outside
BOOKS

W. W. NORTON & COMPANY
NEW YORK • LONDON

For information about permission to reproduce selections from this book, write to
Permissions, W. W. Norton & Company, Inc.
500 Fifth Avenue, New York, NY 10110

The text of this book is composed in Perpetua
with the display set in Monkey
Project Management by Julie Stillman
Composition by Sylvie Vidrine
Manufacturing by Dai Nippon Printing Company
Map illustrations by Janet Fredericks

Book design by Bill Harvey

Library of Congress Cataloging-in-Publication Data

Oliver, Peter, 1953-
    Skiing and boarding / Peter Oliver.
    p. cm. -- (Outside adventure travel)
    "An Outside book."
    Includes bibliographical references and index.

    1. Skis and skiing—Guidebooks. 2. Snowboard—Guidebooks.
    3. Winter resorts—Guidebooks. I. Title. II. Series.

GV854.O49 2001
910'.202--dc21
                                                2001032956

ISBN 0-393-32264-5 (pbk.)

W. W. Norton & Company, Inc., 500 Fifth Avenue, New York, N.Y. 10110
www.wwnorton.com

W. W. Norton & Company Ltd., Castle House, 75/76 Wells Street, London W1T 3QT, England

1 2 3 4 5 6 7 8 9 0

ACKNOWLEDGMENTS

If there is to be any sort of dedication in this book, it should go to my father, Jack Oliver, who has always been supportive of and interested in this business of writing and traveling that has become my life. He actually owns, I believe, all the books I have written and has even read them, and there are very few people on this earth who can make a similar claim.

Thanks to all those people who have contributed their insights and anecdotes to help fill in some of the blind spots in my own skiing experience. I'd like to give special thanks to Rick Armstrong, Rob Boyd, Dean Cummings, Chris Davenport, John Egan, Alison Gannett, Hans and Nancy Johnstone, Doug Lewis, Charlotte Moats, Jeremy Nobis, Paul Fremont Smith, and Gordon Wiltsie. My thanks also go to Lee Carlson, Eric DesLauriers, Shane McConkey, Eric Pehota, Kina Pickett, Daron Rahlves, Scot Schmidt, and Jeff and Julie Zell.

It is always very helpful to have allies at resorts who seem to have facts and figures at their fingertips and possess a special talent for smoothing out potential logistical problems. In particular, I'd like to thank Susan Darch at Whistler, Wilma Himmelfreundpointner at St. Anton, Gina Kroft at Crested Butte, Anna Olson at Jackson, and Brian Schott at the Big Mountain.

Thanks, of course, to John Barstow, project editor at W. W. Norton. By being unwaveringly positive and supportive, John made the transition from raw manuscript to finished book nothing but smooth sailing.

And finally, I'd like to offer a spiritual salute to Hans Gmoser. Hans is the guy who started using helicopters in the '60s to transport skiers into the wild. In doing so, he changed adventure skiing dramatically and forever. For all of us who appreciate standing on a snow-covered mountaintop in the middle of nowhere just minutes after finishing a breakfast omelet in a warm lodge, Hans is a patron saint.

CONTENTS

INTRODUCTION

I f you were of the right, young age and living on the eastern seaboard of America in the 1960s, you more than likely were captivated by the Great American Automotive Dream: the road trip westward. Maybe the dream rose out of some new manifest destiny urging on a generation raised on muscular 8-cylinder cars and gas at less than 30 cents a gallon. Maybe it was inspired by Jack Kerouac, whose *On the Road*, first published in 1957, was the road tripper's Bhagavad Gita. Or maybe the dreamers were just enthralled by the idea of this big old continent sprawling out there and waiting to be met. Drive to Colorado, drive to California. Blow across the plains and become a psychic part of the frontier.

Something else happened concurrently in the '60s that was probably not unrelated: Ski resort development boomed in western America. Vail was born in 1962. Jackson Hole followed in 1965, Snowmass in 1967, and Snowbird in 1969. Squaw Valley had been around since 1949, but it was the Winter Olympics of 1960 that really put Squaw on the map. And a host of other areas, including places like Taos and Mammoth Mountain, came into being only a few years earlier in the late 1950s. All of this winter sport bounty was there for the taking if you had wheels and a wild streak and a flaming desire to get it on with the raw, brawny terrain of the Rockies and the Sierras.

I was among those who dreamed the dream of the big mountains of the West. The Rockies and Sierras were emblematic of the one thing I wanted most in skiing— adventure. Adventure as in steep, long runs. . .powder up to my armpits. . .the call of the mountain wild. . .high-alpine vistas of searing, unsullied beauty. Now, many years and many westward trips later, I have had a taste of all that, and I continue to want more. It is alluring, addictive stuff, this business of winter adventure. I will continue to seek it out in the West or wherever in the world a harmonic convergence of natural phenomena— mountains and snow—allows me to do so.

I am thankful, then, that the metaphoric road trip of the 21st century has taken on dimensions that the whimsical gypsies of the '60s would never have dared contemplate. The horizon of winter adventure is much bigger and more complex now—much wilder, more intriguing, and more beguiling than it ever was. Starting with the ever-expanding scope of what's possible in North America and moving outward, Europe and the Alps are squarely and realistically in focus. (Let us praise quick, cheap, and efficient air travel.) So too are worlds far beyond that, from Greenland to Antarctica.

Opposite: The heli landing, Aiguille du Tour, Chamonix, French Alps. Above: Evergreen grove, Alta, Utah.

Kazakhstan, Kamchatka, Ecuador, Iran, the Himalayas, Morocco—the stories of skiing adventures come in from all over. In October of 2000, a Slovenian named Davo Karnicar skied 11,500 continuous vertical feet from the summit of Mount Everest, the first person to make a ski descent of substantial length from the top of the world's highest mountain. If Everest is on the new horizon, wouldn't it seem, at least symbolically, that all the world's mountains are now there for the taking?

Thus the inspiration for the winter traveler of this century can no longer be a guy like Kerouac. Too restrictively American, that fellow. We need instead to look to somebody more like Phileas Fogg, with global imaginings.

That said, let's still start our look at this bigger, wilder winter world with the American West. If we allow ourselves to dream only of exotic, faraway places, we'll miss out on a critical new reality in the mountains closer to home. The reality is this: The possibilities of where to go and what to do—within the boundaries and in the nearby backcountry of major North American resorts—have multiplied exponentially in the last decade or so.

New lifts have opened easy access to huge chunks of new terrain. Policies restricting off-trail and backcountry exploration are relaxing throughout North America. The growing talent, stamina, imagination, and daring of skiers and snowboarders in exploring new lines—in going where no one has gone before—have become astonishing.

As a result, we're now obliged to look at a resort's layout as if the designated trail network were not much more than a crude and rudimentary scaffolding upon which the really good stuff is draped. From this perspective, the entire sweep of the mountain terrain comes into play, morphing into a vascular organism—a webbed plexus of a thousand capillaries through the trees, over ridges, through the rocks, into gullies, among glacial seracs, and so on. All of these capillaries can be perceived as possible routes of descent.

I see tracks in the snow—through couloirs, over cliffs, on impossible steep faces, in distant bowls—at places like Jackson and Whistler, and I'm amazed and inspired. Inspired not necessarily by the idea that I might follow in those tracks (my own inclinations and abilities determine where I'll go) but by a vicarious satisfaction in confirming that a renegade edge of adventure continues to be nudged outward. The evidence is literally etched on mountainsides throughout the Rockies and the Sierras.

The Europeans might insist that this is nothing new. They'd say that adventuring beyond accepted boundaries (skiing *off-piste* in the Alpine lexicon) has been a staple of the Alpine experience since the 1920s, predating lifts. I'll give them that, but only up to a point. Off-piste in Europe has become dramatically redefined, too. Ever since a fellow named Sylvain Saudan (under the self-annointed, self-promoting title of *Le Skieur de l'Impossible*) began skiing previously unskied couloirs and 50-degree faces in the late '70s, people began looking at the Alps differently. When *l'impossible* was made to seem possible, and when you were already starting out with mountains exceeding 7,000 vertical feet and resorts covering

Opposite: Skiing fresh powder at La Flégère with Les Drus in the background, Chamonix, French Alps.

25,000 acres or more, the doors of perception were thrust wide open.

But now even *that* concept of adventuring has proved to be limited in scope, thanks to the helicopter. Exploiting the versatility of helicopters to access hard-to-reach places, skiers and snowboarders in the late '80s and '90s began racking up so-called first descents in Alaska and other remote locations with such regularity that the concept quickly lost much of its expeditionary cachet. I've asked well-known extreme skiers such as Eric Pehota and Jeremy Nobis how many first descents they have to their credit, and they can't come up with answers. How many? Who knows?

That's largely because in the world way out

there, in the big mountains that only helicopters can reach with ease, there are still thousands upon thousands of lines—indeed whole mountains and even mountain ranges—that haven't been skied yet. Now in praising the helicopter, I don't mean to dismiss one's own two feet as a time-honored means of backcountry transportation. Hiking and climbing remain important parts of the backcountry equation; there is something deeply satisfying about spending hours on an ascent to earn what might be only a few minutes of descending. Yet the helicopter, being the speedy bird it is, has rushed us into an arena of exploration that heretofore would have been impossibly time-consuming to tackle on foot.

In sum, it is a free world out there, in which you're freer than ever to do whatever your imagination urges you to do, within resorts and in the backcountry near and far. The mountain world has been growing freer by the minute, at least if freedom implies the shedding of limits and an expanding range of opportunities. The still largely unexplored winter wilderness of Alaska, the open backcountry of Jackson Hole, the famous glaciers of Chamonix and their antipodal cousins in New Zealand—a wild and wide-open field of dreams awaits. Formulate an image of what you want to do, and you can make it happen.

THE PREMISE: ADVENTURE

If the world is so free to explore and so wide open—if the entire globe is there for the taking—why is this book limited to just 20 locations? It's a fair question. Freedom, after all, is an expansive concept, whereas selecting 20 locations around the world might seem inherently and severely reductive.

On the other hand, having had the opportunity to travel widely around the world in the name of winter sport, I am most frequently asked the following question: "What is your favorite place to ski?" I'm not asked for a top-20 list; people want to know what's number 1. So if you look at it from that perspective, selecting 20 locations might be overkill.

It is a subjective and debatable selection, of course. It would be easy to create a worthy list of omitted others. Ought not places like Taos or Mammoth Mountain or Big Sky or Stowe or Portillo or Les Trois Vallées belong in the mix? Maybe so. Yet when I talk to others who travel widely in the world of winter, the same names—the same locations—seem to come up. Subjective as this selection might be, it's one that I believe will find general agreement among well-traveled skiers and snowboarders.

Or at least there should be agreement regarding the major resorts of North America and Europe, which are covered in Parts One and Two. In Part Three, The Discovery Zone, I have included resorts that, at least by size and reputation, might not, prima facie, deserve ranking among the world's best. Yet the most adventurous and satisfying skiing is not necessarily found in the biggest, most famous resorts. At lesser-known places like La Grave or Crystal Mountain or Crested Butte, I am particularly drawn to an aura of unreconstructed ruggedness—a raw spirit of adventure—that has yet to be softened or homogenized by major resort development. These places still

Opposite: Mountains and snow: a harmonic convergence in the Chugach Range of Alaska.

incubate a free-spirited youthfulness that pushes the envelope of winter sport, creating perhaps an atavistic connection with those ski bums who rushed westward four decades ago. If you're looking for crowd-free, hype-free adventure—if you want to branch away from the mainstream and get in touch with the soul of the sport—I'd say the resorts in Part Three deserve to be at the head of the pack.

In Part Four, Beyond Boundaries, I have reached toward the distant horizon, beyond the convention and limitations of lift-serviced skiing. But I've also tried to be realistic: Even in a free world there are limits, at least for the great majority of us. From acquaintances in the world of skiing, I hear all the time of trips to remote and wild locations, where the skiing is unquestionably spectacular. Yet such trips require considerable logistical planning and often require a high level of ski-mountaineering skill. Perhaps more to the point, they are, as logistically complex expeditions, anything but free financially speaking. (I've made one exception—Antarctica—because it seems, literally at the end of the world, to be the final station in all of our wilderness dreams.)

What's more, politics sometimes intrudes upon freedom, too. At one time, heli-skiing in Kashmir was a robust enterprise, and it's hard to imagine a more likely place for mountain adventure than the Himalayas. But civil strife has put that on hold. I've heard of entrepreneurs trying to get ski resorts going in Macedonia, but given the recent political unruliness in the Balkans, I suspect they'll need a good bit of luck.

There are no specific criteria, no precisely quantifiable standards, that had to be met in the choice of the 20 locations. To be sure, some specifics—terrain size, snow quantity, relative accessibility—needed to be taken into account. Yet ultimately, the chosen few made the cut in being measured by a standard less tangible: a supreme level of adventure and freedom in the exploration of mountains in winter.

An assimilated consideration of several subjective factors was at the heart of the matter: the challenge and variety of the terrain, the quality and reliability of the snow, the scenery, the local history and tradition. I also factored in the quality and accessibility of the off-piste or backcountry terrain.

Most of this book focuses on lift-serviced resorts. For many of us, that's where our exploration of the mountains in winter begins (and perhaps ends). But it would be incorrect to think (as some backcountry purists are inclined to do) that lift-serviced skiing is, ipso facto, not adventurous. I dare anyone to characterize the lift-serviced skiing at Chamonix or Jackson Hole or Crested Butte, or any other resort covered in this book, as lacking in adventure.

In assessing mountainous terrain, it is easy to equate adventurousness with steepness. Indeed, for any resort to be considered among the best in the world, it must deliver the highest level of challenge to any skier or snowboarder. You've got to have the scary stuff. Yet steepness alone as a measure of adventure is too simplistic. Blackcomb Glacier at Whistler, for example, isn't particularly steep at all. But in terms of the scenery, the quirks of the glacial terrain, and the aura of wildness well away from the lifts, it can be as adventurous as any 50-degree chute.

If there is a common characteristic of the terrain at all of these resorts, it is complexity. The range, variety, and sheer amount of terrain and variations in exposure, contour, and steepness all paint a picture of beautiful complication. They present a mental puzzle as well as a physical challenge, and I like that. Failure to resolve the terrain puzzle adequately can lead, most benignly, to boredom (a flat, uninspiring run) or, more dangerously, to extreme hazards (cliffs, crevasses, avalanches). On the other hand, the reward in satisfactorily solving the puzzle might be an undiscovered line through the trees or 100 turns in an untracked bowl of powder snow.

Terrain complexity also means an avoidance of repetition, and I like that, too. Every time I return to Jackson or Aspen or Verbier, or any of the great resorts of the world, I come upon lines that previously I never knew existed. Or I re-ski lines that have taken on an entirely new character because of a change in the snow—perhaps corn one time, powder the next.

Finally, there are the mountains themselves. Let's not forget that we ski with our eyes and our bodies; we come to the mountains to be in beautiful surroundings, to admire the art and architecture of the mountainous world. Hans Gmoser, the man who invented helicopter skiing in British Columbia in the '60s, once said to me, "If the pure act of skiing alone were all there were to it, I would be bored with it. But to be on top of a ridge, surrounded by all these vistas and the different moods of the mountains—I am still very appreciative of what can be experienced out there." As long as I continue to share in that appreciation, I will continue to return to the mountains in winter.

THE THING WE DO

In the 21st century, we have entered a period of ecumenical détente. After the internecine squabbling between skiers and snowboarders that marked snowboarding's meteoric rise through the '80s and '90s, the two camps are at last at relative peace with each other in the shared experience of descending mountains. Though there might be some terrain for which a snowboard is preferable to skis (tight trees), and some terrain where skis are preferable (long flats), on almost all mountainous terrain the two types of equipment perform with equal effectiveness. It turns out, then, that skiers and snowboarders aren't so different after all, and this book is for both.

We're left, however, in a nettlesome semantic quandary. What do we call what we do? In their parallel, separate-but-equal universes, snowboarding and skiing have developed their own nomenclatures, their own syntax. To celebrate and confirm the growing spirit of common brotherhood, we need a common language.

Now, the inventing of language is nothing new to winter sport. I began skiing in a time and place—in the early '60s, in Europe—when there was nothing but skiing, known only as *skiing*. A few word inventions popped up from time to time to describe stylistic variations—*wedels*,

Opposite: Jim Conway jumps off a rock in the Alta backcountry.

christies, *schusses*, and so on. But otherwise when it came to explaining what we were doing, *skiing* alone sufficed.

That began changing with the hyperexpressive, antiestablishment sentiments of the late '60s. Enter *hotdogging*, replete with the signature elements of the flower power era: unabashed exhibitionism, loud music, tie-dyed Day-Glo clothing, and unknown quantities of illegal drugs. *Hotdogging*—performing ballet on snow, executing breathtaking double and triple flips, adding a powerful new flair to mogul skiing—took skiing into a new realm, a new style, that it had never known.

By the '70s, however, with the excesses of the '60s lifestyle in decline, hotdogging was

rechristened *freestyle*. *Hotdogging* didn't exactly have a morally virtuous, Olympic ring to it, and most freestylers lusted after full medal Olympic acceptance, which came in 1992.

Meanwhile at the cusp of the avant-garde curve, a new, cinegenic thing called extreme skiing was coming into vogue. From the mid-'80s on, guys began jumping from 100-foot cliffs and skiing impossible steep faces and tearing up terrain where no one had gone before. If hotdogging made people look at skiing differently, extreme skiing made people look at *mountains* differently. The envelope of possibility was radically pushed by a host of cliff-jumping, powder-ripping, steep-skiing commandos.

Unfortunately, *extreme* had such magnetically evocative powers that it couldn't help but get in its own way. Ski cinematographers and marketeers couldn't resist abusing it, and even skiers got caught up in the act, willing to perform hairball stuff for movies or to perk sponsor interest. In one of extreme skiing's grislier moments, a fellow named Paul Ruff promoted what he billed would be the world-record cliff jump at Kirkwood, California, on March 23, 1993. Ruff figured he could sell the film footage of the 200-foot jump for a half million dollars or more. Instead, he crashed on the rocks and was dead within 45 minutes.

No wonder extreme skiers who took their sport seriously sought to distance themselves from the encumbrances of *extreme*—the camera-hogging daredevilry, the brainless risk taking, the subliminal hucksterism, the marketing hype. Call us freeskiers, they said. The coinage of the new term was not only a means of liberation from *extreme* but also a means of celebrating the expanding freedom to explore the mountains of the world.

Freeskiing was fine as far as it went, but it probably wasn't far enough. A growing number of snowboarders were also venturing deep into the big-mountain world, breaking away from what had become the structured confines of snowboarding's signature event, the halfpipe. But snowboarders weren't skiers, they were *riders*. And so the millennium closed with *freeriding* as the word du jour to embrace all of *snowsport*, another relatively new portmanteau word to describe both skiing and snowboarding.

Now I like *freeriding*, or at least I like the idea it intends to convey. It is an equal opportunity concept, for both skiers and snowboarders are, literally, riders of sorts. Unlike *extreme skiing*, it doesn't suggest an activity beyond the abilities or chutzpah of ordinary, soberly sensible people. Instead, it speaks simply of freedom, of the breaking down of barriers, of an expansion of opportunity. I also think that, like *hotdogging* and *extreme skiing*, it represents a kind of semantic heads up—a signal that the sport is changing importantly. In this case, the bonding of skiers and snowboarders into one more-or-less happy family is a change we ought to salute in whatever way possible.

All that said, however, I'm not comfortable yet with the liberal usage of *freeriding*. Perhaps it is still too much of a neologism—laudable in concept but still untested as a lasting component of common language. So, although I accept (and endorse) the premise and intent of the word, throughout this book I return in most cases to my roots. With apologies to snowboarders, I revert to *skiing* to refer to both skiing and snowboarding. As one snowboarder said to me recently, "It's all skiing now." For the sake of semantic simplicity, I will allow him to be right, at least until *freeriding* gains full acceptance.

ADVICE BEFORE YOU GO

In this newly complex and unfettered world of winter, where adventurous opportunities are more abundant than ever before, a lot of things can go wrong. Blame it on so many variables: terrain, snow conditions, weather, physical ability and stamina, and so on. Some of those variables are obviously beyond anyone's control or manipulation. You can't change the weather, as the saying goes. Still, there are a few steps you can take to maximize your chances of having the best experience possible.

I offer up the following guidelines and suggestions derived as much as anything from my own screwups in more than four decades of skiing. There is no better way of learning how to do something right—how to act sensibly—than to have done it wrong. Failure is a brilliant teacher; make a mistake once and (one hopes) you won't repeat it.

Opposite: Backcountry skiing in a bowl above Whitetooth resort, Golden, British Columbia, Canada.
Above: Spring skiing at Squaw Valley, the Sierra Nevada, California.

Be avalanche smart. Avalanches scare the daylights out of me. I've been caught once in a small slide and buried up to my chest, an episode that completely and permanently sobered me to the dangers involved. The snow was packed so tightly around me that, even though my arms were free, I was unable to dig myself out. I needed the help of my skiing partners.

Learning the nuances of reading snow stability can take a lifetime. So many factors are involved: the structure of the snowpack, the depth of the snow, the nature of the snow crystals, wind, sun, temperature, slope angle, exposure, and so on. A tiny change can turn a safe slope into a dangerous one. And even the most astute avalanche experts, after assessing all of these factors carefully, must ultimately rely on common sense, intuition, and accumulated knowledge to determine if a slope is stable.

Every time I ski in a potentially avalanche-prone area with a guide or someone more knowledgeable than I am, I do everything I can to absorb as much information as possible. Knowledge in this case can be power. Still I always abide by my own cardinal rule, derived from gut feelings: When in doubt, get out. To me, the thrill of a few turns in untracked powder does not have life-or-death value.

Never ski off-piste or in the backcountry alone. The most obvious reason for this is safety. Getting into trouble in the mountains when there is no one else around to help can literally be life threatening. If you happen to get caught in a snow slide or fall into a *tree well* (the deep, wind-sculpted troughs in the snow around trees), you could be a goner without others around to pull you out.

In addition, critical decisions in the backcountry are almost always better made by more than one mind and one set of eyes. Is the snow stable? Will the weather hold for an extended excursion? Or most simply: Where to go? It is astonishingly easy to get lost in the mountains, particularly when the weather and visibility are poor.

Have the right safety gear. When skiing within ski area boundaries, I rarely bring with me much more than lip balm, sunblock, and a $10 bill. In the backcountry, where more self-reliance is essential, it's a whole different story. An avalanche beacon, an avalanche probe pole, and a light shovel are the three principal items to bring along on any backcountry outing. A first-aid kit, extra clothing, light snacks and water, a compass, a multi-tool knife, duct tape, matches, and a bivouac sack are other items to consider for a more extended daytrip into the backcountry.

If you expect to do much backcountry skiing, a good daypack, one that fits snugly and conforms comfortably to the shape of your back, will be necessary for carrying your gear. In particular, I like three features in any pack: a wide waist band that helps secure the pack to my back and prevents it from shifting as I ski; a system of cinch straps to customize the fit of the pack to my back; and external attachments for carrying such items as a shovel, caribiners, an ice ax, and skis or a snowboard.

Finally, a helmet is also something to consider. More and more skiers and snowboarders are helmet-heads these days. There are plenty of helmets to choose from now, so you ought to be able to find one that fits reasonably well, is warm, and doesn't cramp your stylish sense of fashion.

Learn to read the snow surface. I'm not talking necessarily here about avalanche issues.

Being able to assess the texture of the snow from above a slope or from afar can mean the difference between a stupendous run and an agonizing run. Snow comes in many forms: light powder, heavy powder, wind- or sun-crusted snow, breakable crust, corn, ice, and so on. Some cues to go by are the color and sheen of the snow surface, striations caused by wind, and exposure.

As a rule, the snow on north-facing slopes tends to be driest because it is the least exposed to the sun, whereas snow on south-facing slopes can be more variable (mush, ice, and so forth) because of the sun's effects. More subtly, just a slight change in exposure can mean a significant change in the texture of the snow. On many occasions when skiing big open bowls, I've found significantly softer, more tractable snow by traversing just a hundred yards.

Get a comfortable pair of boots. I nearly gave up on skiing many years ago because of the agony caused by a painfully ill-fitting pair of boots. When I finally got a pair that fit comfortably, the sensation was a revelation. My foot relaxed within the boot, giving me a much better feel for the contact between my skis and the snow and greatly increasing my performance. (Incidentally, snowboarders might have the edge on skiers here: Finding a comfortable pair of snowboarding boots—at least the more widely used soft boots—is much easier than finding a comfortable pair of hard-shelled ski boots.)

Performance-minded skiers often worry—rightfully so—that getting boots that are *too* soft and comfortable can mean a significant sacrifice in performance. The trick, then, is finding boots that

Opposite: The Pearly Gates: Upper Rock Springs boundary gate, Jackson Hole, Wyoming.

perform well and still provide a comfortable fit. This might entail trying on many different pairs or enlisting the help of a custom boot fitter, particularly if you have an unusually difficult foot to fit. The extra time (or money) spent, however, is well worth it.

I'll offer one suggestion here: Don't let a salesman talk you into thinking that a boot that causes discomfort in the store will miraculously become comfortable on the mountain. Usually the opposite is true. Once the boot and foot are put in motion, shifting and possible chafing are likely to exacerbate fitting problems. In addition, almost all plastics harden in cold temperatures.

Keep equipment well tuned. I'm spoiled now. For several years I've been testing skis for a skiing magazine, and ski companies always deliver their skis to the tests impeccably prepared. The edges are sharp, and the bases smooth and waxed. That taught me a lesson: well-prepared skis far outperform the scarred-up, neglected gear I used before I began testing. A well-tuned ski (or snowboard) runs smoothly over the snow, turns when you expect it to, maintains its turn shape, and grips evenly and predictably on ice and hard snow.

In many cases well-tuned gear can promote safety as well as performance. For example, standing above an icy, 50-degree couloir and knowing my edges are dull and damaged is not the sort of thing that instills the confidence to ski with vitally necessary precision. I know some people—mostly racers or people with racing backgrounds—who tune their skis every night after skiing. I'm not that obsessed. But a $25 tune job before a big trip is definitely money well spent.

Bring extra goggles and gloves. Good vision —provided by good, fog-free goggles—is the foundation of all good skiing. How comforting it is to have extra goggles should you lose or break a pair. Gloves tend to get lost, torn, or wet. Although I've used the same solidly constructed pair of ski pants for three years, and any decently made ski parka will do, I go through gloves and goggles on a regular basis. I can't imagine being without them, so that's why I always have extras.

Drink more water than you think you should. Winter can play tricks on your body signals. Thirst tends not to kick in the way it does in the heat of summer, yet the typically drier air of winter quickly saps water from your system. (The physiological explanation: Your lungs must draw moisture from your system to make up for the lack of moisture in the air.)

Dehydration can cause a significant decrease in performance. According to physiologists, a 2 percent level of dehydration can cause a drop in performance of 10 to 20 percent. More important, dehydration can lead to cramping, fatigue, and hypothermia. So even if you aren't thirsty, drink.

Relax and enjoy. It's all about quality, not quantity. One perfect run in a day is far better than ten harried, imperfect runs. To be sure, there are days (after nights of heavy snowfall) when you want to get to the mountain early, to experience the untracked snow at its best. But for me, rushing never seems to improve the experience. A new snowfall can sometimes create a frenzy among the powder faithful, who, in their hurry, can become physically abusive of one another just for the ephemeral pleasure of getting first tracks on a popular slope. What's the point?

Take your time, especially when off-piste or in the backcountry. A little extra hiking—usually no more than an extra five or ten minutes along a mountain ridge—almost always produces an

Opposite: Jumping off a cornice at Las Lenas, high in the Argentine Andes. Above: Sailing off a cliff into the setting sun, backcountry Alta, Utah.

untracked line to ski. A great powder run is more likely the product of a little extra effort than a manic rush to get ahead of the crowd.

Finally, take the time to look around. I remember a serious mountain climber once telling me that he rarely got a chance to appreciate the beauty of the mountains he was climbing; his entire mind-set was focused on conquering fear. To me, that seems absurd self-deprivation. Just being in the snow-cloaked mountains in winter—to be able to appreciate

the exquisite beauty of the environment—is at least half of what skiing is all about.

GETTING GUIDANCE

As I mention repeatedly throughout this book, if you're planning to head into the backcountry or off-piste, it is an exceedingly wise move to hire a guide. Particularly at larger resorts and especially in Europe, having a good guide can be an enormous advantage, both in terms of safety and in discovering the best terrain a mountain has to offer. But how do you go about hiring a guide? What should you expect from a guide? And how do you make the most of the experience?

At most resorts in North America, guides can be hired through the ski school, at least if your aim is to venture immediately beyond ski area boundaries rather than deep into the backcountry. If the ski school itself does not offer guide service, it will usually be able to recommend other services or individuals. In Europe, the situation is usually more decentralized; in a place like Val d'Isère, there might be more than a half-dozen reliable services. (In the Resources section at the end of each chapter, I've included mention of reliable guide services.) Even so, the ski school is a good place to start; the local tourist office can also be a good source of information.

The process of hiring a guide is not unlike signing up for a ski school class. Unless you request the services of a specific guide, you'll either be assigned to a group or, if you're hiring a guide privately, have someone assigned to you. How do you know the guide is qualified? The answer is, you probably don't, although if guides are affiliated with a reliable ski school or service, it is almost certain that they are highly qualified.

Still, if you plan to do lots of off-piste or backcountry skiing (over the course of several days), it's probably worth doing a little pre-trip research. Ask friends who have been to a particular resort for guide recommendations. Learn as much as you can about a particular guide service by checking its website or contacting the resort, before signing on. Find out, if possible, what its safety record is.

A number of organizations (the International Federation of Mountain Guide Associations, the American Mountain Guides Association (AMGA), and the Association of Canadian Mountain Guides) certify guides. On its website (www.amga.com), the AMGA has a listing of ski guides, which makes it possible to contract a guide before your trip. However, certification is generally not required. If guides are not certified by one of these organizations, this doesn't necessarily mean that they are unqualified. Still, certification is at least a start— an indication that a guide is trustworthy. So before hiring anyone, at least ask about certification. The bigger and longer the backcountry excursion, the more meaningful certification probably is.

Perhaps most important, guides should have emergency medical training. They should also be fully versed in avalanche avoidance and rescue. And, optimally, they should carry a radio or cell phone, in case of emergency. On the few occasions when a person in my party has had to be evacuated by helicopter, the radio or phone was essential.

These basic safety issues should be discussed before contracting with any guide. In addition, it is especially helpful if a guide is personable and articulate. This includes being able to communicate clearly and calmly what to expect on your trip out of bounds and what to do when circumstances get dicey. Through gentle persuasion, a good guide can talk you through a range of predicaments: jumping off cornices, squeezing through tight couloirs, and so on.

Opposite: Snowboarder Stephen Koch on the 1999 American ski and snowboard expedition to Vinson Massif, Ellsworth Mountains, Antarctica.

Guides can usually provide instruction as well, particularly guides who are affiliated with a resort's ski school. Keep in mind, however, that a guide should be primarily a guide. If your primary interest is in instruction, hire a ski instructor.

At the world's best resorts—the resorts covered in this book—the backcountry terrain is big and varied. For any backcountry excursion, a good guide ought to be able to choose the terrain to match the skiers' ability. If you are part of a group, the terrain will be matched to the ability of the least skilled skier. (In Europe, it seems, the envelope is pushed a bit more than in North America.) If you want to be sure that you and the terrain are a perfect match, you should probably hire a private guide. In a group setting, don't overstate your ability; not only do you not want to get in over your head, but also you don't want everyone else in the group to be thoroughly annoyed at you for holding things up.

Finally, I suggest you reward your guide for leading you to exciting terrain and excellent snow. Tips are expected; something like $10 a person in a group for a day trip is usually about right, along with the offer of a beer or two at a local watering hole. In addition, be sure to recommend that particular guide to friends who might be interested in a similar outing. Word of mouth remains one of the most important means of furthering the careers of those guides who are really good at what they do.

USING THE BOOK

Each chapter is divided into five sections. The first is a general description, followed by At a Glance, What to Expect, Inside Line, and Resources. Let me explain what I've tried to accomplish in each.

AT A GLANCE

In addition to Location, this section provides a snapshot of each destination, with brief nuggets of information to give you a feeling for how a destination stacks up against others. Unfortunately, I can't assure you of the complete precision of some of these informational nuggets because they may vary from year to year.

Season. I list the months in which a resort is usually open, yet exact opening and closing dates vary according to snow conditions. In general in the Northern Hemisphere, I have found the best snow conditions to be in February and early March, but that doesn't mean you can't have great skiing—even great powder skiing—in November or April. Early in the year, however, when the snowpack is not yet well established, the conditions are usually the most iffy; I wouldn't plan far in advance for a November trip.

Ratings. I've rated the resorts on a scale from 1 to 5, with 5 being the highest rating possible. These ratings apply to the terrain and to the snow. In rating terrain, I've differentiated between in-bounds, and backcountry or off-piste terrain. The latter terms refer to any terrain not technically within the ski area boundaries. Rating, of course, is an entirely subjective process, so take my opinion for what it's worth. Also, keep in mind that the destinations in this book are already, simply by their inclusion, deemed to be a notch above the rest of the pack. So the ratings are for the purpose of comparing destinations within the book and don't indicate how a resort rates among all of the world's skiing destinations.

Terrain Acreage. This figure is notoriously derived by approximation (even if it might be a number officially given by a resort), but it will at least give you an idea of a resort's size in relation to other resorts. In general, it refers only to a resort's in-bounds acreage, although in Europe some terrain that is technically off-piste might be included.

Vertical Rise. Of all figures included in At a Glance, this is probably the most accurate. It is the differential between the lowest and the highest point at a destination. Don't assume, however, that runs at a resort with more vertical rise are longer than runs at a resort with less vertical rise. The average ski run, if there were such a thing, covers between 1,500 and 3,000 vertical feet, so any resort that meets that minimum standard can offer skiing comparable to a resort with a vertical rise that is far greater. One of the most important features of any mountain is not the vertical rise itself but the continuity of the pitch. In other words, a run of 1,500 vertical feet with a constant pitch of between 30 and 40 degrees is preferable to a run of 4,000 vertical feet with lots of flat spots and pitch interruptions.

Average Annual Snowfall. This measurement can be as imprecise as Terrain Acreage. Or to be more accurate: It can be, as an average, not particularly indicative of the snow conditions at any particular time. Alta and Snowbird, for example, might receive an average of 500 inches a year, but it's always possible that you might arrive during a snow drought. A 400-inch average could mean that it snowed 200 inches one year and 600 the next. So take the averages for what they are: a general picture of where snow falls and in what quantities, but not a guarantee of quality snow conditions.

WHAT TO EXPECT AND INSIDE LINE

In What to Expect I've tried to flesh out the general descriptions with a few nuts-and-bolts specifics about the terrain and snow—in-bounds and backcountry or off-piste—at a destination.

Inside Line offers up a few tidbits of local knowledge—lodging, après-ski—gleaned from both personal experience and the experiences of other seasoned travelers.

In both cases, I'm hoping to provide enough basic information to enable you to hit the ground running when you arrive at a destination.

RESOURCES

Resources is the who-ya-gonna-call section. I've tried not to overdo it here; this isn't supposed to be a Yellow Pages. Instead, Resources is intended as a starter kit to enable you to do pre-trip research and make plans. In most cases, the phone numbers and websites listed are the main conduits to the logistical mother lode on how to get there, where to stay, what it costs, and so on.

WHAT IT COSTS

Ski industry marketeers, in a chronic state of denial, are forever trying to convince us that skiing is not an expensive sport. They are inclined to insist that when you add up plane fare and the cost of lodging, lift tickets, food, equipment, and winter clothing, your budget will feel no pain. So here are the numbers. You decide.

Start with the average discounted, round-trip airfare, which comes in at roughly $500 for most trips. After that, you can expect to pay at least $50 per person a night for lodging, although $500 a night in a high-end place during the high season (usually Christmas through New Year's and

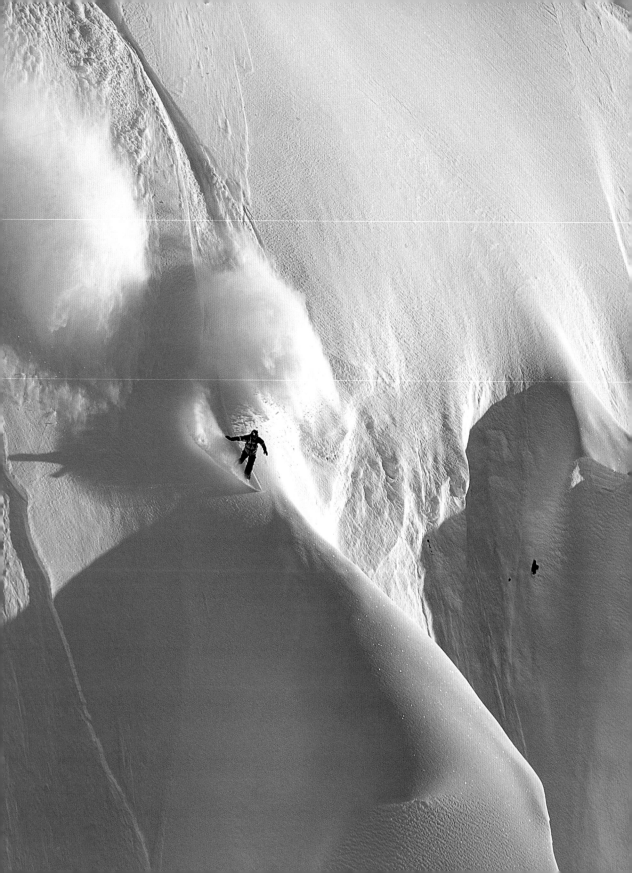

early March) is not out of the question. Lift tickets typically range between $30 and $65 a day. High-performance equipment rentals come in at around $50 a day. If you buy your equipment (as most skiers and snowboarders do), it's easy to spend $1,500 or more for skis, boots, bindings, and poles.

Unlike golf, a recreation that the ski industry likes to turn to for comparison, special clothing is required for skiing. The good stuff—good as in functional, not necessarily fancy—does not come cheaply. My favorite ski pants, for example, cost $400 (though because of quality materials and construction, they've lasted a while). You could spend plenty more if you feel a need to be really fashionable. A good pair of goggles alone costs $60 or more.

At this point, we haven't even considered high-end amenities. A private guide will cost you $200 a day or more. A day of helicopter skiing typically runs around $400 to $500 per person; snowcat skiing comes in at around $150 to $300 a day.

The bottom line. On a shoestring budget, you could probably get by on $1,200 per person for a typical week of skiing. But that kind of budget rules out a plush place like Aspen, where everything from a breakfast bagel on up comes at a premium. And you're certainly not going to be heli-skiing in British Columbia, where a week during the high season of February and March will cost you the better part of $5,000, airfare not included.

All of this is not to suggest that a week of skiing must necessarily be outrageously expensive.

Through a mishmash of discounting schemes that make airfare pricing seem like simplicity itself, ski resorts are forever trying to drum up business during nonpeak periods—weeks in January and April, for example. So shop around. If you steer clear of the high season, you can probably find a decently priced, all-inclusive package.

In addition, in recent years Europe has become surprisingly affordable, Austria in particular. In February of 2001, I flew round-trip between Boston and Zurich for less than $400. At last look, a daily lift ticket in St. Anton was going for about $30, and it's possible in St. Anton to find a very habitable bed-and-breakfast for $30 or thereabouts a night.

Finally, keep in mind that the main expense of skiing is in the cost of lifts and lodging. If you want to embark on a true backcountry adventure—climbing for your skiing, staying in huts, and dining on such epicurean delicacies as oatmeal and macaroni and cheese—you can really go on the cheap. For example, you can reserve a space in a hut in the Fred Braun Hut System near Aspen for $25 a night or less, and of course no lift ticket is required. For the small price of a little high-altitude huffing and puffing, you can reward yourself with skiing that's just about as good as it gets.

Opposite: A boarder finds the perfect, safe seam on a steep, avalanche-prone slope, Chugach Mountains, Alaska.
Overleaf: The immense solitude of glacier skiing, Sheila Glacier, Mount Cook, New Zealand.

NORTH AMERICAN CLASSICS

Aspen

The really good stuff—the immense backcountry—is hardly touched at all

Aspen is the heart of decadence, the notorious Gomorrah of the Rockies. It is a national receptacle for both our envy and ridicule, made so by all the tabloid headlines about $20-million homes, private jets, celebrity tiffs, cocaine sniffing, faux-Euro chicness, and outrageously conspicuous consumption. It is the place where folks like Streisand, Nicholson, The Donald, and so many incalculably wealthy North American and European Brahmins (along with spouses and/or mistresses, all arrestingly haute couture) hang out. It is Rodeo Drive at 8,000 feet. Perhaps Aspen's most famed year-round resident is Hunter S. Thompson, literary America's clown prince of substance abuse.

Aspen is like a stage, where people have a way of dressing theatrically, whether for skiing, après-skiing, or simply to be noticed. It can be likened to a costume drama or opéra bouffe. One vivid image sticks in my mind: a couple walking

Aspen Highlands with the vast and challenging Maroon Bells backcountry stretching out beyond.

Denver ✪

Rocky Mountains

Grand Junction • ⊙ ASPEN

COLORADO

through downtown Aspen, he in a full-length, fur-fringed leather coat, she dressed head to toe in white fur. She was wearing boots that looked like a pair of bichon frise puppies strapped to her feet. Anti-fur sentiment in Aspen was raging through the national news at the time, so you had to admire the unabashed, in-your-face obliviousness (or arrogance) of those two furballs strutting their stuff.

From such absurdity Aspen's national reputation has been formed, a reputation that makes it easy to believe that that's all there is to Aspen—a bunch of rich people often behaving badly. It seems almost beside the point to look at Aspen in any other light. Yet contradictory as it might seem, there is no place better than Aspen for serious, big-mountain skiing in Colorado. Because of that, as local resident Chris Davenport, the 1996 World Extreme Skiing Champion, says, "There is a group of mountain enthusiasts who call Aspen home who pay absolutely zero attention to all the glitz. It's the mountains that keep us here."

The mountains to which Davenport refers are not just the four mountain resorts of Aspen: Aspen (aka Ajax) Mountain, which rises from the town; Aspen Highlands, 2 miles southeast of town; Buttermilk, which is Highlands' neighbor; and Snowmass, 8 miles down the valley. Combining for more than 5,000 acres, the skiing terrain they represent is no small potatoes. But what Davenport has in mind is primarily a vast, undeveloped backcountry, much of it in the 181,000 acre Maroon Bells–Snowmass Wilderness that is literally right out Aspen's back door. Within a few miles of downtown, high-end, decadent Aspen you can land yourself, as Davenport puts it, in the midst of "steep, craggy, gnarly terrain that makes you feel like you're in the Alps."

A few years ago, in researching a story for *Aspen* magazine, I joined a group from The North Face, the outdoor equipment company. The idea was to scramble on climbing skins up a 5-mile trail to the Tagert and Green Wilson huts near Pearl Pass. There we would do a little backcountry skiing and snowboarding, try out some new North Face prototypes, and bone up on avalanche safety basics with an Alaskan avalanche expert named Bill Gluede. The trailhead was about a 20-minute drive from Aspen up the Castle Creek drainage, where the Ashcroft Ski Touring Center

---

AT A GLANCE

LOCATION 150 miles southwest of Denver	**TERRAIN ACREAGE** Roughly 5,000 acres in four areas:
SEASON November–early April	Aspen Mountain, Aspen Highlands, Snowmass, and
IN-BOUNDS 1 2 ③ 4 5	Buttermilk
BACKCOUNTRY 1 2 3 4 ⑤	**VERTICAL RISE** Aspen Mountain: 3,267 feet;
SNOW 1 2 ③ 4 5	Aspen Highlands: 3,635 feet; Snowmass: 4,406 feet;
	Buttermilk: 2,030 feet
	AVERAGE ANNUAL SNOWFALL 300 inches

occupies one of the most stunningly beautiful high-alpine basins imaginable.

The trip was such a good idea that it attracted a crowd, as you might expect when the weather turns sunny and warm in March and word of a backcountry excursion circulates. There were about two dozen of us, more than the two huts could accommodate. As a result, I spent the night suffering in a tent—a North Face tent, of course —with a thin layer of frozen condensation beneath my sleeping bag as the air temperate above 11,000 feet under the star-filled sky plummeted to near zero.

But during the day, as the temperature soared with the rising sun, we climbed above the huts to ski and snowboard a succession of chutes, open slopes, and meadows that rolled down off the high ridgeline. We baked under the intensity of the sun, stripping to our shirtsleeves for each climb of 30 to 45 minutes but still sweating as if under the sun of a desert noon.

At some point, upon reaching a ridgeline— affording a view southward to the town of Crested Butte—or on some prominent breadloaf roll in the landscape, the climb would be over. We'd strip our skis and boards of climbing skins, ingest copious amounts of water, allow our body temperatures to settle back into a normal zone, and then relinquish ourselves to the force of gravity. It is one of the miracles of being at altitudes between 11,000 and 13,000 feet that even as you feel your ski burn under the intense early spring sun, the snow won't melt. And so we would come blasting down through the layers of crisp, dry powder that had formed into wind-created, wave-like patterns known as *sastrugas*.

It is among Aspen's many ironies that much of the best skiing and snowboarding, both in the backcountry and in-bounds, is made better by a reputation that emphasizes almost everything else. The mountains tend to be overlooked, shadows washed out in the headlights of all the glamour, wealth, and glitz. The stereotypical Aspen visitor is someone who dresses for the slopes in a $1,500 Bogner one-piece outfit, takes a few leisurely midday runs (and only if the weather is good), then basks in the afternoon sun with a glass of Pouilly-Fuissé among equally stylish friends.

Nothing wrong with that, of course. But the result is that the *really* good stuff—all the steeps and powder and immense backcountry—is hardly touched at all. It is left to a considerable minority, a few locals and a handful of more adventurous visitors who know a good thing when they see it. I remember once rushing to the base of the Aspen mountain gondola for the 9 A.M. opening after an overnight snowstorm, expecting to be moshing my way through an impatient pack of powder-crazed wackos. That's the usual resort scene on a powder day. But not so in Aspen; the place was incongruously deserted. Most people apparently were sleeping in, or were lingering over breakfast, or were simply uninspired by the gray weather.

Davenport sees the same thing all the time. "That's one of the great things about this place," he says. "On a powder morning, it's nothing like Jackson or Crested Butte or Squaw, with

Above: Deep powder in the Y Zones, Highland Bowl. Opposite: 1996 Extreme Skiing Champion Chris Davenport hiking to a run in the Five Fingers backcountry behind Highland Mountain.

hundreds of guys in Gore-Tex and with fat skis waiting for the lifts to open. In a certain way, it makes everything more pristine."

In many ways, that pristine character is epitomized in Aspen Highlands, the antihero of Aspen ski areas. With terrain too challenging and/or too raw to appeal to the Bogner-and-Pouilly-Fuissé crowd, Highlands is Aspen's shunned stepchild, where on an average day fewer than a thousand skiers show up. That's less than a fifth of the number that Snowmass claims.

It's not just the steepness of Steeplechase and Olympic Bowl, some of the finest expert terrain in Colorado, that scares people away, nor the complete absence of long, easy runs. There is also Highland Bowl, an enormous, starkly exposed, mostly treeless swath of high-alpine terrain, only recently opened to legal skiing even if locals had been poaching it for years.

Highland Bowl is at the core of a classic Aspen paradigm: Locals love it, almost everybody else won't get near it. I've skied in Highland Bowl and can understand why people might shy away. It's intimidating not just because of the steepness or the depth of the snow; the bowl imposes a profound sense of isolation upon you, the unsettling feeling of being out there clinging to the edge of the world at 12,000 feet with nothing but the uncompromising, untamed elements to keep you company.

No more perfect avalanche zone can be imagined—perfectly pitched and perfectly shaped, a narrowing V from the summit ridge to a choke zone 3,000 feet below. In March of 1984, three ski patrolmen died in an enormous avalanche in Highland Bowl, so the dangers are demonstrably real. At the same time, no more perfect powder zone can be imagined either, with the pitch of the slope, at an average of about 40 degrees, just right for deep-snow skiing and extending for a continuous 2,000 vertical feet. In all of in-bounds Aspen, there is nothing more pristine or frightening than Highland Bowl.

Aspen's real crowd pleaser is Snowmass, with its preponderance of wide and easily manageable slopes, its famed Big Burn in particular. This sweeping patch of open turf and widely spaced trees, cleared by a forest fire some years back, is perhaps the definitive intermediate run in America. I've skied the Burn countless times and can attest to its inherent assets: its many lines, the opportunity to charge ahead through a series of fast, big-arcing turns, the intensity of the high-altitude sun. And as a generalization, if you just want to ski long, long, easy runs, Snowmass is one of the best places in America to do so.

But like almost everything else about Aspen, Snowmass is not all it appears to be. There are buttelike protuberances in Snowmass's topography that hide a number of steep chutes leading into pocket valleys that barely see any skier traffic at all. I'm talking of chutes like KT Gully, AMF, and Gowdy's, which drop off the edge of the Big Burn plateau, or Baby Ruth and Possible, which drop into the magnificent gladed steeps of Hanging Valley. Possible is flanked by a neighboring chute not included on the official Snowmass trail map. It is called Impossible.

Adventurous types also come to Snowmass because of its easily accessible backcountry. Immediately beyond the boundary line lies a big and serious mountain world, the almost-Alps that Davenport speaks of. It's so serious, in fact, that access gates through the boundary lines have skull-and-crossbones icons on them, and the warning is absolutely appropriate. From the periphery of the Big Burn, I've looked over the edge into the East Snowmass Creek drainage, where rock-lined couloirs drop away for 4,000 feet. Just standing there, I could feel my toes grip inside my boots and my knees become rubbery. Guys like Davenport think this kind of dangerous terrain is great fun, but it exacts serious consequences upon anyone without the proper skills and mountain smarts to take it on. For example, the Snowmass ski patrol told me of a guy who skied over a cliff in Sand Chute above East Snowmass Creek, and survived only because he was wearing a helmet after suffering a concussion in a serious fall a few days earlier. Sometimes luck blesses the foolhardy.

If I plan to venture beyond the Snowmass boundary, I head in the other direction, beyond the High Alpine lift into West Willow Basin. The terrain is still steep and raw, but the consequences of screwing up aren't as severe. Heck, I've made the five-minute hike from the top of High Alpine to the top of West Willow just for the view—the sprawl of high, open country leading to still higher peaks and ridges and beckoning with all-but-limitless backcountry possibility. "Who would ever think that Snowmass, blue-run [intermediate] paradise, would harbor such intense terrain?" says Davenport.

Yes, how utterly unlikely it is. But that's Aspen for you, a lot more and a lot different than its reputation makes it out to be.

WHAT TO EXPECT
IN-BOUNDS

Aspen Mountain rises right out of the town of Aspen itself. One of its great assets is a base-to-summit gondola that rushes you to the top without having to change lifts. Intermediate skiers tend to stick to the top third of the mountain, which features mostly mellow, groomed (though short) runs. Ski a few runs here; pull out a deck chair and bask in the sun at the summit; lunch on the sundeck at Bonnie's Restaurant about a third of the way down the mountain—a classic, laid-back day at Aspen Mountain.

Two main ridges—Ruthie's and Gentlemen's Ridge—form the basic topography of Aspen Mountain. For experts, steep runs descend to either side, most notably Walsh's, perhaps Aspen Mountain's steepest pitch, on the high

RICH MAN, POOR MAN

Nowhere is the contrast between the adventuring minority and the vacationing majority more pronounced than in recent developments at Aspen Highlands. For years Highlands was regarded as the locals' area of Aspen, a fashionably retro-chic place where you skied like a maniac and chugged beers with your pals at day's end.

But by the turn of the millennium, the first giant steps had been taken in a radical transformation of Highlands. A sumptuous base village was on its way to completion, and surrounding home lots were reportedly going for $2 million and more. It seemed inevitable that a new wealthy clientele would supplant the mostly local ski bums, most of whom probably couldn't afford a down payment on a broom closet in the new Highlands Village.

Yet the displacement hasn't happened, for in the late '90s the Aspen Skiing Company replaced antiquated lifts at Highlands with fast, new, high-capacity lifts and began steadily pushing out the boundary lines into Highland Bowl. This only made the best expert skiing in Aspen more accessible and more extensive.

Thus does Highlands move schizophrenically into the future. On the mountain are Aspen's hardcore, the serious-skiing worshippers of the steep and deep. At the base are the Ralph Lauren and Gucci folk, frequenting the village's chichi boutiques and restaurants and probably doing most of their skiing at Snowmass. It's an odd duality, but it seems somehow to work.

western slope of Gentlemen's Ridge, and a series of narrow runs on the western slope of Ruthie's known collectively as "the Dumps." Bell Mountain, which protrudes in-between the two ridges, is the heart of Aspen's mogul country. Aspen Mountain's main drawback is that most runs feed into aortal Spar Gulch, and toward day's end there can be a chaos of skier and snowboarder traffic trying to get back to town.

A single, narrow ridge forms the basic spine of Aspen Highlands, a spine that essentially extends beyond the top of the lifts as the ridgeline above Highland Bowl. By sticking to the ridge, you can find a few decent intermediate runs, but expert terrain is really what Highlands is all about.

Steeplechase, on the east side of the ridge, is a series of five or six runs where big moguls seem to form readily. On the west side, Olympic Bowl runs are usually less bumpy, but because of a generally western exposure, the snow can sometimes be either crusty (on cloudy days) or supersoft (on sunny days).

Weather and snow conditions determine the feasibility of entering Highland Bowl. On a snowy day, the first few lines, through an area called Temerity, are in the trees and represent your best option for both visibility and stable snow. On good weather days, you might get lucky and hitch a ride on a snowcat with the ski patrol to carry you up the ridgeline to ski the open bowl. The patrol, in fact, would like to see more skiers and snowboarders out there, believing that more traffic helps to compact and consolidate the snow, hence

Opposite: Chris Davenport on Hanging Valley Wall, a 15-minute hike from the High Alpine Lift at Snowmass.
Above: Pyramid Peak rises above Maroon Bowl and its stash of backcountry powder.

Riding deep powder in the Y Zones, Highland Bowl.

find it in two main areas—the Cirque and Hanging Valley—both of which typically feature short but very steep chutes that feed into tree-mottled slopes that often cache powder long after a storm. The last time I skied Snowmass, during a 10-inch snowstorm, I ventured with Steve Sewell of the Snowmass ski patrol through a chute called Baby Ruth and on into Hanging Valley, where the snow was piling up in mushroom tufts on spruce tree branches. We skied the run once, and then came back and skied it again, and all the while we never saw another person. That's one of the beauties of Snowmass' more challenging stuff —the combination of snowy weather and steeps tends to discourage the typical Snowmass intermediate.

Buttermilk, as its mellow name might imply, is the easiest of the four Aspen mountains. Yet in many ways, Buttermilk is a beautiful thing, an area that courts a relaxed lack of pretension that is otherwise hard to find around Aspen. When the weight of relentlessly stylish Aspen begins to bear down on you, come to Buttermilk for an antidote.

BACKCOUNTRY

Where to begin? Probably on Richmond Ridge, which extends from the summit of the Aspen Mountain gondola. It's both easily accessible and relatively unintimidating terrain. Work your way down through a succession of meadows and open trees and eventually hit roads that lead to the valley floor, where you should be able to hitch a ride back to town. Or be prepared and leave a car. Or bring your own snowmobile to shuttle back to the ridge, as some locals do. Or join up with the cat-skiing operation run by the Aspen Skiing Company.

For backcountry rambling, the Pearl Pass area is superb, with something for all ability levels. But it has its limitations. For one thing, the huts are relatively small, and reservations well in advance are pretty much essential. The terrain itself is almost all above tree line and exposed,

making it more stable and resistant to avalanches.

Snowmass is the big daddy of Aspen skiing, with the highest vertical rise and the most terrain acreage. It has the reputation of being Aspen's family mountain, and for good reason. Easy terrain, plenty of on-mountain accommodations, and a big ski school are all family-friendly ingredients. The wide-open Big Burn is Snowmass' signature run, absolute cruising nirvana, but there's also plenty of good intermediate terrain at Elk Camp and Sam's Knob.

Given Snowmass' reputation as intermediate never-never land, it's somewhat surprising how much first-rate expert terrain it offers. You'll

rendering it out of the question when the weather's bad and prone to snow stability problems. When the weather and conditions are right, it can be pure magic.

The terrain along the 10th Mountain hut system, which extends from Aspen to Vail, is more protected and more doable when the weather is stormy. But the terrain itself, at least for anyone seeking a steep and deep experience, is less inspiring. This system is best for hut-to-hut touring, with the occasional powder run tossed in. Again, plan ahead; hut reservations are snapped up quickly.

The big mountains of the Maroon Bells–Snowmass Wilderness are serious stuff. The possibilities are infinite and the dangers (steeps, avalanches, high exposure) considerable. I suggest trying a few runs just beyond the ski area boundaries—West Willow at Snowmass or Maroon Bowl on the back side of Highland Bowl at Aspen Highland—to determine if you're ready to venture into the great beyond. Above all, get a guide, even for runs immediately beyond the ski area boundaries. This is high-alpine country that does not abide deficiencies in either ability or judgment.

INSIDE LINE

A condo at the Boomerang Lodge (800-992-8852, www.bomeranglodge.com) in downtown Aspen is reasonably priced, at least by pricey Aspen standards. And thanks to an excellent and mostly free public bus system, you'll save in not needing to rent a car. For high-end lodging, the Hotel Jerome is historic, handsome, great for people-watching, and ridiculously expensive, with rooms starting at around $500 a night.

The Aspen scene is governed by a familiar catch-22: Once a place becomes cool, it's no longer cool. The forever-restless "in crowd" is always impatient to establish the next cool thing. A few places, however, manage to weather all the trendiness. Woody Creek Tavern (970-923-4585),

Aspen nightlife: live music at The Double Diamond.

about a 15-minute drive from Aspen toward Snowmass, remains a place where celebrities come for beer and burritos, and to escape the glitz and rub blue-collar elbows with a local crowd. On the other side of the coin, the Caribou Club in town is the place to go to rub elbows with martini-drinking, cigar-smoking big shots, if you can figure out how to get in—it's theoretically a members-only place.

For gear shopping—especially backcountry gear—the place to go is Ute Mountaineer (308 S. Mill Street; 970-925-2849).

RESOURCES

General information and snow report: 800-525-6200 or 970-925-1220. Central reservations: 800-290-1325 (Aspen); 800-215-7669 (Snowmass). Website: www.skiaspen.com. Backcountry guide service: Aspen Expeditions (970-925-7625) guides trips and instructional clinics in the Aspen backcountry.

Alta & Snowbird

A time-honored, backcountry serenity takes hold here

It was the morning after two full days of continuous snowfall, a storm cell so intense that it forced the road leading from Salt Lake City into Little Cottonwood Canyon to be closed. An avalanche had steamrolled down the notorious White Pine chutes and deposited a barrier of snow and debris several feet deep across the road. That left a good many people trapped at the end of the canyon, at the contiguous resorts of Alta and Snowbird. Unable to return to Salt Lake City and without a place to spend the night, people camped on the hallway floors of Snowbird's Cliff Lodge, using table linens for bedding.

I was among those fortunate enough to have accommodations in the lodge, and at about 9 A.M. the phone in my prized room rang. Mark Schelde, organizer of the King of the Mountain downhill race scheduled to take place the next day at

Into the blue yonder, Gad Chutes, Snowbird, where you'll find more than 1,500 vertical feet tilted up at something like a 40-degree pitch, without interruption.

UTAH

Great Salt Lake

WYOMING

Salt Lake City • Park City

**ALTA &
SNOWBIRD**

Snowbird, was calling. The mountain was entirely closed to the public, he reported, but the ski patrol had agreed to take the captains of the race teams up in the aerial tram to check out the status of the course. Would I, as a privileged member of the media, like to come along? Well, of course I would.

I soon found myself in the Snowbird tram with Schelde, two ski patrolmen, and four of the great legends of ski racing: Franz Klammer, Bill Johnson, Pirmin Zurbriggen, and Steve Podborski—three Olympic gold medalists and a bronze medalist, respectively. With the sky still spitting and threatening another outburst, four feet of new snow lay below us, both inviting and frightening (given the White Pine avalanche).

The patrolmen were edgy about the outing, choosing a relatively avalanche-safe route from the top of Hidden Peak to the top of the racecourse, about a third of the way down the mountain. The route avoided most of Snowbird's famous steeps—the Cirque, Silver Fox, and Great Scott, sweetly and ominously mantled in untracked snow.

Yet once we began to move and the snow began to fly in our faces, we all became like kids at the seashore, oblivious to potential hazards and high on the rare thrill of being alone on a mountain of untrammeled snow in the eerie gray light between storm pulses. At one point, as I blasted through an opaque curtain of snow, the front of my skis crossed over the tails of Steve Podborski's skis. I hadn't seen Podborski until I was a foot away from running him over.

Snow is what made Little Cottonwood Canyon famous. The average annual snowfall at Alta and Snowbird is somewhere between 500 and 550 inches, but in the history of snow, averages are not nearly as sexy as epic aberrations in meteorological history. Take the winter of 1983 to 1984, for example, when Alta officially recorded 761 inches—more than 63 feet. Skiers took to wearing surgical masks over their mouths to prevent suffocation from flying snow, and by April volunteers were sandbagging to hold back the Great Salt Lake, which was overflowing with snowmelt into Salt Lake City's streets. Or take the series of storm cells that rolled through Little Cottonwood in January of 1996, producing 14 feet of snow in 16 days. It was in the midst of that event, in fact, that I experienced the rare thrill of skiing with four great Olympians in the bottomless, untracked snows of a closed Snowbird.

Given the abundant snow, it's not surprising

AT A GLANCE

LOCATION 12 miles southeast of Salt Lake City	**TERRAIN ACREAGE** Alta: 2,200 acres; Snowbird: 2,500 acres
SEASON November–April	
IN-BOUNDS 1 2 3 ④ 5	**VERTICAL RISE** Alta: 2,100 feet; Snowbird: 3,240 feet
BACKCOUNTRY 1 ② 3 4 5	**AVERAGE ANNUAL SNOWFALL** 500–550 inches
SNOW 1 2 3 4 ⑤	

that the Cottonwood Canyons—Little Cottonwood and Big Cottonwood, just to the north and home to the Brighton and Solitude ski areas—mark the historical beginnings of Utah skiing. Norwegian-born Alf Engen, the great ski-jumping champion of the '20s and '30s, first began looking at Little Cottonwood Canyon in 1935 as the possible site for a ski area. The country's first ski lift, a rope tow installed in Woodstock, Vermont, had appeared a year earlier, and the idea of building lift-serviced ski areas was coming into vogue. Soon a new lift at Sun Valley in Idaho would be up and running, and the first lift in Utah would be installed at Brighton in 1936.

The first lift at Alta went up in 1939, with a day pass going for a buck-fifty. Since then, the area has become associated with some of the great names in powder skiing and the development of powder skiing technique. Prominent among them have been Engen and his brother, Sverre, Dick Durrance, and Junior Bounous, with the torch passing from one generation to the next.

I had the good fortune to share a powder day with Junior, when we traversed and hiked from the top of the Snowbird tram to the top of Mount Baldy, which rises to 11,068 feet above both Alta and Snowbird. It had snowed about 10 inches overnight, and we skied the open face of Baldy down to the periphery of Alta, cut along a ridgeline, and then dropped into Snowbird by way of a chute known as the Keyhole. From there, we worked our way back to the Snowbird base through a series of chutes and steep, open slopes, with Junior expertly leading the way around potential hazards (such as cliffs) and conversing in his high, singsong voice. It was, in a way, the essential Little Cottonwood experience—fresh tracks through unmarked terrain in the company of a man directly linked to the lineage of powder skiing in America.

Alta, separated from Snowbird by a long ridge extending from Mount Baldy, is today virtually a living monument to the kind of improvisational experience I shared with Junior. As such it can be a joy, an anachronism, an ever-expanding cosmos of exploration and discovery, and a total pain in the ass. My general opinion of the place after my first few visits was the latter, particularly in light of the reverential buildup I'd heard from members of Alta's fold of loyal believers, who love the place like a religion. What were they thinking?

Trail signage is minimal to the point of being almost useless, and the best stuff isn't marked at all. Lifts are old and oddly situated, and lift lines, particularly at the popular Germania lift, can be ridiculously long. The trail layout is full of obnoxious flat spots. Snowboarding, that nouveau folly, is not permitted. And you dare not complain. Suggest any imperfections to the Alta faithful (who are usually identifiable in their dressed-down, weather-beaten, time-tested attire), and you feel as if you have spit in the temple. Alta, you must know, is pure and righteous.

Actually, Alta just takes a while to figure out, and you're wise to enlist the help of the faithful, who have developed a familiarity with Alta's terrain

Opposite: Skiing off a cornice on a powder day at Catherine's Pass in the Alta backcountry. Above: The Snowbird aerial tram.

that borders on instinct. Rather than simply head downward from the top of any lift, you must traverse or hike or forage about until suddenly, as if the blinds have been thrown open to let in the bright morning light, some breathtaking run reveals itself as a shimmery path of pure Alta snow.

Nothing like that ever happened to me in my first three or four visits to Alta. But then I hooked up with a patrolman named Dave Madeara, who guided me out along the ridge that divides Alta into its two, constituent parts: Albion Basin and the Wildcat area. We bounced along the bumpy traverse, and gradually the metaphoric curtain slid away to reveal what makes Alta the legend it is. To one side, West Rustler and Alf's High Rustler dropped steeply away for 1,200 or more vertical feet. To the right, if you could find the seemingly inconsequential slots through the rock

Opposite: Dave Swanwick jumps off a rock in Wilbere Bowl at Snowbird.

THE STORY OF SNOW

The meteorological rationale for all the snow in Little Cottonwood has been explained to me by people who ought to know—guys like Alta general manager Onno Wieringa and Liam Fitzgerald, former snow safety (avalanche control) director at Snowbird. Little Cottonwood (as well as its neighbor, Big Cottonwood Canyon, which ironically is home to the two *smaller* resorts of Brighton and Solitude) sits at the convergence of two major storm tracks.

Maritime storms come straight out of the west, bearing Pacific moisture, whereas colder continental storms drop down from the northwest by way of Alaska and British Columbia. They tend to bide their time over the arid deserts west of the Wasatch mountains, suck up added moisture from the Great Salt Lake, and get squeezed into the narrow Cottonwood Canyons.

Next comes the process of orographic lift, in which the storms must lighten their load in order to rise over the mountains and continue their passage east. In winter, that lightening occurs as an expulsion of snow. This weather phenomenon is geographically very specific; resorts immediately to the north (Park City), receive only about 300 inches of snow a year, as does the small resort of Sundance to the south. Meanwhile Salt Lake City, 15 miles to the west, receives less than 60 inches of snow in an average year. But more than 500 inches fall each winter in the Cottonwood Canyons—good reason for their claim to powder-skiing fame.

Fresh powder in Grizzly Gulch, Alta backcountry. Alta averages 500 inches of snow a winter.

introduction to the true soul of Alta. Alta is not just about the skiing and the snow, but about the process of finding the skiing and the snow. It is among Alta's charming oddities that the lifts don't take you to the best skiing. Traversing and hiking—to Greeley, or West Rustler, or Devil's Castle, an area named for the rock wall that is its most prominent feature—are required to complete the journey to where the skiing can begin.

The point is this: If you prioritize convenience, you are missing the point at Alta. All the hiking and traversing are what protect Alta snow from becoming skied up quickly and packed out into obnoxious moguls that might wreck the fluidity of a classic powder run. An old-fashioned, time-honored, backcountry-like serenity takes hold here, away from the mechanization of lifts and the claustrophobia of crowds. Alta rests its case on requiring of its constituents a willingness to make an extra effort, to venture from the mainstream, in which case you will be amply rewarded.

The accessibility of the terrain is perhaps the main thing that differentiates Snowbird from Alta. For my money, Snowbird's terrain is fundamentally better. The pitch in general is steeper, a welcome feature on deep-snow days when the extra pull of gravity helps to generate momentum. The fall line is generally more continuous. I've skied lines between the Gad Chutes and Wilbere Bowl that have absolutely beaten me up, with more than 1,500 vertical feet tilted up at something like a 40-degree pitch, without interruption. Snowbird's total vertical rise is 3,240 feet; Alta's is just 2,100. With the tram and the fast chairlifts, I'm sure you could record twice as much vertical footage in an average day at Snowbird than in a day at Alta, if maximizing vertical footage is your ambition.

Yet it's a double-edged sword. Ride the tram and virtually all of Snowbird is revealed below you. There is little of the hidden mystery that characterizes Alta. And it's all pretty easy to get to

outcroppings, were the wide-open spaces of Greeley Bowl and East Greeley. And if you continued on, sneaking through the trees and making a few unmarked zigs and zags, you might find the open trees of Eagle's Nest. Or, if you happened to be following some in-the-know ski patrolman, you might luck into a sequestered powder stash known locally as Bombay Chute.

It was all a revelation to me, a jump-start

Braly Joy explodes through fresh snow at the top of the Gad Chutes, Snowbird.

from the top of the tram—only a bit of traversing and very little hiking. So on an average fresh-powder morning, all the untracked snow at Snowbird is pretty much gone by noon (depending on the rate at which terrain is opened after avalanche control work), whereas there are still stashes to be found at Alta—if you're willing to hike and you know where to find them—a day or more after a storm.

Fortunately, there are still places to poke around and find unfound powder, if you're lucky enough to be under the guidance of someone like Junior Bounous. And in some ways, I actually enjoy Snowbird more when the powder is all tracked out, because the fresh-snow frenzy subsides, and guess what? The snow is still great, so soft and easy to bury an edge into. There are still great lines to be found at Snowbird when the powder is gone, on runs like STH (aka Steeper than Hell) through the trees or in the wide-open spaces of the Cirque.

I've skied at Alta on a partly cloudy day that somehow produced six new inches, from whatever innocuous or invisible clouds. I've skied at Alta immediately after the passing of a morning thunderstorm, complete with lightning bouncing on the mountaintops, that deposited nearly a foot of snow on the mountain. The phenomenon of snow in Little Cottonwood Canyon is a miracle—maybe not fish turning to loaves or seas parting, but I've seen enough to believe that the faith of Alta's true believers is properly placed. After all, I've been at Snowbird in one of the epic snowstorms of all time.

WHAT TO EXPECT IN-BOUNDS

Alta is divided into two main parts, Albion Basin and the Wildcat side. The gentle, lower slopes of Albion Basin make it one of the great places for novice and intermediate skiers to learn the art of powder skiing. The higher you go on the mountain,

Snowboarding through fresh powder, Wilbere Bowl, Snowbird. Alta still forbids snowboarding.

The best skiing at Alta is from the central ridge dividing Wildcat and Albion, accessible mainly from the Germania lift on the Wildcat side. You can ski either side of the ridge, but be prepared for a bumpy ride getting to the line of your choice; the traverse is invariably rough and rutted. I prefer the skiing on the Albion side—in East Greeley and Greeley Bowl—wide-open faces that end in a series of nifty little gullies near the bottom. But there are plenty of great lines down the other side of the ridge in an area called West Rustler; they're just shorter, that's all. My least-favorite terrain here is the most famous—Alf's High Rustler, at the end of the ridge. It seems to get skied the most and can have moguls, and to me, mogul skiing is just not what powdery Alta is supposed to be all about.

Snowbird, like Alta, is divided in two main parts, the Gad side and the Peruvian side. It is for the most part an experts mountain, with a few decent intermediate runs and almost no novice terrain. To me, learning to ski at Snowbird has always seemed equivalent to learning to drive at the Indy 500. Intermediates can take Chips from the top of the tram, a long top-to-bottom cruiser, but even Chips has a couple of pitches toward the end that might unnerve a timid intermediate.

A handful of good but short intermediate runs are on the Gad side, from the Gad Two lift; confident intermediates might want to head up to Little Cloud Bowl and traverse all the way out to where the pitch eases off.

For steep powder skiing, it doesn't get any better than Snowbird. Drop to either side of the Cirque Traverse from the top of the tram, and amazing possibilities unfold. Silver Fox, Great Scott, and the Upper Cirque are all exceptionally steep—40 degrees or more in places—but continue farther out on the traverse, and the pitch eases off somewhat in the main Cirque. All of these options are on the Peruvian side; I prefer lines that feed from the traverse down into the Gad side—runs like Barry, Barry Steep (and steep

the more the pitch steepens, with some good intermediate terrain off the Sugarloaf chair. Powder-minded experts will want to hike from the top of Sugarloaf to the steeps of Devil's Castle.

For days when the visibility is poor, the lower slopes of the Wildcat side feature some of Alta's best tree skiing. Another good place to ski when the weather is stormy is in the trees beneath the Germania lift. The runs aren't long, but the pitch is perfect for powder skiing and the snow is invariably good.

it is)—because there are more trees, and I happen to like the company of trees.

Tree-lined shots like STH, Tiger Tail, and Black Forest, from the Gad Two chair, are among my favorite steep runs at Snowbird, even though they're a bit short. Little Cloud Bowl is a popular spot for powder but tends to get skied out quickly. Perhaps the recent opening of Mineral Basin on Snowbird's back side, bringing another 500 acres of mostly advanced terrain into the Snowbird fold, will relieve some of the pressure on Little Cloud.

Although Alta and Snowbird are contiguous, you can't ski both on the same lift ticket.

BACKCOUNTRY

The White Pine area, to the west (and down-canyon) from the Snowbird boundary line, is probably the most popular area for backcountry touring. Snowbird has sought in the past to expand into White Pine, but strong resistance from backcountry enthusiasts and environmentalists has squelched that plan. Skiers and riders are permitted to cross through gates in the Snowbird boundary line (unless the ski patrol has closed the gates due to unsafe conditions). But White Pine is an avalanche-prone area, and beacons and shovels are essential.

There is also good backcountry terrain down the back side of Snowbird and Alta through Mineral Basin and on down to the valley floor in American Fork. But because this leaves you far, far away from the base of the ski areas, you need to make arrangements for pickup and transportation at the end of the run.

There are two other pay-to-play backcountry options worth considering. Ski Utah leads something called the Interconnect Tour, starting in Park City and ending in Snowbird. The tour is a combination of both in-bounds and backcountry skiing, and is suitable for intermediates and up. There is also heli-skiing with Wasatch Powderbird Guides, an experience best reserved for advanced and expert skiers and riders.

INSIDE LINE

If you're staying in the canyon, try Alta Lodge (800-707-ALTA). It's older and has much more character than Snowbird's high-rise Cliff Lodge (800-453-3000). If you're staying in Salt Lake, ride the Utah Transit Authority bus (schedule: 801-743-3882) to avoid the worries of driving on the snow-packed canyon road.

Hanging out over beers around the rooftop pool at the Cliff Lodge is a reasonably cool après-ski scene if you happen to be staying there. Or get a massage and then have a beer—a great, soporific combination if ever there was one. Otherwise, do what most locals do—head back into the city for après-ski beers.

Much is made in the national media of Utah's restrictive liquor laws, but don't sweat it. Getting a beer in Salt Lake City (or Little Cottonwood Canyon) is no more difficult than it is anywhere else in America—except perhaps in New Orleans during Mardi Gras.

Side trips: Check out Brighton (801-532-4731) and Solitude (800-748-4754) in neighboring Big Cottonwood Canyon. And for the big resort experience, head to Park City, one canyon north of Big Cottonwood and home to Park City Resort, Deer Valley, and the Canyons.

RESOURCES

ALTA General information: 801-359-1078. Central reservations: 888-782-9258. Website: www.altaskiarea.com.

SNOWBIRD General information: 800-232-9542. Central reservations: 800-453-3000. Website: www.snowbird.com. Backcountry guide service: For heli-skiing, contact Wasatch Powderbird Guides (801-742-2800; heliskiwasatch.com). For the Interconnect Tour, contact Ski Utah (801-534-1907).

Jackson Hole

*For those inspired by a free-form mountain
ruggedness, there is Jackson*

In the pitch black of early morning on February 16, 1996, Hans Johnstone snuck quietly out of his house in Jackson, Wyoming, without telling his wife Nancy where he was going. No reason to worry her or give her a chance to veto his plan: to climb to the summit of the Grand Teton with his partner, Mark Newcomb, and ski down the treacherous Hassock-MacGowan Couloir on the mountain's north face. "If she had known, it would have ruined her day," says Johnstone.

It was a hairy idea if ever there was one. The route had never before been attempted on skis, and for good reason. The couloir was just over 2,000 vertical feet at over 52 degrees, and in four places unskiable rock and ice bands would require short rappels. Johnstone and Newcomb planned to freeski the couloir—that is, without ropes to anchor them to the mountainside as a safety precaution. Any small slip would almost certainly

Hiking up the Headwall and access to narrow, rocky north-facing chutes and couloirs.

cause catastrophic injury or death. "A little sluff of snow could knock you right over a cliff," says Hans. In addition to running the couloir, they would have to ski 800 vertical feet of highly exposed skiing terrain just to reach the entrance to the couloir from the summit, and another 4,000 vertical feet worth of glacier and mountain would still have to be negotiated to seal the deal.

The Grand suffers neither fools nor the faint of heart, and Hans Johnstone is no timid fool. He is a great athlete and superb skier—a former U.S. Olympian as a Nordic skier and now a mountaineering and helicopter-skiing guide. He knew what he was doing in planning to ski a route no one had skied before. In fact, he and Newcomb had climbed the Grand before with plans to ski the couloir, only to turn away and climb down when they deemed the snow conditions to be unreliable. But on that February 16, the conditions were just right, with a chalky, dry snow plastered to the couloir, and the two completed the perilous descent without mishap.

Hans Johnstone is an incurable lover of mountains, and in Jackson he has plenty of company. When you've got the Tetons sitting right in your backyard—more than 7,000 vertical feet worth of granite, ice, and snow exploding from the valley floor to the 13,770-foot summit of the Grand—you'd have to have cold water running in your veins not to be inspired just by the sight of it all. People like Hans Johnstone—hardcore climbers, skiers, snowboarders, ice climbers—congregate in Jackson, "because they want to live the Alpinist lifestyle, to ski and climb and have that be their focus," Johnstone says. For the Alpinist lifestyle, no place in America surpasses Jackson.

Nevertheless, the Jackson of Alpinist passion makes hardly a blip on the lifestyle radar screen of mainstream America. In big-picture America, Jackson and the Tetons are probably best known as a photo op for summer tourists on their RV- and car-bound pilgrimage to or from Yellowstone National Park, about a two-hour drive north. In fact, after the leaves come down in fall, more than a few motels and lodges shut down, and how odd it is to walk the streets of a ski town in winter and see "Closed for the Season" signs on many a door.

AT A GLANCE

LOCATION Western Wyoming, 250 miles north of Salt Lake City, Utah

SEASON November–April; February is the biggest snow month

IN-BOUNDS	1 2 3 4 (5)
BACKCOUNTRY	1 2 3 4 (5)
SNOW	1 2 (3) 4 5

TERRAIN ACREAGE More than 2,500 acres

VERTICAL RISE 4,139 feet

AVERAGE ANNUAL SNOWFALL 400 inches

Pro rider John Griber arcs a turn off Cody Peak at Jackson Hole.

A crafty California radio ad salesman named Paul McCollister came to Jackson in the early '60s with an idea to change that. McCollister envisioned a ski resort on the eastern slopes of the Tetons, and he knew the sales pitch most likely to secure approval from the federal government, which owned (and still owns) most of the land on which the proposed ski area would be created. Why not do something to give the dormant winter economy a kick in the pants? A major ski resort would be perfect. The feds agreed.

An ambitious man, McCollister had in mind a resort to rival the great resorts of the Alps, and he figured that the Tetons were about the only place in America where that would be possible. The topography awed him. Here was a series of high-alpine bowls—soon to be named Rendezvous Bowl, Cheyenne Bowl, Laramie Bowl, Tensleep Bowl, and so on—framed by stark granite walls and rising above a series of humpbacked, tree-dappled ridges that had serious powder skiing possibilities written all over them. And so, in 1965, Jackson Hole Mountain Resort was born, with a tram servicing the biggest lift-serviced vertical rise in America at that time.

In the long run, the scheme to save the winter economy probably didn't work out quite as well as McCollister and the government might have hoped. The ski resort now records somewhere around 400,000 skier (and snowboarder) days every winter, a fairly modest number alongside the million-plus skier days recorded annually at a more mainstream resort like Vail. And the total number of winter visitors to the ski area, about 125,000, is even more modest when compared with the more than 3 million people who pass through the Jackson valley in summer.

Part of that is due to Jackson's relative remoteness, but a big part has to do with the fundamental challenge of the terrain. It's not all breathtaking, fear-inducing steeps—not all runs like Corbet's Couloir, the big gutter through the cliffs below Jackson's aerial tram that is the resort's most famed (or infamous) in-bounds descent. It is certainly not like skiing the north face of the Grand. Still there's not a whole lot to entice a public insistent on well-groomed and gentle proceedings. For that majority, there is Vail. For the minority inspired by a free-form mountain ruggedness, there is Jackson.

Look from across the valley at the Teton front and it is very difficult, even if you know where you should be looking, to pick out the ski-area layout. It fits seamlessly into the mottled facade of granite, limestone, spruce thickets, and open slopes, jumbled together at all different

THE TOWN HILL

Long before there was a tram up Rendezvous Mountain, more than 30 years before there was a ski resort on the east slope of the Tetons to bring national attention to Jackson, there was Snow King. In the history of lift-serviced skiing in the United States, places like Alta in Utah, Woodstock in Vermont, and Sun Valley in Idaho now hold legendary status. Yet Snow King, the small ski area rising steeply out of the town of Jackson, deserves a rightful place in that company.

People were climbing up and skiing down Snow King as early as the 1920s, on ash and hickory skis almost 10 feet long and sometimes with their mukluks simply nailed right to the skis. Who needed bindings? In the '30s, the Hoback Boys, an enterprising team of local skiers, put on exhibitions on the hill. They dressed up in cowboy garb and performed tricks on skis, such as jumping through flaming hoops. The hill was also the site of regular competitions.

The first tow was installed in 1939, made of an old oil drilling cable driven by an old Ford tractor. The first chairlift was installed in 1941.

Like Woodstock (and unlike Sun Valley and Alta), Snow King never made it to the big leagues of American skiing. It was too small, now at just over 1,500 vertical feet, and probably too steep for the average skier; 60 percent of its terrain is now rated expert. But it has continued to record

footnotes in skiing history. For many years, its ski school director was the iconoclastic Bill Briggs, who in 1971 became the first man to ski down the Grand Teton. And in the spring of 2000, the slalom competition at the U.S. Alpine championships was contested at Snow King.

Long live the King.

angles and exposures. The rocky muscularity of the Tetons—a muscularity that, just a few miles north along the range from the ski area, rises so magnificently to the summit of the Grand—has been left intact as the singular element that differentiates Jackson from every other ski resort in America.

A few years ago I came to Jackson, on a magazine assignment, to compete in the Grand National Powder-8 Championships with a guy named Jeff Zell. (Powder-8 competitions involve teams of two skiers who, by skiing synchronously, try to form perfectly braided, figure-8 patterns in powder snow.) Zell had become available as a partner a couple of days before the competition when his original partner, the two-time World Extreme Skiing Champion Doug Coombs, was hijacked by Disney to be a stunt skier for the forgettable movie *Aspen Extreme*.

A slightly built man with a crooked, self-effacing smile, Zell didn't have the look of a guy who could rip up a mountain with a powerful, silky athleticism. Yet when I'd see ski tracks on the mountain in the most impossible-to-ski places—in near-vertical slots through the rocks, over cliff bands, on faces so steep you'd assume the edge of a ski would fail to gain purchase—I'd ask who was responsible, and invariably the answer was: "Must have been Zell."

As it turned out, Zell and I never did compete together. The snow on the competition slope, in Cody Bowl just beyond the ski area boundary, was wiped away by an avalanche when explosive charges were detonated to test the snow stability. But we did spend a couple of days skiing together in what for me became an education on the art of skiing Jackson.

Zell would turn a run into something of his own creation, connecting parts of the mountain via routes that had little or nothing to do with

Top: Jackson Hole Ski Patrol gunner Jerry Balint fires a 75mm recoilless rifle during morning avalanche control following a storm. Above: Antlers stacked to make an archway in the center of downtown Jackson.

what was indicated on the trail map. He might slip away to an untracked cache of powder hidden in the trees on the north periphery of Rendezvous Bowl, cleverly avoiding the rough-cut moguls in the heart of the bowl. From there he might then cut back to the south-facing slopes of Cheyenne Bowl, although that was entirely a matter of timing; he knew that there was a critical half hour in the morning when the composition of the snow

Opposite: Rick Armstrong skies the Cave Line, an 80- to 100-foot drop into Corbet's Couloir, while Micah Black looks on. This line has never again been skied and is forbidden.

surface was in a state of transition, producing just the right texture for skiing. Any earlier and the snow would be frozen and teeth-chattering; any later and it would be soup.

And so on, down the mountain. The whole process of creation—of imagining and then executing your own kind of run, of putting your signature on the mountain—is what attracts people like Zell to Jackson. In fact, it attracted the rest of his family, too, including his sister Julie, a three-time World Extreme Snowboarding Champion, and his brother Jim, who twice finished second in the World Extreme Skiing Championships. Says Julie: "I live in Jackson Hole because it offers me the best of the things that I love: plenty of snow, steeps, and accessible terrain with an open-gate policy into the backcountry."

Ah, yes—the open-gate policy. It made news a while back when Jackson decided to allow skiers and snowboarders to venture beyond boundary ropes into the backcountry. After all, as backcountry guide Chris Leveroni said to me, "We've got 2,500 acres in-bounds and 120 square miles of backcountry." In other words, the ski area proper isn't much more than a big grain of sand surrounded by a backcountry beach.

Personally I'm not moved by a great urgency to rush out-of-bounds at Jackson. Although 2,500 acres might seem a pittance compared with 120 square miles, it's still an awful lot of terrain. Big chunks of mostly untracked snow end up rotting in the sun for lack of skier and snowboarder traffic. Even in-bounds, there can be a kind of wildness; I have a vivid memory of stopping in the middle of one in-bounds Jackson run to observe a bald eagle who was observing me, circling above me as if I were its prey.

Still, the backcountry siren sings loudly to guys like extreme skier Kina Pickett, who told me that he lives in Jackson primarily for the opportunity "to explore the backcountry scaring myself." Hardcore locals had been clamoring for an open-boundary policy for years, and in 1999 the resort management made it happen.

The Teton County Sheriff's Office, responsible for backcountry search and rescue, braced for chaos. In the Jackson backcountry, all the classic Teton hazards come into play: big cliffs, potentially unstable snow, steep drops, tight couloirs, and so on. Laurie Davis Shepard, a backcountry guide for more than 15 years, told me of her own difficulties in navigating through the rock-and-tree labyrinth of the Spock chutes, on the back side of Apres Vous Mountain. Getting caught in a cul-de-sac, with cliffs below, trees right and left, and a steep, hard-to-climb slope above is very easy. Getting out is not—even, apparently, for someone who knows where she's going.

But the boundary opening did not turn into an immediate search-and-rescue nightmare, and that's largely due, I think, to the aura of mountain savvy that permeates the culture of Jackson skiers and snowboarders. To be disrespectful of the mountains, to do something stupid like getting lost or triggering an avalanche, would be considered unconscionably bad form.

Furthermore, there is also, I believe, a higher skill level at Jackson than almost anywhere else in the United States, embodied in the likes of the Jeff Zell, Hans Johnstone, Doug Coombs, Laurie Davis Shepard, and Kina Pickett. It is one of the main reasons to visit the place—to appreciate the feats of such people, to witness advances in the state of the art in big-mountain skiing and snowboarding. These people take their mountains seriously, and that's the way it is around Jackson, where the Alpinist lifestyle rules.

WHAT TO EXPECT
IN-BOUNDS

Officially, 50 percent of Jackson's terrain is rated as expert, while 10 percent is rated beginner. These statistics portray a clear picture of what Jackson is all about, and I'd say even that minimal 10 percent of beginner terrain is probably an exaggeration. There are a handful of long, groomed

Atop a south-facing, very steep couloir on the South Teton, Grand Teton National Park. Such backcountry skiing requires mountaineering skills and three or more hours of hiking.

runs for intermediates, most noteworthy among them being Gros Ventre, which drops 2,700 vertical feet at a steady pitch and is one of the best intermediate runs in America. For intermediates as well as experts, however, the soul of Jackson is found in exploration, not in a rigid adherence to following trails marked on the map.

The resort covers two main mountains—10,450-foot Rendezvous Mountain and 8,481-foot Apres Vous Mountain. Of the two, Apres Vous certainly offers the more mellow terrain. The pitch is intermediate with a few steeper drops here and there. Among the nice features of Apres Vous are areas of widely spaced trees, particularly in the section called Saratoga Bowl. It's great terrain for powder days when Rendezvous Mountain is shrouded in clouds and storminess. If you're an

intermediate with an exploratory mentality, you could probably spend several days on Apres Vous without skiing the same line twice. In addition, Apres Vous is a good place to go to avoid crowds, although its generally southeastern exposure can cause the snow to be either mushy or crusty.

The Bridger gondola, between Apres Vous and Rendezvous, also provides access to good intermediate terrain, with an overall pitch that is slightly steeper than the pitch of Apres Vous. All wannabe racers should get to the gondola first thing in the morning to rip a few fast runs down Gros Ventre while the groomed snow is at its best. But if it's a serious powder day, you'll want to head straight for the Rendezvous Mountain tram instead.

I have made several visits to Jackson over the

Sunrise illuminates the Tetons as fog hangs over the Snake River.

years and logged several hundred thousand vertical feet, yet I'm sure I haven't come near to skiing every possible line that is skiable on Rendezvous Mountain. From the top of the tram, you have two choices—Rendezvous Bowl or Corbet's Couloir, with the former being vastly more popular than the latter. Like any couloir, Corbet's is extremely steep and rock-lined, but the real challenge is getting into it in the first place.

Depending on the level of the snowpack, you might have to jump as much as 25 feet before making your first turn. I watched Daron Rahlves, a top downhill racer, simply airmail the lip at the top during a day off at the 2000 U.S. Alpine Championships, landing perhaps 80 feet below in the heart of the couloir. So, if you've got a similarly high level of skill and daring, the Corbet's entry is not a problem. For almost all others, the jump into Corbet's is reason to head instead for Rendezvous Bowl.

Because the overwhelming majority of the tram traffic heads for the bowl, the surface tends to become as roughed up as a giant mogul field. I prefer to stick to the edges of the bowl, where the snow is usually softer and less bumpy. Once you're through the bowl, the mountain seems to expand with exponential possibilities. In the middle third of the mountain, the best snow is usually on the north-facing slopes, although many of these—including the Alta Chutes, the Expert Chutes, and Tower Three Chute—are exceedingly steep.

The bottom third of the mountain fans out across the Colter and Sublette Ridges and an area called the Hobacks. The snow here, exposed to the sun and lower in elevation, can often be soft and punishingly difficult to ski. But on a powder day, with thousands of possible lines to ski, it is fabulous terrain. In fact the Hobacks are generally skied only when there's fresh powder.

BACKCOUNTRY

The most accessible backcountry terrain is in Cody Bowl, just south of Rendezvous Bowl. The main face of Cody Bowl, with its northerly exposure, features superb open-bowl powder skiing, although the run is relatively short. More skilled skiers and snowboarders head higher on the Cody Bowl ridge to the faces of Four Shadows or No Shadows or, if they have extreme inclinations, to the hair-raisingly treacherous Central Couloir.

If you're willing to do some hiking by heading in a generally southerly direction from Rendezvous Peak, a world of backcountry possibilities opens up. Beyond Cody Bowl are Pinedale Canyon, No Name Canyon, and Jensen Canyon, all featuring combinations of open bowls, rock-lined chutes, and well-spaced trees. In many ways, the hiking, often along narrow, exposed ridges, can be as challenging as the skiing itself.

Hiking up the Headwall to the north of Rendezvous Bowl provides access to a variety of north-facing chutes and couloirs leading into Granite Canyon. It's steep stuff that can become very narrow and rocky in places, so it's not an area to venture into without someone who knows where they're going. In fact, the same can be said for pretty much anywhere in Jackson's backcountry.

Beyond the resort, the Teton backcountry rolls on, as Chris Leveroni suggested to me, for 120 square miles. Teton Pass, southwest of Jackson, has many fine, long runs—both open bowls and lines through the trees—and is popular because the drive to the top of the pass lessens the amount of climbing time on skis. Somewhat less traveled are the mountains of Grand Teton National Park—rugged, inspiring stuff if you happen to be fit and possess at least rudimentary mountaineering savvy. But there is a price to pay. Most of the good stuff requires something along the order of a three-hour or more climb.

Get the right safety equipment and hire a guide. The imperatives of backcountry exploration that apply anywhere in the world of mountains apply in capitalized letters and boldface in the backcountry around Jackson.

INSIDE LINE

Jackson Hole is one of the few resorts left in America with a hostel (307-733-3415) at the base of the mountain for those on a budget. As little as 17 bucks gets you a bed for the night.

In town, check in at the Alpine House (800-753-1421), a well-kept and attractively furnished B&B run by Hans and Nancy Johnstone. These two former U.S. Ski Teamers know the Jackson Hole backcountry like nobody's business.

Sunday night is bluegrass night at the Saloon in the Inn at Jackson Hole, and it draws a big crowd of locals with well-worn baseball caps and weather-worn faces, all of which look like they've each logged at least 100 days on the mountain.

Arrange for a guide the afternoon before if it looks like a powder day is in store for the following day. This ensures that you'll get the first tram up the mountain in the morning for first tracks in the fresh snow.

Side trip: Head west over Teton Pass to Grand Targhee. It's a much smaller resort than Jackson and the terrain isn't as challenging, but with an average annual snowfall of 550 inches a year, it's one of the great powder stashes in North America.

RESOURCES

General information: 307-733-2292. Central reservations: 800-443-8613. Snow report: 888-DEEP-SNO. Website: www.jacksonhole.com. Backcountry guide service: The resort offers its own guide service (800-450-0477). For guiding beyond the resort, contact Exum Mountain Guides (307-733-2297). Also for hut-to-hut skiing in the Jedediah Smith Wilderness south and west of Jackson, contact Rendezvous Ski Tours (877-754-4887).

Squaw Valley

"It's all about the acceleration you get there,
like jumping off a plane."

T he 1960 Olympics might have made Squaw Valley famous, but it was Scot Schmidt who made it sexy as hell. In the mid-'80s, Schmidt jumped 100 feet from the Palisades, the cliff band that tops 8,900-foot Squaw Peak, and maybe he was or maybe he wasn't the first guy to do something that wacky at Squaw. But the cameras of ski filmmaker Warren Miller captured the moment, and when it made its way onto the big screen, to the jaw-dropping amaze-ment of audiences across the country, extreme skiing, American-style, was born with Squaw Valley as its birthplace.

It might have happened elsewhere—Mammoth Mountain, let's say, or Crested Butte, or even Squaw's neighbor, Alpine Meadows. Squaw wasn't the only place in America where you could jump big cliffs and ski seemingly impossible steeps, and it certainly wasn't the biggest, with a vertical rise of under 3,000 feet.

Squaw is famous for its steeps and for the freeriding skiers and boarders they attract.

But the celluloid heroics of Schmidt gave Squaw a cachet it could never lose.

Actually, Schmidt wasn't the first guy to try and stamp his signature on the Palisades, or on Squaw in general. In the '60s and '70s, less heralded talents like Rick Sylvester, Bob Burns, and Greg Beck were skiing crazy lines through the rocks, too. In fact Beck had gone crazy for the ski movie cameras a decade before Schmidt arrived, in a cult classic called *Daydreams*. After that came guys like Steve McKinney, Mike Slattery, and Tom Day. And then Schmidt arrived in the '80s, to be captured on film with his breakthrough leap, and the doors were thrown open. The freeriders, on both skis and snowboards, began coming as extreme pilgrims, to show that they could do what Schmidt could do, and maybe do it even better.

Squaw has thus has been dubbed Squawllywood, not always kindly but not without just cause. Since the '90s, it has been perhaps the first port of call for any young buck who thinks he (or she, for that matter) has the goods to become an extreme, freeriding superhero. Like doe-eyed starlets trying to impress studio execs, the young freeriders descend upon Squaw, because that's where the action is. It is very likely that more ski film and still photo action have been shot at Squaw than anywhere else in the known freeriding universe.

Many of the starlets become stars, too, because the list of Squaw graduates is long and distinguished: Schmidt, Shane McConkey, Jonny Moseley, Eric DesLauriers, Scott Gaffney, Darian Boyle, Steve McKinney, Brad Holmes, and on and on. You might not know all the names, but if you've watched a ski film or two or even flipped casually through a ski or snowboard magazine, you have seen their images.

The Palisades are the most famous of Squaw's extreme terrain, but there is a lot more to Squaw than the Palisades. Before the Palisades became famous there was KT-22, which has since become the heart and soul of Squaw's powderskiing bounty. KT-22 earned its name because it was so steep that it took Sandy Poulsen, one of the original visionaries in the development of Squaw, 22 kick turns to make it down safely.

After the Palisades grew to prominence, places like Mainline Pocket, Adrenaline Rock,

---

AT A GLANCE

LOCATION North shore of Lake Tahoe, 45 miles west of Reno, Nevada

SEASON November–May; February is the biggest snow month

IN-BOUNDS 1	2	3	4	(5)
BACKCOUNTRY 1	(2)	3	4	5
SNOW 1	2	3	(4)	5

TERRAIN ACREAGE 4,000 acres

VERTICAL RISE 2,850 feet

AVERAGE ANNUAL SNOWFALL 400 inches

Granite Chief, and the Fingers made their way into Squaw legend. If you're among the lucky few extremists who make a name for yourself at Squaw, if fame comes from what you do, you might even have a line (which will never appear on the trail map) named after you. Like Schmidiot's, named after you-know-who.

In the freeriding lore of Squaw, all of these places have an unwritten chronicle—of so-and-so performing such-and-such a stunt using Schmidiots or Adrenaline Rock or wherever as a stage. The tales from this ongoing oral chronicle are the stuff that spills out over beers, probably at some bar in the nearby towns of Truckee or Tahoe City, when the young bucks gather at day's end to exchange battle stories and assess their collective achievement. Spend any length of time at Squaw among the extreme crowd, and you'll become inundated with a raft of anecdotal data about who has skied what lines under what circumstances and so on.

I first came to Squaw in the late '80s, not knowing the specifics about Squaw's legend of extremism. I'd heard the word, of course, circulating in the community of skiing, and I'd seen Schmidt's famous jump on film. I knew about the 1960 Olympics. So I knew enough to know that Squaw was cool, but I didn't really know much about what actually was there.

I drove up to Squaw in a snowstorm, leaving behind the overdeveloped tackiness that gambling wrought upon the community of South Lake Tahoe. I drove through enchanted forests and past achingly beautiful Emerald Bay along the lake's western shore. As I entered Squaw Valley itself, situated just a few miles from the lake's northwestern shore, the storm clouds began to part, as if some divinity were making a welcoming gesture. The mountains shimmered in their new coat of snow.

What struck me immediately about Squaw, however, wasn't the ethereal spectacle. Instead, I was immediately taken by the sheer scope of it all—a big place with a lot of lifts. Six mountains in all—Red Dog, KT-22, Squaw Peak, Broken Arrow, Emigrant Peak, and Granite Peak—and more than 4,000 acres of rumpled terrain. And lifts everywhere, something close to 30 in all, give or take a few, which was something I discovered that Squaw founder, Alex Cushing, had a fondness for. Cushing, an often irascible and insistent East Coast transplant with a penchant for jumping fast on new technology, continues to carry a reputation as a guy who never met a lift he didn't like.

The topography had little of the fiercely vertical angularity of the Alps but was instead more classically Sierran, with humpbacked ridges, fault-line seams of granite and red rock, and evergreen trees that seemed a shade or two greener than anywhere else in America. Winter comes to Squaw primarily as a function of elevation rather than latitude or climate; to the west are Sacramento and San Francisco, where it never snows, and to the east are the deserts of Nevada. As a result, I got a peculiar feeling—maybe it was just the quality of light or the color of the trees and rock—that even with a 10-foot base of snow, summer was right around the corner, ready to break out at any moment.

Above: Granite slalom course on Broken Arrow. Opposite: Arcing a perfect turn on the Palisades.

Adrenaline Rock, one of Squaw's several proving grounds for extreme freeriders.

basins, all sorts of prominent outcroppings, the Palisades being most prominent among them. Almost everything was visible from one lift or another; you could plan your course of action on your uphill ride. See a cliff, figure out exactly how to approach it, calculate the angle and softness of the landing area, and so on, and by the time you'd reached the top, you had essentially briefed yourself in the necessities of putting your plan into action. And because almost everything was visible from the lifts, you had witnesses.

All of that, I think, has contributed to the making of Squawllywood. Squaw skiing, particularly after a typically dense and copious Sierra snowstorm, can be an exercise in exuberant slam-dunking. Skiers are out there launching off everything, straightlining the Palisades, crashing through the trees, doing backflips off rock faces, all to the oohs and aahs of lift-borne admirers. The state of the art in skiing and riding gets pushed at Squaw like almost nowhere else in the country. "You see people doing stuff and you get pushed hard by your peers," says McConkey. "It seems like *everybody* is really good—everybody is stepping it up all over the mountain."

Well I'm not about to do backflips off anything anytime soon, but I will say that after that first visit to Squaw and several later visits, the terrain is special. It is expansive rather than constrictive, which is to say, its jumbled, crazy-quilt layout screams with opportunities to do things you wouldn't think of doing elsewhere. The nuances of the terrain change constantly—the pitch, the exposure, the trees, the rocks, the snow consistency, and so on—that you could probably make a run at Squaw and never execute the same kind of turn twice.

Despite its extreme reputation, Squaw isn't all steeps and cliffs; 70 percent of the terrain is rated intermediate or easier, and that's probably accurate. But even much of the easier terrain is augmented by the insistent enticement to venture off-trail for a few turns, to explore in the woods,

It became almost immediately clear why Squaw was the new hotbed of extremism. The terrain was put together as if the sculpting hand of geomorphology had been indecisive, failing to settle upon a single, coherent pattern. Cliffs over here, trees over there, steep pitches, flat-bottom

to find a private moment or space away from the crowds. Put it this way: Squaw demands to be explored.

And it's more than just the exploratory quality of the terrain that is unique at Squaw; it's the combination of terrain and snow. Lito Tejada-Flores, a ski writer who once taught skiing at Squaw, once said that you could ski steeps after a storm at Squaw that would scare you senseless elsewhere, because the depth and density of the Squaw snow slowed you down, providing a medium of control. He's absolutely right—the dense snow sticks to the steeps, and you stick to the dense snow, and that's that.

I sense that an era might be passing at Squaw, that the frenzy that once swirled around Squaw and made it the capital of extreme is subsiding. Squaw regulars lament that every line has been done now; there are no more unskied Schmidiot's out there, because Squaw, big as it is, is only so big. With the emergence of Whistler, with the growing number of heli-skiing operators in Alaska, with the wild world in general becoming more accessible, Squaw has serious challengers in the fight to maintain its prominence as the main portal into freeriding fame. There's bigger and hairier stuff out there now, with more people able to ski it, and with equipment (fat skis) better suited for the task.

That makes some experienced locals now look at Squaw with somewhat less awe than in years past. "It's a good training ground for the big stuff," is the way McConkey describes it, meaning Squaw is a good warm-up for Alaska and the Alps. The steeps at Squaw, says McConkey, are shorter and the run-outs safer, and the consequence of screwing up is correspondingly reduced.

The people skiing crazy lines at Squaw are no longer a small, select cadre, no longer the chosen few at the very peak of the freeriding pyramid. Says Schmidt: "When I came to Squaw, there were maybe a dozen guys skiing the lines we skied. Now there are hundreds." Not only has the number of Squaw freeriders increased, they're doing stuff that the likes of Schmidt thought unimaginable—throwing backflips and freestyle tricks on terrain that the previous generation would have been happy just to survive unscathed. It is as if the terrain has become a playground rather than a proving ground.

Nevertheless, Squaw is still Squaw, and just mouthing the name comes close to saying *wow*— a word that adequately captures the spirit of the place. Even for those who ski it regularly, it still delivers thrills. "I've had so many good memories of skiing the Palisades," says McConkey. "It's all about the acceleration you get there, like jumping off a plane." Squaw might not be at the very top of the extreme pyramid anymore, but it is still center stage, a place to see and be seen. For the foreseeable future, it will remain Squawllywood. In the realm of extreme, if you can make it here, you can make it anywhere.

WHAT TO EXPECT

IN-BOUNDS

With its 6 mountains and 30 lifts (give or take a couple) and 4,000 acres, Squaw offers a lot of choice. What's more, almost all of the area is skiable, so designated runs on the trail map are really only suggestions. It helps, then, to approach Squaw with a wide-open mind: Almost anything you see is there for the taking if you've got the ability and imagination to pull it off.

For sustained steeps at Squaw, it's hard to beat KT-22, which rises close to 1,800 vertical feet without a flat spot. On a powder day, KT is the place to head for first. That's not just because its steep continuous pitch is perfect for long powder runs, but also because KT is often opened first, whereas avalanche control is still being done higher on the mountain. As a result, the powder at KT gets skied up in a hurry. Wait too long and you'll be skiing moguls.

Otherwise, some of my favorite steep terrain at Squaw is from Granite Chief, which at

Classic Sierra backcountry near Donner Summit: weatherworn rocks and sun-baked snow.

9,050 feet is the highest of Squaw's six mountains. One reason why the terrain here is so good is that it doesn't see that much traffic; it takes a few lift rides to get to the summit of Granite Chief, and many people aren't willing to make the extra effort. In addition, there's no easy way down, so if you don't want steeps, you don't want to deal with Granite Chief. One bonus at Granite Chief is that if you're willing to hike a bit along the high ridge, you can almost always find something that's hardly been skied.

For intermediate and novice skiing, Squaw is something of an upside-down area—the best stuff is high on the mountain. At most resorts, lower-level skiers and riders are restricted to the lower third of the mountain, never getting to experience the thrill of higher elevations and the scenery they offer.

Two complexes, Gold Coast and High Camp, function as high-mountain base areas, in the heart of an enormous basin served by a dozen lifts. Because both complexes are served by lifts (a so-called Funitel and an aerial tram) that are easy to ride back to the bottom, those who are uncertain of their skills needn't worry about a long, terrifying run to the bottom at day's end. The drawback to this high basin, big as it is, is that it can become congested. For novices and intermediates, there's really nowhere else to go.

When it snows at Squaw, it really snows. Dense storms come in from the Pacific and have been known to dump seven to eight feet of snow at a time. The Squaw ski patrol are superb at controlling avalanches and getting the mountain open in a hurry, but don't be surprised if you have to endure a few hours of down time after a big explosion of snow. Also, on a powder day at Squaw it helps to be strong. The mountains of California are notorious for so-called Sierra cement, a snow much heavier and wetter than you'll find in Colorado or Utah. I've never found it as unmanageable as it's made out to be; if you're light, you can simply surf the top layer of snow. I will say this, though: If you fall in that stuff, it can be one sweaty chore digging yourself out and getting back on your feet.

BACKCOUNTRY

Backcountry opportunities immediately beyond the Squaw boundary lines are limited. Better backcountry terrain is accessible from neighboring Alpine Meadows, itself a worthy resort with terrain very similar to that at Squaw. Beyond Squaw, Mount Tallac, which rises to 9,735 feet near Emerald Bay, is a popular backcountry climb and descent on Lake Tahoe's north shore. Otherwise, there are only a handful of quality backcountry descents in the area. Opportunities exist for good touring from various access points along the roads around Lake Tahoe. All in all, however, Squaw ranks behind places like Jackson, Whistler, and Aspen for backcountry options. But when you consider that much of Squaw's in-bounds terrain has an unprocessed, off-piste quality, and when you toss in 2,000 acres of similar terrain at Alpine, perhaps a big, brawny backcountry isn't necessary.

INSIDE LINE

Of all the small hamlets near Tahoe's north shore, the funkiest is Truckee. It still bears the approximate look of a 19th-century railroad town, and in fact trains still pass through—noisily—on a regular basis. There are several fine restaurants in Truckee—try Pianeta for high-end Italian—but for real Truckee flavor, drop in for breakfast at the Paradise Deli and Grocery. Get a cup of coffee, a bagel, a newspaper, and a sandwich to go for lunch, and mingle at small bistro tables with a mix of locals and tourists.

A few miles down the road, Tahoe City is more functional: a good place for cheap lodging and food, and an excellent place for gear shopping. A decent place to stay for a decent rate is the Pepper Tree Inn (800-624-8590), which also offers reasonably priced ski packages.

For high-end lodging, the Resort at Squaw Creek (800-403-4434) has a lift right out the back door; you can get to the fresh snow in a hurry.

Side trips: It's hard to go to Squaw and not

In the mid-'80s, Scot Schmidt jumped 100 feet from the Palisades, and Squaw became the hot resort among extreme skiers.

spend at least a day or two at Alpine Meadows, right next door. In all there are 12 ski areas in the Lake Tahoe area. Of these probably those most worthy of a side trip are Kirkwood, about two hours south of Squaw, and Sugar Bowl, about 20 minutes away, near Donner Pass.

RESOURCES

General information: 800-441-4423. Central reservations: 800-949-5296. Snow report: 530-581-8374. Website: www.squaw.com. Backcountry guide service: Alpine Skills International (530-426-9108), based on Donner Pass west of Squaw, conducts tours and multiday seminars for touring, telemarking, and ski mountaineering.

Whistler & Blackcomb

"…they come here to run with the big dogs, because this is the place."

Black Tusk at dusk, seen from Blackcomb Mountain.

It's the Big Show now, the North American circus of the stars. All the big-name freeriders come here, for film or photo shoots or to gain sponsor and media exposure, because Whistler is *the* place to come. But just 20 years ago, it wasn't like that at all.

Whistler was nothing back then—or not much more than nothing—on the road map of winter sport. It was an unknown, an inconsequential hamlet of slapped-together bungalows tucked into a seam in the Coast Mountains a couple of hours north of Vancouver. In the early '80s, nobody was talking about going to Whistler to rip up the biggest lift-serviced vertical drop in North America, to go big in a way (in a lift-serviced way) that was otherwise possible only in the Alps.

Whistler's winter populus consisted mainly of hardcore ski enthusiasts living around what had once been a garbage dump, because that's where today's Whistler village was born—on the site of the old town dump.

But that was another time, before the developers arrived in earnest and initiated the most radical transformation of a mountain town since the birth of Vail in the '60s, before the whispers began circulating of this big-mountain Shangri-La. I came to Whistler for the first time in the late spring of 1994, and even then the place was still in its relative nascency as the king of North American winter resorts.

I was on assignment to cover something called the World Technical Skiing Championships, a multiskill contest that would supposedly determine the world's best all-round skier. An all-star cast from all walks of the sport had been assembled—Steve Mahre and Tamara McKinney, two of the greatest names in U.S. ski racing; Doug Coombs, the two-time World Extreme Skiing Champion; Franz Weber, the one-time world speed-skiing record holder; Wayne Wong, the freestyle pioneer; and so on. And Whistler was a fitting place to come, because here was a mountain with every kind of terrain for putting the best skiers in the world to the test.

It turned out to be a private party. The slopes were all but deserted, except for people involved in the event and the occasional bear wandering out of the woods to pry into garbage dumpsters. The competition was held on Blackcomb, which rises 5,280 vertical feet on one side of Fitzsimmons Creek, because Whistler, which rises 5,020 vertical feet on the other side of the creek, was closed. No point, so late in the season with so few customers, in keeping two giant ski areas running.

Six years later I was back, and the growth of the event, now rechristened the World Ski and Snowboard Festival and now two weeks worth of competition and musical, megapartying mayhem, was a sign of the times. Whistler had busted loose. Mid-April, and there was hardly an empty room to be found in the village, which had roughly tripled in size since my first visit. To say that Whistler had put itself on the North American map of winter sport would have been an understatement. It had become ground zero.

An enormous black sound stage stood in the middle of the central plaza from which lifts diverged in one direction up Blackcomb and in the other up Whistler. At three or so in the afternoon, a flood of humanity came down the mountain.

AT A GLANCE

LOCATION 70 miles north of Vancouver, British Columbia	**TERRAIN ACREAGE** Whistler: 3,600 acres; Blackcomb: 3,500 acres
SEASON November–July; great late-spring skiing	**VERTICAL RISE** Whistler: 5,020 feet; Blackcomb: 5,280 feet
IN-BOUNDS 1 2 3 4 ⑤	**AVERAGE ANNUAL SNOWFALL** 360 inches
BACKCOUNTRY 1 2 3 4 ⑤	
SNOW 1 2 ③ 4 5	

On the sound stage, the music roared. A guitarist named Alpha Yaya Diallo led his West African band through a thunderously rhythmical session that had a throng of sweat hogs in T-shirts and ski boots writhing before the stage in spring-feverish delirium.

On the terraces of bars and restaurants along the plaza periphery, every seat was filled. The beer flowed, and through the crowds, the freeriding gladiators—the Herculean studs who were there either to compete or to be photographed or filmed—strutted around with their fat skis slung over their shoulders and their eyes masked by $150 wrap-around shades and their whole, collective being radiating an aura of big-mountain, high-adventure confidence and cool. The festival was the embodiment of what Whistler had become: the center of the freeriding universe.

The coming of age of Whistler isn't surprising. In this case, size does matter: More than 5,000 vertical feet, more than 7,000 acres, and who knows how much backcountry. Seven-mile-long runs. A maritime weather pattern that bombs the Coast Range with snow-laden storminess—officially 360 inches a year on average, although in the 1998 to 1999 season, it snowed 644 inches. The numbers don't lie; in lift-serviced North America, Whistler is as big as it gets.

Off-slope, Whistler has got the goods, too: a smartly designed "village" (small city is more like

it) where pedestrians rule over vehicular traffic. It's a killer party town, where debauchery smolders deep into the night with an urban intensity, with all the young freeriding stars and wannabes slamming vodkas and smoking cigars and lusting hopefully for the miniskirted bartenders at Garfinkel's or the go-go girls at Tommy Africa's.

But ultimately it's all about the mountains. For all of its newfound urbanity, Whistler is still, in an almost literal way, a frontier town. Drive about 15 miles north of Whistler, and the road all but ends in Pemberton, where the real heart of the Coast Range asserts itself as a virtually impenetrable mass of rock and glacier, sprawling to the northwest for 200 miles and capped by 13,338 foot Mount Waddington. That kind of wilderness can make even the peaks of Whistler and Blackcomb, which top out at 8,000 feet, seem small by comparison, and small is a word not usually mentioned in the same sentence as Whistler. In short, it is an intense mountain world, both daunting and inspiring. Eric Pehota, Whistler resident and renowned ski mountaineer, put it in simplest terms: "Being in the mountains is at the core of why we are here."

I got a taste of that one night during the World Ski and Snowboard Festival when I dropped in at Merlin's, a popular locals' hangout, for a slide show featuring the work of local photographers. The place was packed, a convocation

Above: Skiing fresh tracks in the backcountry behind Whistler Peak. Opposite: The backcountry is a vast array of glaciers, couloirs, chutes, bowls, ridges, and peaks that roll on and on.

Top: Extreme star Charlotte Moats. Above: Whistler village was created in the '80s, and the resort soon became the largest in North America.

of Whistler's hardcore. As each image flashed upon the screen—of a skier, or snowboarder, or mountain biker, or rock climber—the room would swell with a chorus of *aahs*, like a mantric response from the congregation at a revival meeting. Extroverted athleticism against a rugged mountain backdrop—it is the vital substance that drives Whistler life.

In that respect, Whistler hasn't changed all that much since the predevelopment days. Rob Boyd, a two-time Olympic downhiller, moved to Whistler in 1982, and in those days he and his ski partners would hike up to Blackcomb's Saudan Couloir (since renamed the Couloir Extreme), or to even scarier lines like Whistler's Friday the 13th or Don't Miss, where skiing is no longer permitted (even if poachers track them up on a regular basis). "Blackcomb in particular was so young and unexplored then that you could go over there three days after a storm and find just *tons* of powder," says Boyd. "It was just a riot.

"It wasn't until the mid-'90s that the rippers began coming from all over. Now you've got to really plan your day, because everything gets tracked out a lot faster. The number of high-caliber skiers and riders is incredible. I guess they come here to run with the big dogs, because this is the place. It became an international scene."

An international scene indeed, though not just in the way Boyd suggests—not just for the high-end rippers who come primarily to be camera fodder for magazines and film. Regular old tourists come, too, and plenty of them—from Europe, North America, Japan, Argentina, Australia, and other points around the globe. This might have something to do with Whistler's geographic centrality, for *Whistler* happens to be the answer to the trivia question: What major winter resort is approximately equidistant, give or take a couple of thousand miles, from Paris, Tokyo, and Buenos Aires? But more likely, the international scene converges here simply because Whistler has more of everything for everybody than pretty much any other resort on the planet.

To be sure, there's all the scary stuff that attracts the international rippers and makes for dramatic photos. In fact it can be downright dangerous. I remember coming into Jersey Cream Bowl at Blackcomb via a tricky little entrance along Chainsaw Ridge, to the left of the Couloir Extreme. The entrance required a couple of quick little turns and then a jog to the left onto an open face; miss the jog, and you'd literally be on the rocks and in a heap of trouble. I made the jog successfully, but a few minutes later, a woman taking the same line did not. She tumbled over a cliff and got seriously banged up—a helicopter was summoned to evacuate her.

So if you want to scare or hurt yourself, opportunities abound at Whistler. On the far side of the coin, however, there is the big easy of Symphony Bowl on the back side of Whistler—all soft, mellow rolls of wide-open, child-friendly terrain with magnificent views of the Coast Mountains to the north and east. And as the bowl funnels gradually into the trees, you can ride a novice run all the way to the base of the mountain, more than 4,000 vertical feet and more than five miles in all.

Or at Blackcomb you can cruise for miles down Blackcomb Glacier, which is within a provincial park, and be far away from the sight and sounds of all the lifts. With walls of granite and snow rising forcefully to either side of the glacier, a contrarian, urban illusion might form—of traveling down a wide, wide avenue of snow through a succession of tall buildings. You can look up to your left to the steeps of Sapphire, Garnet, Ruby, and Diamond Bowls, accessible only via an exposed, vertigo-inducing scramble up a ridge known as Spanky's Ladder. But to appreciate the wild beauty of the glacier itself, you need have nothing to do with Spanky and friends.

The new Shangri-La is not a perfect place. In any utopia, it should never rain—not a cold, miserable, foggy rain, at any rate—and it rains at Whistler. The base elevation (2,214 feet) is low, and the ocean is close, and the Coast Mountains

BEARS AT WHISTLER

I've seen it with my own eyes in spring—bears still apparently drowsy from hibernation wandering across lower slopes and scavenging for food. And I've heard a few pretty good bear stories. One involves a kitchen worker who went out to dispose of a few bags of trash in a nearby dumpster one morning. Little did he know that a bear, who had managed to pry his way into the dumpster overnight, had become trapped inside. So you can imagine the surprise, both human and ursine, when that dumpster hatch was thrown open.

According to Whistler naturalists, there are eight bear families living within the ski area boundaries. They're attracted to the area not only by the wealth of garbage (seemingly a staple of the modern bear diet), but also by berries on the mountain. With the tree canopy thinned out by glade and trail cutting, more sunlight reaches the ground, and berries have flourished.

But it is the bears' appetite for garbage that is of primary concern. The proclivity to raid dumpsters has spawned a small science project in Whistler: the design of bear-proof garbage containers. Several prototypes were tested until a satisfactory design was achieved, at considerable cost. If you want a twin set of bear-proof garbage cans (photo above) at Whistler, it's going to run you about $2,500.

Fresh powder stash in the trees off Whistler Peak.

on the mountain, or at least as high as the weather and visibility (or lack of same) will permit.

Or you do as does a guy like Rob Boyd, a powerful enough skier not to be worried by variable snow textures, because he can make his way through snow thick and thin. He'll look out his window and see that it's a powder morning, and he'll head for the hills. He'll ski the steep West Cirque from the summit of Whistler, then dip into Frog Hollow and work his way through the trees all the way to the base. Then he'll go up and do it again and again and again—when you've got 5,000 vertical to work with, eight runs in a day is an impressive total, and that's what Boyd shoots for. And you love the fact that there's at least some gooeyness to the snow, because it sticks to the steep slopes and is less likely to slide or sluff.

After that, you stop in at Dusty's Den at the Creekside base, where locals have been coming together for years after an epic day on the mountain. Except that it's not the same Dusty's anymore, having recently been replaced by something newer and swishier as the development of Whistler rushes onward. Whistler, like an impatient adolescent, can't wait to get on with the future.

WHAT TO EXPECT

IN-BOUNDS

Local folks have told me that if they had their choice between the two, Whistler or Blackcomb, Whistler's their place. Blackcomb, they say, is more crowded and attracts more of a tourist clientele, and to be a local and mingle among the tourist hoi polloi is bad form. The local opinion also has it that Whistler has better tree skiing for powder days, when it's snowing like hell and the visibility is so terrible in the high-alpine bowls that the trees are the only option. But I don't know. Seems to me that Blackcomb's more than 3,000 acres provide plenty of space in which to distance yourself from the plebeian crowds, and those 3,000 acres don't include some very serious backcountry just beyond the Blackcomb periphery.

are the first range to be assaulted by relatively warm storms pulsing in from the Pacific. Those storms might produce snow at higher elevations, but rain in the valley is not uncommon. What does it tell you when a ski resort produces trail maps that are weatherproof? It speaks of moisture, that's what. Even if that moisture isn't in the form of rain, it can come as a heavy, gooey, barely navigable snow. I've seen it happen; I have struggled through the muck.

But I've also seen what more than 5,000 vertical feet can do to the composition of snow: goo near the base, smoke-light powder near the summit. When the snow falls like that, you stay high

A short hike from the top of Blackcomb leads to amazing steeps and powder on what locals have named Diseased Ridge, with chutes called Gonorrhea, Syphilis, and the like.

If the terrain can be divided into two laterally —Whistler to one side and Blackcomb to the other—it can also be divided vertically, between the high-alpine terrain and the sub-alpine trees. The decision of which to choose—Whistler or Blackcomb—is usually a toss-up, but the decision between the high-alpine terrain and the trees is usually dictated by the weather. When the weather socks in—as it is inclined to do from time to time—and the visibility diminishes to near zero high on the mountain, you are essentially compelled to ski lower down, where the trees provide visual references and contrast.

For high-alpine steeps, the best runs are from the Peak chair, which leads to the top of Whistler and a series of couloirs and bowls. You can ski a variety of exposures here, so snow conditions can vary considerably depending on the snow, the temperature, and the wind. At Blackcomb, the best steep runs in the high-alpine zone are those accessed via Spanky's Ladder, with a northerly exposure that shields the snow from direct solar radiation. If you're looking for dry, light conditions in late spring, this is a good place to find it.

For high-alpine intermediate terrain, I'd head first to Harmony Bowl at Whistler. There are some steeper pitches here and the occasional mogul field, but none of the pitches is long or scary, and I like the transitions from easy to steep to easy. Probably the most popular intermediate terrain, however, is Seventh Heaven at Blackcomb—half of it wide-open, high-alpine country; the rest runs through the trees. If you don't care about challenge, if it's a sunny day and all you want is an easy ride and a great view, Symphony Bowl at Whistler is hard to beat.

On a stormy day, I've had good luck skiing in the trees on north-facing slopes accessible from the Harmony Express lift at Whistler. If the visibility is really bad, however, traversing across the high-alpine terrain to get to those slopes can be a tough chore. On the south side of Blackcomb, a series of glade runs descend below the road leading to the Seventh Heaven lift; they tend to be overlooked, I think, and hence usually have relatively untracked snow.

For flat-out, intermediate cruising, I'd opt for the Jersey Cream Express lift at Blackcomb. It's easy, it's groomed, and the trails are wide. If your ego has been bruised elsewhere on the mountain, this is a good place to come to restore it.

If there's a drawback to Whistler-Blackcomb skiing, it's that runs tend to bottleneck toward the bottom of the mountain. At the end of the day, that can mean a traffic jam, with hundreds rushing to the bottom to make whatever cool après scene they're trying to make. It might seem like wimping out, but riding the lift down at day's end is a smart choice. And a popular one, too—if you download, you will definitely not be alone.

You can ski both Whistler and Blackcomb on the same lift ticket, but you can't ski from one to the other without skiing down to the base.

BACKCOUNTRY

Backcountry seems almost too benign a word to describe the vast array of glaciers, couloirs, chutes, bowls, ridges, and peaks that roll on and on once you cross beyond the boundary ropes. I asked a ski patrolwoman one morning, while having breakfast in the Crystal Hut high up on Blackcomb during a snowstorm, just what the out-of-bounds policy at Whistler was. Given the daunting caliber of the terrain, I assumed that the policy would be relatively restrictive, erring on the side of safety. But rather than answer, she just look at me a bit dumbfounded. Policy? There was no policy at all. The boundaries were yours to cross and Godspeed at that point, for your life was in your own hands.

Let me put it in simplest terms: It's a big world out there. Probably the most easily accessible backcountry is off the back of Whistler Peak and various points along Blackcomb Glacier, where maybe 20 minutes of hiking can reward you with as much as 800 vertical feet of untracked powder. In addition, a relatively short hike from the top of Blackcomb leads to what Rob Boyd calls "pretty amazing steep skiing and powder" on what locals have named Diseased Ridge, with chutes called Gonorrhea, Syphilis, and the like.

A short hike from Whistler leads to the small but beautiful little mountains called Picolo and Flute overlooking Symphony Bowl—rife with avalanche danger when the snow is unstable, but great for fresh tracks when conditions are safe. Also at Whistler, a run rough-cut for future expansion leads from the bottom of West Bowl to the Creekside base. On a powder, day the so-called Peak-to-Creek run offers 4,000 vertical feet of something unusual—out-of-bounds trail skiing.

Anyone who is really ambitious can head out from the top of Blackcomb to the Decker Glacier,

The back side of Whistler Peak offers some of the resort's most accessible backcountry.

whence starts the three-day Spearhead Traverse that eventually leads back to Whistler. It is a wildly beautiful trip, but a trip through a glaciated, big-mountain environment that is not to be taken lightly.

All of this is the most meager of introductions, and I dare not speak much more. The mountains are big, as are the temptations, and the corresponding risks are even larger. Hire a guide.

INSIDE LINE

For high-end lodging, the Chateau Whistler (604-938-8000, chateauwhistlerresort@fairmount.com) is nearly as grand and imposing as the ski area itself. For more modestly priced lodging, a well-appointed studio in the Alpenglow (877-598-1312) goes for under $200 Canadian a night, or less than $130 at recent exchange rates.

The Girabaldi Lift Company at the base of Whistler, Merlin's at the base of Blackcomb, and Dusty's at the Creekside base are the principal après-ski watering holes for local folk.

Sushi Village might not serve the best Japanese food in the world (though it's very good), but in the culture of Whistler freeriding, it is a place to see and be seen.

Showcase Snowboards on the Village Plaza takes salesmanship to a new level. Riders come here just to hang, to be part of the scene, which sometimes includes go-go girls dancing in the windows. For whatever back-to-the-'60s reason, go-go girls have become a big thing at Whistler.

RESOURCES

General information: 800-766-0449. Central reservations: 800-766-0449. Snow report: 604-932-4211. Website: www.whistler-blackcomb.com. Backcountry guide service: Can be arranged through the resort's ski school or through Xtremeley Canadian (604-938-9656). Also try Whistler Alpine Guides (604-938-9242) or Whistler Heli-Skiing (888-HELISKI).

EUROPEAN CLASSICS

Chamonix

On the couloir-riddled flanks of the Mont Blanc massif, extreme skiing reputations are forged

Coming into Chamonix is like walking right onto a giant stage set, amidst props deliberately oversized for dramatic emphasis. The glaciated dome of Mont Blanc looms over the town like an enormous lampshade, an effect that is enhanced when the mountain is illuminated in the morning light, before the sun has reached the valley floor. The Mont Blanc summit is more than 12,000 vertical feet above the town, so that anyone looking up at that giant lampshade faces a vertical relief greater than that which climbers face at Everest base camp upon surveying the world's highest mountain.

Alongside Mont Blanc, the Aiguille du Midi punctures the sky like a 9,000-foot granite steeple. A cable car, shooting almost straight up out of town to a restaurant at the peak of the Aiguille (meaning *needle* in French), provides a terrifying ride if ever there was one. The Aiguille du Midi cable car is among the most impressive

The traverse to the infamous Belvedere run at Les Grands Montets, favorite playground of extreme skiers.

mountain lifts in the world, and it certainly represents an engineering feat that stretches the limits of technical feasibility and human imagination. The Vallée Blanche, which descends from the Aiguille du Midi over the Glacier du Géant and the Mer de Glace for more than 12 miles and 9,300 vertical feet is, quite possibly, the longest, most famous ski run in the world.

Chamonix is big both in topography and reputation, for it is the undisputed crossroads of the mountaineering universe. It is mountaineering's Times Square, through which almost all climbers, extreme skiers and snowboarders, and anyone with dreams of mountain conquest eventually must (or at least ought to) pass. On the couloir-riddled flanks of the Mont Blanc massif and in the mountains surrounding Chamonix, extreme skiing reputations are forged.

The hagiography of winter extreme is filled with the names of those who first made their mark in Chamonix. It is here that the now-legendary likes of Sylvain Saudan (the self-styled *Skieur de l'Impossible*) and Pierre Tardivel, along with the late Patrick Vallencent and the extreme snowboarder, Bernard Gouvy, first earned fame. Every year, a new generation of hopefuls arrives, for no matter where you've been or what you've done, making your mark in Chamonix is the quickest and surest route to acceptance into the community of extreme.

Chamonix is the birthplace of modern mountaineering, according to those eager to assert whatever imprecise standards can be used to validate the claim. At least one standard might apply: The world's oldest mountain guide organization, La Compagnie des Guides de Chamonix, was founded here in 1821. On the map of the mountaineering world, Chamonix is like the New York of the famous Saul Steinberg drawing—a dwarfing geographical entity, with the rest of the world correspondingly diminished.

A campuslike atmosphere prevails on the streets of Chamonix, teeming with students of the mountains. They are a polyglot bunch, most sporting the youthful, half-shaven, scruffy look that is mountaineering chic and hailing from as near as Chamonix itself and as far away as South America and Australia. They mill about in the late-day sun

AT A GLANCE

LOCATION 50 miles southeast of Geneva, Switzerland	**TERRAIN ACREAGE** 30,000 acres in 13 separate areas
SEASON December–May	**VERTICAL RISE** 9,000 or more feet
IN-BOUNDS 1 2 ③ 4 5	**AVERAGE ANNUAL SNOWFALL** Approximately 300 inches
OFF-PISTE 1 2 3 4 ⑤	
SNOW 1 2 ③ 4 5	

after coming down from the mountains that are their open-air classroom, and they talk the talk of mountaineering, ice climbing, skiing, and snowboarding in a half-dozen or more languages. They sip strong coffee in the many restaurants and

Hiking for turns in the Vallée Blanche. At 12 miles and 9,300 vertical feet, it is quite possibly the longest, most famous ski run in the world.

patisseries in town, their fingers idly toying with a cigarette or a carabiner. They project an air of mountain-cool confidence.

They live not only for the mountains but also for the chance to live among others who live for the mountains, and Chamonix is unquestionably the place for that. In the subculture of mountaineering, oral history and lore—the anecdotal interchange of success and failure, the talk of legendary feats and tragic consequences—take on a life of their own. So if you take your mountains seriously, you must come to Chamonix at least to listen, if for no other reason.

I have made the mistake of showing up in Chamonix in the fall, after the summer climbing season had ended and before the winter ski season had begun. It was a ghost town, the streets empty

except for a group of Japanese shutterbugs. I ate alone in a deserted restaurant and watched a rainstorm gradually turn to snow by evening, a phenomenon that coated the trees and mountain ridges with a gilded fringe when the sun rose the next morning. It was a lonely place, a deserted campus when school was not in session.

But I've been there in midwinter, too, and that's a whole different story. Chamonix, as a winter sports area, is the sort of place that can suck in thousands of visitors with the allure of sheer numbers. There is, foremost, Mont Blanc itself, the highest mountain in western Europe at 15,771 feet. But there's a lot more than just the big mountain alone, for there are 13 ski areas in all, stretching from Les Houches at the opening of the valley through Chamonix itself and on to Balme and Le Tour at the valley terminus. Some areas, like Les Planards, with just three lifts and three runs, are tiny; others, like Les Grands Montets, with more than 6,000 vertical feet of terrain, are enormous. Big and small, they combine for a total of something like 30,000 skiable acres, give or take a few thousand.

Any discussion of Chamonix ought probably to begin with the Vallée Blanche, for it is the essential Chamonix run, if not the essential Alpine run. It is certainly not the most difficult run in the Alps, or at least it needn't be, for multiple routes are possible. For most people who venture to the Vallée Blanche, the most challenging part of the journey is getting there. You'll see people riding

Opposite: Skiing under Serac Towers, Aiguille du Midi. Meaning needle *in French, the Aiguille punctures the sky like a 9,000-foot granite steeple.*

The Aiguille du Midi cable car, shooting almost straight up out of town to a restaurant at the peak, is among the most impressive mountain lifts in the world.

the Aiguille du Midi cable car with their eyes shut to prevent vertigo, but this behavior only forestalls the inevitable.

Leaving the cable car terminal, a slippery slope leads to a footpath chopped out of the ice, passing precariously above a sheer drop of several thousand feet. Iron stakes supporting cables provide handholds and a fragile sense of security. Guides often rope clients together, just to be sure. Yet incredibly, some of the people who spill from the cable car seem utterly unfazed by the prospect of a single misplaced step courting almost certain death. These bravehearts scramble down the route without apparent fear, moving purposefully like New Yorkers through a subway station on their way to work.

If you can deal with such madness at the brink of death, you can certainly deal with the

Vallée Blanche itself.

The descent takes you through a massive ice sculpture garden, around crevasses and amidst turquoise seracs. To make the 12-mile run with a mind-set focused on the physical experience of skiing is to miss the point. There might indeed be ways of entering the *vallée* that provide heart-stopping thrills—couloirs and such—but eventually all comers end up on a low-angled thoroughfare of the glacier. From there, the idea is to move at a contemplative pace through a glacial world, like a museum goer in a gallery of ice, snow, and sun. It is all something else to behold, though not necessarily the still-life work of natural art it might seem. I've had friends tell me of making a pleasant run down the Vallée Blanche, only to return to find a part of the route they'd previously taken to be covered in the rubble of collapsed seracs. Imagine the disaster if their timing had been different.

Les Grands Montets is the main reason people come to ski Chamonix, that is if the physical rush of speeding downhill is the primary objective. Les Grand Montets is a giant, flared buttress of snow and rock supporting a saw-toothed ridge of *aiguilles* between the Glacier d'Argentière and the Mer de Glace. Its reputation as one of the great off-piste areas in the world is undoubtedly deserved, but not necessarily because of size alone; several ski areas in the Alps are bigger. The renown of Les Grand Montets is elevated in large part by Chamonix's celebrity. So many supremely talented skiers and snowboarders have spent time here that Les Grands Montets is perhaps the European equivalent of Squaw Valley—a stage on which every line, every route of descent, has a dramatic history.

People who talk of Les Grands Montets typically swill the air with superlatives. It is the longest, steepest, deepest, wildest skiing in Europe, they will proclaim rhapsodically, although that's not quite true. There are certainly longer runs and steeper runs. Snow depth is always a matter of meteorological luck, and wildness is a matter of opinion. But factor all of the elements into a combined sum—long, steep, deep, wild—and there is undoubtedly something exceptional about Les Grands Montets.

"The terrain has so many contours, and you can ski every inch of it," says John Egan, a renowned extreme skier who runs guided off-piste camps in Chamonix. "Every inch," of course, is a measure that applies only if you're willing to attempt such wild lines as the face directly beneath the Lognan-Grands Montets cable car. It is a run that can thoroughly entertain anyone like Egan, in search of a rare challenge of the kind that can be found in Chamonix and almost nowhere else. It begins with a jump from a small cornice and continues on a bobsled-run ride right through the bottom of a broad, deep crevasse, from which the skier is eventually jettisoned onto a wide-open face. On powder days, says Egan, "the snow on that face is just filthy good."

THE HAUTE ROUTE

If there is a single experience that stands out as the essential Alpine adventure on skis, it is probably the Haute Route tour, from Chamonix to Zermatt. First pioneered by British mountaineers in 1861 for summer touring, the route is now perhaps more popular for spring ski touring.

The Haute Route—literally translated as "high route"—certainly lives up to its name. Most of the route is well above tree line, reaching elevations above 12,000 feet as it crosses high mountain passes. This is a classic Alpine world—sharp, saw-toothed peaks surrounded by snow-covered glaciers, all of it affirming that, despite considerable resort development throughout the Alps, there is still true wilderness here.

April is prime time for Haute-Route touring—the weather is usually good and the snow conditions more stable than in midwinter. Typically, the entire route can be covered in seven days, with nights spent (and dinners served) in high mountain refuges along the way. This enables skiers to travel with relatively light packs and thus to cover a substantial distance —10 or so miles—each day. Given the nature of the terrain—highly exposed, with potentially high avalanche danger—it's not out of the question that a night might be spent in a snow cave, waiting out a storm.

Actually, to refer to the Haute Route in the singular is potentially misleading. Over the years, a number of variations of the basic route have been

continued on page 88

continued from page 87

developed, including extensions beyond Zermatt into the Saas Valley or into Italy. Regardless of the route chosen, however, the daily activity is much the same. The climbs, using skins on skis or crampons, typically range between 1,500 and 3,000 vertical feet, with comparable descents. Much of the route involves glacial travel (with all of its inherent beauties and dangers) and, depending on the steepness of the slope and the snow conditions, ropes might be used for either climbing or descending. At certain points along the way, ski resort lifts make quick work of the climbing, and depending on the route chosen, bus transfers in some cases can come into play.

A number of guide services (such as La Compagnie des Guides de Chamonix; 011-33-450-530-088; www.cieguides-chamonix.com) lead groups along the Haute Route. Expert skiing skills and mountaineering experience aren't required, but the Haute Route is certainly not for everyone. Given the amount of uphill travel, you must be in excellent shape and able to cope with potentially gnarly snow conditions—ice, breakable crust, etc. And fundamentally, you should be reasonably at ease in an exposed, high-Alpine environment.

The traditional Haute Route, as well as several variations, is well covered in *The Haute Route: Chamonix-Zermatt*, by Peter Cliff (AlpenBooks, 1997). The book is available in both English and French at nearly all the sporting-goods shops in the Chamonix Valley.

The cornice-crevasse-and-face combo might not suit the likes and talents of all skiers, but it is simply one possible line among many on Les Grand Montets, the land of 10,000 dances. The sustained pitch of over 4,000 vertical feet, from the summit (the Aiguille des Grands Montets) to what is effectively the midstation of the mountain (La Croix de Lognan), is a rare find in the mountain world, in Europe or anywhere else. Most descents are interrupted by some flat spot, shelf, traverse, or humpbacked roll, but not Les Grand Montets. It just keeps on keeping on. And in years when the depth of the snowpack is sufficient, you can continue for another 3,000 vertical feet from La Croix de Lognan through the trees to the valley floor and the town of Argentière.

If that's all there were to it, just the filthy, twinned pleasures of deep snow and sustained steeps, then Les Grands Montets might be simply great. But it is the scenery that makes it extraordinary, the sharply cut mountains rising from two great rivers of ice, each of which could reinvent, in glacial terms, Mark Twain's famous description of the Mississippi "rolling its mile-wide tide along, shining in the sun."

In fact, beyond any desire to ski powder or to challenge 50-degree couloirs or to chum about with the stars of extreme life, one comes to Chamonix just to look around. Determining which might be the world's most visually striking mountain is a matter of opinion and debate, a matter certainly discussed in Chamonix on a regular basis among the lords of mountaineering. But you know, many of them travel far and wide, to the Himalayas and South America and so on, and they have a habit of returning here. As perfect as mountains might be elsewhere in the world, it's hard to find anything much better than this.

Opposite: Many extreme legends are born on the steeps of Chamonix.

Dede Rhem makes the first snowboard descent of the Aiguille du Tour, Chamonix.

WHAT TO EXPECT

IN-BOUNDS

Thirteen ski areas covering roughly 30,000 acres might sound like a lot, as indeed it is. Yet only four areas make Chamonix the special place that it is: primarily the Aiguille du Midi (the Vallée Blanche) and Les Grands Montets, and secondarily Le Brévent and La Flégère.

The Vallée Blanche is basically a one-run-in-a-day affair. Aggressive skiers might be able to make the trip more than once, but rushing down the Vallée Blanche to try to squeeze in an extra run is entirely missing the point. Take time, look around, appreciate the glacial surroundings. Depending on snow conditions, the run is open from mid-December through May.

Les Grand Montets is where the powder-mad crowd heads after a storm. The result can be lift lines of epic proportions at the Lognan-Grands Montets cable car, leading to a possible wait of an hour or more. Politeness in European lift lines is not commonly exercised; pushing, leaning, and jostling are the order of the day. Normally you wouldn't ever want to put up with such nonsense, but the descent, once you have successfully been delivered to the cable car summit, is exceptional. So you must weigh the two against one another and decide if dealing with an hour of rude behavior is worth it. The answer will probably be yes.

There are a couple of alternatives to the cable car—an old, slow double chair that covers about 2,000 vertical feet of the cable car's terrain, and a gondola that accesses a cirque to the left of Les Grand Montets summit. The runs from these lifts are shorter, but if the cable car line is ridiculously long, running round-trips on the shorter lifts might be a more sensible strategy.

The terrain at Le Brévent is primarily south facing, so the snow texture might be rough and crusty if there hasn't been fresh snow for a while. But it's a good place to head on a cold, sunny day in January or a warm, sunny day in March, when the snow turns to corn. Most of the terrain is intermediate, but experts favor an area known as the Kitchen Wall, where the pitch is so steep that the corn snow usually peels away under your skis, rarely becoming deep, unmanageable mush.

One important thing to be said about Le Brévent and its neighbor, La Flégère, is that their exposure reveals extraordinary views of the Mont Blanc massif. When in Chamonix, wherever you are skiing, always keep in mind: If you aren't appreciating the scenery, you're missing out on the best part of the whole experience. One last note about Chamonix skiing: The lift systems of the separate ski areas in the Chamonix Valley are not interconnected. The multivalley odyssey you might experience in a place like Val d'Isère or Verbier is not possible at Chamonix.

OFF-PISTE

When is in-bounds no longer in bounds? Chamonix can blur the line as can no other place in the world. Les Grands Montets, for example, is essentially all off-piste, as is Vallée Blanche. At Chamonix, however, the off-piste areas offer long, dramatic runs for skiers of nearly all abilities. There are relatively mellow runs (some routes down the Vallée Blanche), but some couloirs so extreme that they might have been skied no more than a few times, if that. The ethos of "if you fall, you die" extremism, after all, finds its ground zero in Chamonix. One thing to be cautious

The clock tower at the Chamonix Train Station.

about in venturing off-piste around Chamonix is that these mountains are heavily glaciated. Crevasses can be encountered just a few feet off a marked and groomed run. And because crevasses are often covered by thin, collapsible bridges of snow in the winter, the astute eye of an accompanying guide can literally be a lifesaver when you venture off-piste.

Fortunately, guide services abound in Chamonix, and you ought to avail yourself of their expertise. Big is a word that applies appropriately to Chamonix's off-piste environment—big glaciers, big steeps, big drops, and big trouble if you make an error in choosing a route of descent.

INSIDE LINE

Lodging, from modest B&Bs to four-star hotels, is not in short supply in Chamonix. It's your call on how rustic or fancy you want to go; a reasonably priced, middle-tier option is the three-star Vallée Blanche Hotel (011-33-450-530-450, www.vallee-blanche.com), a renovated 18th-century hotel in the heart of town.

If you're into rolling dice and playing cards for money, Chamonix is a great place to visit. Its stately casino is one of the town's landmarks.

Given the international crowd it attracts, Chamonix offers a wide array of restaurants and cuisines. Chamonix can even claim a fairly good Mexican restaurant, La Cantina.

If you want to get wild with the Aussies—who are remarkably well represented at many European ski resorts—head for Wild Wallabies. Or for late-night action, try Bar du Moulin.

A car isn't essential in Chamonix; the public bus service is adequate. But because the trip from Chamonix to Argentière, where Les Grands Montets is located, is several miles, it's nice to have a car and not have to squeeze into a bus invariably crowded at rush hour.

The six-day "Around Mont Blanc" pass allows you to ski a number of resorts in the general Mont Blanc region, including Verbier in Switzerland, Courmayer in Italy, and Chamonix in France.

RESOURCES

General information: 011-33-450-530-024. Web-sites: www.chamonix.net; www.grands-montets.com. Off-piste guide services: The main guiding company is La Compagnie des Guides de Chamonix (011-33-450-530-088; www.cieguides-chamonix.com). American Alpine Adventures (011-33-450-588-354) is run by American (and English-speaking) Francis Kelsey.

Val d'Isère & Tignes

It could never be said of Val d'Isère:
Been there, done that

W e were a relatively compact group—myself, a couple of other Americans, two Italians, and a German. Our guide was a man of pure mountain breeding—a skier, climber, goatherd, and heavy smoker who would roll unfiltered cigarettes in his lips as he smoked them. His drooping mustache, a bulbous thing that seemed to be a living entity, had an ocherous tinge around the edges.

We were preparing to ski a couloir some-where within the enormous domain of mountains and lifts known as l'Espace Killy—the name given to all the terrain in the neighboring and adjoining resorts of Val d'Isère and Tignes. The couloir was a nasty-looking thing, a couple of thousand feet long and lined with threatening walls of rock. What's more, the snow was a thawed, frozen, rethawed, and refrozen mess. The average pitch was close to 50 degrees, and falling (which would have resulted in a long, accelerating, and injurious

Guide with group at the top of the Tour du Charvet, one of Val d'Isère's most famous off-piste routes, reached via the Bellevarde sector.

slide) was out of the question.

To ski it seemed utter folly; why bother when there was better snow elsewhere and a world of terrain to choose from? If there is one thing I have discovered in following off-piste guides in the Alps, it is this: At some point you will almost certainly find yourself in a ridiculous predicament that involves a couloir. Among mountain guides, the most perversely pleasurable aspect of the job, it would seem, is to observe the expressions of clients swept by trepidation and doubt.

A 20-foot vertical icefall at the top of the couloir presented an initial complication, but our man with the biotic mustache had a plan. Using his two ski poles as twin anchors embedded in a ledge of firm snow above the icefall, he tossed down a rope that we would use to rappel, wearing our skis, to a point where there was snow supple enough for our skis to gain purchase.

I was right behind the Italians in descending the rope, and they weren't at all happy. They spoke no English and I spoke no Italian, but the dialect of body language and gesticulation put us on approximately the same wavelength: What we were doing was nuts. But as we worked our way slowly down the first third of the couloir, we somehow managed to put one another at ease. It was the kind of situational camaraderie you might expect to develop among fellow sailors on a leaking boat.

Thank goodness all of Val d'Isère is not like that. But then again, a lot of it *is* like that, simply because there is a lot of everything within l'Espace Killy. It blows away any North American conception of what a large resort is all about. l'Espace Killy alone is said to comprise 25,000 acres, something close to 10 Jackson Holes. There are close to 100 lifts. The vertical rise exceeds 6,000 feet, and off-piste runs covering more than 7,000 feet are possible.

In short, it is essentially too large to be defined—impossible, as far as I can tell, to figure out where it all begins and ends. I discovered that fact several years ago in a weeklong adventure through the Tarentaise region, skiing from one resort to the next in a combined in-bounds/off-piste trip. If you were to ask me now to retrace

---

AT A GLANCE

LOCATION 140 miles east of Lyon, France; 110 miles southeast of Geneva, Switzerland	**TERRAIN ACREAGE** 25,000 acres
SEASON October–August	**VERTICAL RISE** Approximately 6,000 feet
	AVERAGE ANNUAL SNOWFALL 360 inches

IN-BOUNDS 1 2 3 4 ⑤

OFF-PISTE 1 2 3 4 ⑤

SNOW 1 2 ③ 4 5

my steps, I'd be clueless. But the trip confirmed the fact that Méribel, Val Thorens, Courchevel, Les Arcs, and La Plagne, along with Val d'Isère and Tignes, are all roughly interconnected, and a week of touring was a meager introduction. You could probably keep going for an entire winter—up lifts, down into the next valley, through a high col and into another valley, even into another country, and so on—without ever crossing your path.

Actually, it can all be a bit daunting, because how does one choose when there is so much to choose from? It is entirely possible to turn a day at Val d'Isère into a seemingly endless litany of lift riding and traversing of roads, traveling from one *vallon* ("small valley") into the next in search of a satisfying run. I have done just that, and come up almost completely empty. It is also entirely possible to become hopelessly lost or to end up in Tignes when you wanted to be in Val d'Isère, having to call a taxi to resolve the problem of dislocation. I've done that too. Or you could play it safe and stick to a few familiar lifts and runs, but in doing so you'd never come close to tapping into the full bounty that is l'Espace Killy.

All of that is sufficient reason to hire a guide, even if it might result at some point in having to humor the fellow by skiing a frightful couloir. But when everything comes together under knowledgeable guidance, when the lift riding pays off and you stand at the threshold of a miles-long run through supple snow with the severe upthrust of

the Tarentaise Alps as your visual accompaniment, it is astonishing how good it can be.

That is to say, I have been astonished. I have had runs in Val d'Isère and Tignes that rank among the best I have ever experienced. I can remember, for example, one late afternoon in spring, when the sun was just beginning to edge beyond the jagged ridges, and below me the Vallon de l'Iseran was divided into equal parts of light and shadow. I could never indicate on a map what specific line our group took—when you have a guide you tend simply to follow without question—but it was a roller-coaster ride of steep ramps and mellow folds, all in untracked snow for something like 4,000 vertical feet. The lower our descent took us, the more we became absorbed in shadow, and the taller and more imposing the mountains around us seemed to become. We ended up in the village of Le Fornet and from there took a taxi back to Val d'Isère.

I can also remember a run down the back side of Tignes, beyond the ski area boundary into the Parc National de la Vanoise. It was pure spring skiing, the hot sun burning down on a vast, rumpled bed of baked snow, not particularly steep, with 3,000-foot rock walls looming to our left. We continued for 6,000 or more vertical feet until the snow ran out in a meadow of grass and mud. We then lunched in a drooping, stone-walled restaurant, drinking much too much wine, an exercise in gustatory excess that led to my passing out in a bus on the ride back to town. If you ask me, that—the drunkenness included—

Top: Snow threatens to bury a sign announcing Val d'Isère's elevation. Above: Val Thorens, another of several nearby interconnected resorts. Opposite: The north face of the Grande Motte, a crevasse-filled, off-piste glacier route reached by the Grande Motte cable car.

The terrain park in the Bellevarde sector is known for its big-air and skier/boarder cross competitions.

is what skiing in the Alps is all about.

Were it not for skiing, there would be no Tignes. An antiseptic encampment on a tundral plateau above the tree line, it is the epitome of what the French call a "purpose-built resort"—a resort built for the purpose of recreation and not much else. When last I was in Tignes, a considerable amount of construction was in progress, but I doubt its completion will be enough to save the place. Tignes has the architectural complexity of a cinder block, and it's a shame, because its setting is exquisite in an austere, high-Alpine way. At breakfast at the Hotel Diva one morning, I came to realize that the best way to appreciate Tignes is to look away from it rather than toward it—to look out the dining room window at the rising sun

spilling over snow-mantled bulwarks leading up to La Grande Casse, a 12,710-foot pyramid of granite, in the distance. In Tignes, the natural aesthetic effortlessly humbles the crude structures made by man.

Val d'Isère is not such an architectural eyesore. That's mainly because its modern angularity is softened by the impressionistic presence of weathered, stone-and-wood buildings constructed in the 11th century by high-mountain herdsmen who would while away the long winter months by making lace and pungent cheese. Val d'Isère seems now to like touting its medieval roots as an atavistic, cultural substratum that enriches the relatively nouveau frivolity of skiing. The church steeple of St. Bernard de Menthon is the town's much-photographed icon, appearing in all sorts of promotional materials and conveying a sense of a historical authenticity.

Indeed, the area can still claim a few ties to its ancient, pre-skiing past; some mountain pastures are still used for grazing in summer, and there is even an eponymous cattle breed native to the Tarentaise region. But don't be led too far astray by these timeworn, pastoral images; the culture of skiing dominates Val d'Isère. If you want history, you ought to turn more appropriately to the 1992 Winter Olympics or to Jean-Claude Killy, the legendary ski racer and Val d'Isère native.

For the Olympics of '92, renowned race-course designer Bernhard Russi created a diabolical downhill track on the Face de Bellevarde. The idea was not only to create a great downhill course worthy of its magnificent setting—after the Olympics, the postmortem opinion was divided on the subject—but also to create a course visible to thousands of spectators. Indeed, drive into Val d'Isère now and you cannot miss it—the 3,000-vertical-foot Face de Bellevarde, rising abruptly from the town.

In fact, it is something of a deception. When I first came to Val d'Isère in 1993, I wanted to see and ski the course, to experience what I imagined was the essence of Val d'Isère in the afterglow of Olympic glory. Well I did ski it, all right, but only as an afterthought as it turned out. For I discovered that the real Val d'Isère lay beyond, obscured by the mass of the Face de Bellevarde. The real Val d'Isère was not encapsulated in a carefully designed race run but consisted, antithetically, of a vast sprawl of mountain terrain almost entirely

PRESEASON TRAINING

Where do elite ski racers go, like baseballers going to training camp, to prepare for the winter season? They go to Tignes, as I discovered a couple of years ago. If you want to ski in the fall in the Northern Hemisphere, no place has more reliably good snow than Tignes.

I arrived in Tignes in October with two former U.S. Ski Team members—Tommy Moe, the 1994 Olympic Downhill Champion, and Jeremy Nobis. We were coming from Paris, where the boys had wandered about the city streets the night before, unfamiliar with the language and not entirely sober, and they didn't show up at our hotel until sometime in the middle of the next morning. We barely made our train to Lyon, and from there we drove for 2½ hours into the mountains.

The three of us had been assembled by a ski company that wanted us to try out new prototypes on the glacier above Tignes. It's the place to go,

after all, when there's no snow anywhere else, a fact not lost on race teams around the world. The U.S. Ski Team was there, along with the French and Japanese teams and a number of others, and it was quite the scene, with Lycra-clad racers and walkie-talkie-toting coaches and lackeys bearing extra skis.

In the morning we boarded the high-speed funicular railway that bores through the heart of the mountain on its climb to the glacier of La Grande Motte. We emerged into full winter, with fog swirling and snow blowing in a hard wind, and with the near and distant peaks disappearing behind lowering clouds. We managed to get in about two hours of skiing before the fog closed in completely, at which point we joined a mass exodus for the funicular ride back to the base. Not a spectacular day of skiing perhaps, but where else can you ski in October?

One of Tignes' highest off-piste routes, the north face of the Grande Motte offers great dry snow due to its north- to northwest-facing exposure.

(except for lifts and few strategically placed restaurants) in its natural state.

Glaciers, couloirs, well-spaced larch trees, steep faces, gently sloping terraces, massive, open bowls—exposures covering every point of the compass. Val d'Isère even has such geological oddities as alley-wide cracks in the rock, perhaps 80 feet deep, and to ski through something like that, a natural bobsled run, is a rare experience indeed. And if for some inconceivable reason you were ever to tire of Val d'Isère itself, just ski on over to Tignes, a different world despite its proximity to

Val d'Isère. The mountains of Tignes appear more foreboding, rockier, and more muscular, as if assembled from giant blocks of granite and soil.

To experience Val d'Isère in its entirety is to watch the petals of a flower unfurl, with each phase in the process revealing something more amazing and impressive. Upon reaching the summit of a lift on a high ridge, you're apt to discover a valley that had previously been shielded from view. That experience keeps repeating itself—a new ridge a new revelation, and on and on.

That is why the full sweep of Val d'Isère

can't be comprehended in a day or a week, or perhaps even in a lifetime. It could never be said of Val d'Isère: Been there, done that. Just when you think you're getting a handle on the place, a guide will steer you in a new direction, and an entirely unexpected event will unfold. You might even find yourself clinging to a rope over an icefall, an experience so absurd you think you'd never encounter it in your skiing life. But that's Val d'Isère—pushing the limits of possibility well beyond the ordinary.

WHAT TO EXPECT IN-BOUNDS

One of the truly impressive aspects of l'Espace Killy (Val d'Isère and Tignes combined) is that it features abundant terrain for skiers and riders of all abilities. If you want extreme, 50-foot slopes, they're there for the taking; if you've never, ever been on snow before, you can also find happiness. A common complaint I've heard about Val d'Isère is that they do a poor job of trail grooming. I've not encountered that, but then most of my memories of Val d'Isère are of skiing off-piste, where grooming isn't an issue.

One thing that might take some getting used to—regardless of ability—is the exposure, the high-Alpine openness. This is big, sprawling terrain with big peaks, deep valleys, and few trees. Tignes in particular has a raw and exposed character, where the sheer granite bulk of the mountains makes them appear more massive than those in Val d'Isère. If you are used to smaller mountains and the comforting companionship of trees, l'Espace Killy might be disconcerting at first.

Within the sprawl of l'Espace Killy, it is very difficult to single out specific runs that, in and of themselves, are distinctly representative of the entire place. In all, the skiable terrain comprises perhaps a half-dozen small valleys aligned like waves rolling in from the sea. In navigating this

First tracks into the off-piste route of the Pays Desert in the Fornet sector of Val d'Isère.

layout, you will probably find yourself moving laterally almost as much as you'll move vertically. This can be frustrating; you can spend a good amount of time riding lifts, and in some cases even descending on lifts. Be patient; an hour of lift riding is usually rewarded with a run of proportional length.

For expert skiing, however, don't automatically assume that you have to travel far and wide to find the good stuff. In fact, the best tree skiing, what little there is in l'Espace Killy, is within the larches on the flanks of Solaise, just above town. The Face de Bellevarde is accessible via a couple of speedy base-to-summit lifts. But don't be satisfied with that; the best steep-slope powder skiing is on the faces that descend from the several ridges that divide the terrain.

Intermediates have much to choose from, either by sticking to the gently sloping valley

Couloir Number 3, one of the three famous couloirs leading into the Lanches at the base of Tignes' Grande Motte sector.

lift ride to get you over a ridge separating Tignes and Val d'Isère, you can ski intermediate terrain for 6,000 vertical feet back to Val d'Isère. Or, if you prefer, you can descend on the lifts, as many people do.

OFF-PISTE
Within the boundaries of l'Espace Killy, possibilities abound. Such is the size of the area that on virtually any winter day, you'll be rewarded with a powder run if you're willing to do a little hiking and traversing. Guide services in Val d'Isère do a healthy business, and for good reason. If you don't know where you're going, not only can you encounter the usual, serious hazards that the Alps impose—cliffs, avalanches, crevasses—but you can spend a lot of time wasting time, by roaming around without ever finding an extended fall-line descent.

Val d'Isère is also one of the great places in the Alps to begin a multiday, valley-to-valley tour. To the southwest are the resorts of Les Trois Vallées—Courchevel, Val Thorens, Méribel, and others. To the northwest are Les Arcs and La Plagne. To the east is the Aosta region of Italy. I once toured the region for six days, beginning in Les Arcs, continuing through l'Espace Killy, and ending in Val Thorens. It was one of the more memorable weeks of my skiing life. Lifts do most of the uphill work, so you don't have to be an aerobic superstar to participate, though you must be a competent skier. A good guide service will arrange to have your luggage transferred by road from one valley to the next, relieving you of the burden of carrying a heavy pack for a week.

INSIDE LINE
If you don't rent a car, probably the most convenient way to get to Val d'Isère is by bus, from either the Geneva or the Lyon airport. Train connections are poor.

If you want to bed down in style, stay at the four-star Hotel Christiana. It will probably run

floors or by heading into the high country of l'Espace Killy. Both Val d'Isère and Tignes top out with broad glaciers (open for summer skiing) on which the pitch is very mellow. Any skier of intermediate ability ought to head up to the glacier of La Grande Motte in Tignes on a clear day; the view is something special. And from here, with a

Two skiers on the Solaise Red Run, with the town of Val d'Isère below.

you a little over $200 a day, but when you throw in breakfast and dinner, all sorts of amenities (such as a great fitness center), and a central location at the base of the lifts, it's not a bad deal.

No matter where you stay, don't make long-distance phone calls from your hotel room. Get a phone card and call from a public phone, for about a third of the cost.

Dick's Tea Bar is a Val d'Isère institution, and you've got to go there at least once. Because just about everyone who comes to Val d'Isère feels that way, you might find yourself waiting outside. If so, head for Le Petit Danois instead for après-ski.

Don't worry about visiting Val d'Isère if you don't speak English. Its clientele is international, and the locals are reasonably willing to converse in English, lacking some of the linguistic chauvinism you sometimes encounter in a place like Paris.

RESOURCES

General information: 011-33-479-060-660. Website: www.valdisere.com. Off-piste guide service: Several companies in Val d'Isère and Tignes can guide you off-piste. Among the most reliable are the main ski school, École du Ski Français (011-33-479-060-234) and Evolution 2 (011-33-479-411-672). Bon Ski (1-888-9BON-SKI; www.bonski.com) leads guided valley-to-valley excursions.

Verbier

The heli-skiing terrain, like most everything about Verbier, is of the highest order

On a clear day at the summit of Verbier's Mont-Fort, you can pretty much see forever. I stood on the mountaintop with Marcus Bratter, a part-time mountain guide, as the sun burned a hole in a cobalt sky and the harsh light brought every slope contour and rock outcropping into the crystalline focus of an Ansel Adams photograph. A chiaroscuro of blinding white and blue black shadow was brushed across the cirques and basins below us.

To the west stood the shrugged giant of Mont Blanc, its glaciers forming a mirror to the sky. To the east was the swaybacked pyramid of the Matterhorn, and around us the Alps seemed to march on forever toward a 360-degree horizon of saw-toothed peaks. It was the sort of view that you might be willing to cross continents to witness, and in fact Bratter had done pretty much just that. He had moved to Verbier from Australia in the '70s, he said, "when the Swiss franc was cheap

Evening view of Verbier, where the chalet roofs "rise up the mountainsides in herringbone uniformity."

Bern

SWITZERLAND

AUSTRIA

Geneva

VERBIER

Alps

Alps

Alps

FRANCE

Mont Blanc

ITALY

and drugs were plenty." He moved and he stayed, because he figured that if he was going to live his life in the mountains, he'd have to search long and hard to find a place to top Verbier.

I was preparing with Bratter to make my first run at Verbier, and I was only beginning to understand, by looking out at the giant halo of mountains encircling us, the tree dimensions of the place. We first skirted the steep mogul field that spilled down from the summit into the shadows of a deep basin, while above us ribs of rock separated banded chutes of snow. Traversing the basin, we began a steep descent of the Tortin face, puckered with gullies and seams and fed by still more chutes spilling out from between serrated rock buttresses. Far below, the pitch leveled off, but with each turn we didn't seem to come much closer to level ground. It was an illusion that perhaps more than any other feature of the run impressed upon me how big Verbier really is.

And so it went. At last reaching the base of the Tortin aerial tram, we jogged up a couple of short lifts and continued from there to the slopes of Veysonnaz, where the snow had been made

deliberately icy for a recent World Cup race. Eventually we bottomed out in the village of Veysonnaz itself, 6,700 vertical feet below where we had begun.

This was Verbier flexing its muscles openly, demonstrating that if you are looking for long, steep, wide-open runs—descents that, like the view from the top, seem to go on forever—you have certainly come to the right place. Yet Verbier in its entirety reveals itself with far more subtlety than that. Its rock-buttressed ridges conceal an extraordinary number of chutes and couloirs and open faces of untracked snow. Such hidden treasures, secreted amidst walls of seemingly impassible rock, are a big reason why Verbier has gained worldwide renown as a center for off-piste exploration. In places where you think skiing ought to be impossible, where there appears to be nothing but rock, a sliver of snow appears, leading to a wider opening and something wider still, until suddenly you find yourself on a great face of untracked snow. All you can do is marvel at your good fortune and wonder how in the world you got to where you are.

I discovered just how this works a day after skiing with Marcus, when I joined up with a guide

---

AT A GLANCE

LOCATION 110 miles southeast of Geneva, Switzerland

SEASON December–May

IN-BOUNDS 1 2 3 ④ 5

OFF-PISTE 1 2 3 4 ⑤

SNOW 1 2 3 ④ 5

TERRAIN ACREAGE Over 20,000 acres

VERTICAL RISE 5,850 feet in Verbier itself; close to 7,000 feet in the entire resort area

AVERAGE ANNUAL SNOWFALL 300 inches

and a group of French skiers. The guide spoke little English and I spoke little French, so as he explained the plan of action to the group, I was obliged to take on abstract faith that he knew what he was doing and where he was going.

Skiing down from Mont-Gelé, we traversed across a flat basin toward what appeared to be a dead end, a small tabletop plateau of snow surrounded by sharp rocks. We had to scramble on our skis up to the top of the plateau, and when we arrived there our guide again began to deliver further instructions in unintelligible French. The other members of the party appeared to be listening intently, leading me to suspect that we were about to enter a tricky phase in our adventure. Completing his spiel, our leader turned and seemed to disappear into the maw of the rocks.

I slid a bit closer to the vertex of his disappearance and discovered what had happened: He had slipped through a very steep little gutter of snow between the rocks, not much more than 10 feet wide and perhaps 200 feet long. It looked like a back alley set at a 45-degree pitch and seemed to end in a cul-de-sac of granite. We all followed, one at a time, cautiously and somewhat dubiously. Yet once we had navigated that dicey passage, lo and behold—the world opened up. We all stood below the rocks and above a broad, open face of pure, perfect powder, perhaps 1,000 vertical feet in all. Who would have known?

That's classic Verbier for you: From seemingly nothing a great run is made. After completing that run, we proceeded to behave in classically European style—we went to an on-mountain refuge to refresh ourselves with food and drink.

The Cabane du Mont-Fort sits on a rubbled, windswept promontory overlooking the main Mont-Fort basin. It is a refuge in a very literal sense—a haven for mountain travelers in general and those escaping storms in particular. Travelers on the Haute Route from Chamonix to Zermatt often stop here, for it marks an approximate halfway point in the journey. In a pinch—in a particularly vicious storm—the refuge can house as many as 100 lost souls, an accommodation that initially struck me as improbable in surveying the somewhat cramped, dimly lit interior. But everything was designed for a meticulously efficient use of space, including racks for boots beneath the ceiling, to clear floor space. I could imagine that, as a place to spend the night with 99 others, it might actually make for a neatly cozy encampment in which to weather out a storm.

And storms can close in on these mountains with savage and astonishing speed. As we sat around the worn wooden table eating sweet tarts and drinking coffee, descending clouds began to darken the windows with an ominous light. By the time we left, it was snowing hard and the visibility had become so poor that the only way we made it to the bottom was by following what looked like a red beacon—our guide's suit.

Almost immediately after that, the skies caved in, and for two days snow fell, and winds of over 50 miles an hour howled around the mountain summits. The lifts were shut down; the high-Alpine

Above: A backcountry hut on des Pantalons Blanc. Opposite: Verbier is recognized worldwide as a center for lift-serviced off-piste exploration. Overleaf: For way off-piste, check out the back side of Mont-Fort.

visibility was nil and the avalanche danger off the scale. The one escape from this weather madness was gluttony—drinking beer and wine all day and fattening up on raclette, the fonduelike concoction of potato, cheese, and vegetables that is ubiquitous in the high Alps. When I'd literally had my fill of doing that in Verbier, I traveled by train to the charmingly quiescent village of Orsières in a neighboring valley, for more wine drinking in a small café there. Returning to Verbier, I noted that the chalet roofs, rising up the mountainsides in herringbone uniformity, had collected tufts of new snow in a postcard image of hopefulness. If the weather were ever to clear, what a powder day it would be.

In the Alps, inconsistency is the one reliable parameter. The snow can be fabulous, the snow can be dreadful. A beautiful day in the sun can be followed by a two-day, all-encompassing storm. To be sure, that can be true about winter in the mountains the world over, but the swings in the moods of weather and snow seem particularly pronounced in the Alps. I remember, for example, coming to Kitzbühel, Austria, one January when the snowpack was so thin that you could see the grass peeking through it. Three days later, it had snowed ten feet. You never know.

Verbier is not immune to such highs and lows, as the 48-hour storm I experienced proved. But one of the reasons it stands out among Alpine resorts is that, all things considered, its snow conditions are about as reliable as you'll find anywhere in Europe. I'm not sure quite how to explain it; the Alps, with their extraordinary verticality, have a way of fostering meteorological peculiarities. Weather gets trapped, funneled, spun around, warmed and cooled, and subdivided into dozens of microclimates, and the effect on the snow is irregular. Perhaps Verbier is at the core of a mystical, meteorological vortex. Whatever the reason, the snow in Verbier is typically cold, dry, and plentiful and replenished regularly.

The mountain opened gradually after that storm had passed; it would be more than a full day before the avalanche control crew would deem the Mont-Fort summit safe. That might suggest, before the summit opening, a crippling diminution of skiable terrain. But you could still ascend the lifts to Attelas, a 9,150-foot peak, 4,200 vertical feet above Verbier. More than 4,000 vertical is not exactly inconsequential.

The sun returned fiercely again, a force just as intense as it had been on my first day atop Mont-Fort. I rode up to the Attelas summit with a friend, and we set about to find some untracked snow. We made our way along a ridgeline, with spiked rocks protruding like shark's teeth from the snow. The potential for damage to our skis was considerable, but we pressed on. Eventually, we reached a saddle in the ridge, and wouldn't you know it—Verbier rewarded our exploration, as is its tendency. Below us, the surface of a steep chute was a rumpled bed of moguls, clear evidence that we weren't the first to discover this spot. But the chute was a short bottleneck that led to an enormous bowl in which large tracts of barely tracked powder remained to be skied.

We bombed down through the new snow,

Bivouac on des Pantalons Blanc, a vast off-piste area behind Mont-Fort and between Verbier and Zermatt.

Verbier is among the best resorts in the Alps for fresh, dry snow.

jumped off rocks, took photos, and eventually reached the tree line and a groomed run that led to the base of the La Combe chairlift. It doesn't get much better than that: powder and brilliant sunlight, a panoramic view, and a run of perhaps 3,000 or more vertical feet. After wending our way through the lift network back to the Attelas summit, tiptoeing across the rocks, and repeating the run, we certainly did not lament the fact that Mont-Fort was closed.

When we were done, we took the long, winding run through the forest and back to town, a normally festive place that on this particular afternoon seemed especially animated. New snow and sunshine can reinvigorate the spirit of any ski town anywhere in the world. An hour or so later the sun began to set, painting the distant mountains with the pink of alpenglow, and that's the way any day of skiing ought to end—with the memory of a fabulous day, with the last whisper of daylight still on the mountaintops, and with a beer in your hand.

WHAT TO EXPECT
IN-BOUNDS

There is Verbier and there is something called the Four Valleys, and all of it runs together in such a way as to leave entirely unclear what falls under which rubric—where one valley begins and the next ends. When is Verbier officially not Verbier? It's hard to say. It makes more sense to me to think of Verbier as one monolithic resort connected by lifts and accessible from several different towns within a 20-mile radius. Verbier itself is just one town—the largest, to be sure—among 10 or more towns from which you can access the terrain.

Despite its size, Verbier is not a difficult resort (at least by often confusing Alpine standards) in which to find your way around. One of the reasons for the relatively easy navigation is that Verbier, unlike many other multi-valley resorts in Europe, rises to a single, central peak, the 10,989 foot Mont-Fort. Mont-Fort serves well as a focal reference from which the resort fans out.

Verbier is known for the good quality of its snow, and at least two reasons might account for this. Shielded from the sun by steep, rocky ridges, many of Verbier's best runs are not exposed to direct solar warmth, under which snow can deteriorate quickly. In addition, the layout of the terrain is such that it is relatively easy to choose exposures where the snow is at its best. At most resorts, with a single, predominant exposure, that's more difficult.

Mont-Fort, Verbier's high point, might be the resort's best-known geographical feature, but whether this is the place to find the best steep skiing is debatable. The main face of Mont-Fort tends to turn into a giant mogul field—fine when the snow is soft, but a chore at other times. For my money, some of the best steeps in Verbier lead down from Mont-Gelé and Chassoure to the Tortin base. The runs here have everything—steep chutes, open powder fields, a few flat spots for relief, and a little tree skiing thrown in at the end.

There's not much tree skiing in Verbier itself, but on snowy days, local experts often head across the valley to Bruson. Not only does this area feature fine, steep lines through the trees, but it's also overlooked by most visitors, so fresh tracks are relatively easy to find.

Verbier's reputation for steep off-piste terrain is justified, but there's plenty of in-bounds stuff here for less skilled skiers, too. Both the Lac des Vaux and La Chaux areas have a number of gentle runs, all above tree line—great for a sunny day. The drawback is that the runs are relatively short given Verbier's size. There's also decent intermediate skiing at Veysonnaz and Thyon, good choices on low-visibility days, when you want to stay below the tree line. The drawback here can be the low elevation and hence less assurance of quality snow.

A good place for intermediates to escape crowds is the Savoleyres area just above Verbier itself. Whereas most skiers rush to go up the main Ruinette lifts, the first stage in ascending to Mont-Fort, Savoleyres is often overlooked. But like Veysonnaz and Thyon, its elevation is lower, and hence the snow is less-reliable than higher on the mountain, particularly early and late in the season.

Verbier for novices? The concept is not quite oxymoronic, but there are certainly better places in the world to learn to ski or snowboard.

One note to all who venture out into the vastness of Verbier: Leave plenty of time to make your way back to Verbier or wherever you began the day. Being stranded in the wrong valley when the lifts have closed at day's end isn't the worst predicament, but it can result in an expensive taxi ride home.

OFF-PISTE

Within the resort proper, opportunities abound. The trick is finding the good stuff. Often you can see a line that looks great from afar, but figuring out how to get there is another story. As mentioned, access to some of the best lines is often a hidden slot through the rocks. If you can find the opening, you're golden; if not, you could be in big trouble. The characteristic off-piste run at Verbier involves a steep, short chute through the rocks, leading to a long, open face covered with fresh powder. To wit: Barry's Bowl, visible from the Cabane du Mont-Fort. You might find yourself hopscotching over rocks barely covered by snow as you pick your way through the introductory chute. But once into the bowl itself, the skiing is absolutely glorious.

There is off-piste and then there's *way* off-piste. For the latter, the main route at Verbier begins as a series of couloirs and chutes down the back side of Mont-Fort. It's very steep stuff, but after a couple of thousand feet, the pitch mellows out in an enormous, treeless plateau called le Grand Desert. This route leads to a frozen lake, Lac de Clueson, and eventually back to the ski area—a long, long run far away from the lifts. It's spectacular, high-Alpine terrain, in which getting lost is relatively easy. Be sure to go with a guide.

If that's not wildly off-piste enough, there is one other option. Verbier is among the few resorts in Europe that offer helicopter skiing. If you have stood at the top of Mont-Fort on a clear day and looked at the mountains around you, you know that the heli-skiing terrain, like most everything about Verbier, is of the highest order.

INSIDE LINE

A great place to stay in Verbier is the Hotel Montpelier (027-771-6131, hotelmontpelier.ch). It's quiet, attractive, and has an excellent restaurant. Unfortunately, like most things in Switzerland, it's not especially cheap—close to $200 per person, with breakfast and dinner included.

At day's end, the English-speaking freeriding crowd tends to congregate at Le Pub Mont-Fort, simply known as Le Pub. If you're looking for insider information on where the best snow is, this is a great place to get it.

The Swiss seem to like robustly filling food. If you want to eat like a local, feast on highly caloric fondue, raclette, and *rosti*, a kind of potato hash that is German-speaking Switzerland's national dish. And wash it all down with inexpensive wine from the Valais region or with *genepe*, a potent, regional liqueur distilled from the mash of Alpine flowers.

The six-day "Around Mont Blanc" lift pass allows you to ski a number of resorts in the general Mont Blanc region, including Verbier in Switzerland, Courmayer in Italy, and Chamonix in France.

Verbier is such an international resort that it's sometimes hard to tell you're actually in

Heli-skiers track virgin powder. Verbier is among the few resorts in Europe that offer helicopter skiing.

Switzerland. English (particularly with an Australian accent) is widely spoken, and the Swiss, for the most part, are multilingual. Generally speaking, the Swiss who live in Verbier are a far looser bunch than the more orderly, sober types you tend to meet in a place like Geneva.

RESOURCES

General information: 011-41-27-775-3888. Websites: www.verbier.ch, www.televerbier.ch.; www.skiswitzerland.com. Off-piste guide service: Contact the ski school (011-41-27-775-3363) or the Bureau des Guides La Fantastique (011-41-27-771-4141). La Fantastique can also arrange heli-skiing.

St. Anton

There is an edge of daring in the air,
an urgency to take things to the edge of adventure

T he snow wouldn't stop when I last visited St. Anton, in March of the year 2000. For six days and six nights, the stuff kept piling up on the mountains of the Arlberg region and the streets of town, turning the place into both a land of enchantment and a war zone.

Every morning at seven o'clock sharp, the avalanche control work would begin as the booming of an invisible battle being waged beyond the smoky veil of falling snow. Detonations would reverberate from one side of the valley to the other before dissolving into a faint, throbbing blur of dissonance and, finally, eerie silence.

The trains to and from Zurich and Innsbruck continued to come and go, more or less on schedule, but otherwise travel through the Arlberg region was almost completely shut down. From time to time, given the heightened avalanche risk, much of the skiing terrain was shut down, too.

Evening run. St. Anton receives more snow than anywhere else in the Alps.

Such circumstances, however, didn't faze most of the vacationers in St. Anton. The surfeit of snow might have cut into their skiing opportunities, but so what? There's more to St. Anton than sliding downhill. St. Anton is extremely popular among Britons and Scandinavians, both of whom come in no small part because the cost of a drink in Austria is far, far cheaper than it is back home.

One evening, with the snow thick on the town's main street, a fellow on skis went gliding past me and slammed into a lamppost. He fell to the ground, apparently unhurt, and cheerfully asked if I might be kind enough to help him back to his feet. He was only slightly less inebriated than a well-kempt blonde woman, in an all-white ski outfit and still on skis, who made quite a spectacle of herself at the town's main railroad crossing. With her skis hung up on the snowless steel of the tracks, she screamed for help from her boyfriend, who had somehow made the crossing successfully. "I need another drink!" she yelled, as if alcoholic fortification might provide some magical propulsion.

Make no mistake about it: Many people

come to St. Anton for social engagement as much as for winter sport. It's been that way for at least a half century, even if the tone and mood of the times has changed. Ferdl Nöbl, a St. Anton native and former ski instructor to the rich and famous, told me how different things were in the '50s. The partying was more urbane, even stately, back then. Such quaint institutions as five-o'clock tea were observed, and evenings brought live swing bands in hotel lobbies, champagne, and tuxedos.

The atmosphere is considerably rowdier and dressed-down now. People tend to quit their skiing at around three in the afternoon and, rather than retire to afternoon tea, they head for raucous places like the Krazy Kanguruh, a chalet bar on the lower slopes of the main ski area.

There they drink, dance, and sing until well after nightfall, at which point they attempt to ski back to town, in the darkness and often in a state of considerable intoxication. It's comic and dangerous and people do get hurt, which seems, perversely, to be part of all the fun. So that's how you can end up, at a respectable dinner hour, with a woman stuck on her skis on the train tracks and

---

AT A GLANCE

LOCATION About 120 miles southeast of Zurich, Switzerland	**TERRAIN ACREAGE** 12,000 acres
SEASON December–April	**VERTICAL RISE** Roughly 5,000 feet
IN-BOUNDS 1 2 3 ④ 5	**AVERAGE ANNUAL SNOWFALL** 330 inches
OFF-PISTE 1 2 3 ④ 5	
SNOW 1 2 3 4 ⑤	

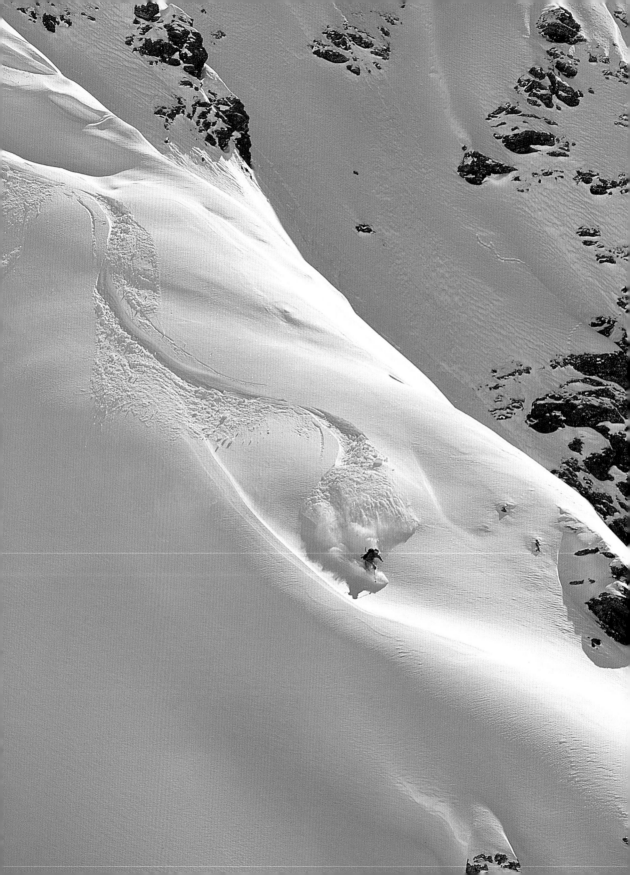

some guy skiing into a lamppost.

But for all of that, St. Anton is foremost an impressive place to ski, not the least reason being that it receives more snow than pretty much anywhere else in the Alps. As the snow fell and fell during my week in March, I ventured up onto the mountain with a guide named Wolfgang Birkl, to poke around blindly in the maelstrom in an effort to find safe and satisfying skiing.

The snow limited our options, but that didn't keep Wolfgang from painting a verbal picture of what was possible, of the things we wouldn't be able to do. Wolfgang had much to say about Valluga, at 9,276 feet, the highest peak in the St. Anton area. The off-piste possibilities, Wolfgang said, were all but limitless— wide-open bowls, steep chutes, fabulous snow, long runs. On Valluga, you could ski pretty much forever.

A week earlier, he'd been doing just that. In the final days of a long warm stretch preceding the storm, Wolfgang had led clients on long, fast descents on slopes of perfect corn snow. It was a different story on my first day in St. Anton. I had boarded the cable car that ascends Valluga, and rose up into a cloud of fog and snow. Only a half-dozen or so others were along for the ride, and we eyed one another warily, like card players trying to call a bluff. Would any of us really ski down in this utter whiteout? A couple decided they would, but I was in the majority in taking the safe ride back down in the tram. The next day, with the storm intensifying, the Valluga lift was shut down.

That's why Wolfgang and I headed instead for an area called Schöngraben, literally "beautiful

little valley," although to appreciate this, at least at first, required powers of visualization. With the snow falling and the clouds closing around us, we were skiing in a cocoon of all-white nothingness. This is what can happen in the high Alps, when weather moves in over treeless slopes, and all natural features and contours fold into a single, seamless sheet of white.

Wolfgang navigated brilliantly through knee-deep snow and the void, armed with an intuitive feel for the mountains, honed by years of growing up and guiding in the Arlberg. He was familiar with every small roll and drop-off and change in pitch and fall line, and I simply followed his hazy silhouette, investing in him and his orienteering skills a complete and (almost literally) blind trust.

Upon reaching a small ridge, we came to a stand of fir and larch trees, all ragged looking without their needles. We could make out through the snowy haze the features of the valley we were skiing; at the tree line, where the clouds and fog had thinned, I could make out a series of steep chutes that fed from both sides through the trees into open snowfields, narrowing into a streambed far below. In all, I was looking at 3,000 vertical feet, as a guess, with 5 feet of new snow and not a single other human being in sight. A beautiful little valley indeed.

So we skied it, steep at first before gradually leveling out along the banks of the half-frozen stream. What began as light powder became a dense porridge at lower elevations. We skied all the way into the outskirts of St. Anton and stopped for lunch at a small restaurant on a vacated side street. For a moment, amidst the aromas and *gemütlichkeit*

Opposite: A one- to two-hour hike up the valley beyond Rendl brings you to high-Alpine off-piste skiing. But don't set out for this country before hiring an experienced guide. Above: Time out to catch some rays.

Making turns at Stuben. The interconnected resorts of St. Anton, Lech, Zürs, St. Christoph, and Stuben comprise 85 lifts and 250 miles of marked runs.

of an eatery no self-guided tourist would likely ever find, I felt that I was part of the inner circle, the salt of the St. Anton earth. Wolfgang devoured an enormous plate of roast pork, gravy, and noodles; mountain intuition and a healthy appetite are typically a guide's most outstanding attributes. As we ate, our ski jackets, hanging on a coatrack behind us, steamed from the warming residue of melting snow. We then went up and skied the beautiful little valley all over again.

There are many reasons to think of St. Anton—or the Arlberg in general, including the interconnected resorts of Lech, Zürs, St. Christoph, and Stuben—as representing the soul of Austrian skiing. The enormity of the area—85 lifts and 250 miles of marked runs—is as good a reason as any. The numbers reflect only a

fragment of the possibilities. Unmarked runs, like Schöngraben or the big slopes of Valluga, expand opportunities exponentially.

And if you are game for high-Alpine touring—strapping climbing skins to your skis or snowboard and going for a long hike high and deep in the mountains—the possibilities continue to multiply. Touring is at the core of Arlberg winter life, embedded deeply in its history. The Arlberg Ski Club was founded in 1901, decades before there were lifts. Six local fellows, attired in wool suits and ties and slogging along on heavy hickory skis, made their way overland through the snow from St. Anton to the neighboring village of St. Christoph. After doing so, they became inspired. "Delighted by nature's beauty. . ." and "dedicated to sports," the gentlemen founders wrote, a club would be established "for all fellow enthusiasts of this noble art." No doubt a glass or two of beer or *glühwein* was raised to commemorate the occasion.

Thus does touring in the mountains of the Arlberg become a shared experience with fellow enthusiasts both past and present. The slopes between St. Anton and St. Christoph are all lift serviced now, but an uncountable number of other backcountry excursions still exists. A classic, certainly, involves a one- to two-hour hike up the valley beyond Rendl, the ski lift complex to the southwest of town. Hike up, linger over a picnic lunch, then set off on a long run of 5,000 vertical feet, through the Moostal (the valley of the Moos River), that eventually leads back into town. It is a severe, rugged, and wild world only just beyond the periphery of civilized, urbane St. Anton.

Snow, of course, makes the Arlberg special; the region seems to suck in snowstorms with more regularity and voluminous effect than other areas of the Alps. A day before joining up with Wolfgang, I had skied the open slopes of Rendl in snow that can best be described as perfect—deep, soft, and exploding from my ski tips like bursts of talcum powder with each turn. At lower elevations, the new snow clung to the tall evergreens that resembled an idealized picture in a children's book.

But as much as anything, I like the history of St. Anton. The Arlberg in general and St. Anton in particular stand out importantly in the evolution of skiing; the first real downhill race, the Arlberg Kandahar, was held in St. Anton in 1928. More significantly, Alpine skiing technique—the art of making a ski turn smoothly and efficiently while going downhill—was first developed in St. Anton in the 1920s (see box below).

Of course, as Ferdl Nöbl suggested, things in St. Anton aren't quite what they used to be. Back in the days when people came to St. Anton for a month at a time with their steamer trunks packed with fur coats and black-tie attire, the idea was mainly to spend time in the mountains. No more and no less than that, and the pace was very laid back. You came to the Arlberg to breathe the clean air and soak in the views and maybe go for a long, relaxed ski tour.

Today, in addition to the more youthful and raucous party atmosphere, there is an enhanced edge of daring in the air, a subliminal urgency to take things to the edge of adventure. Guides like Wolfgang Birkl worry about that—about skiers and snowboarders venturing into terrain that is either beyond their ability or in which the snow is dangerously unstable. There's plenty of that kind of terrain and snow around, and the consequences can be severe if you don't know where you're going or what you're doing.

I had my own small moment, skiing alone in an off-piste area near the Kapall lift. At one point the open slope steepened briefly, and as my skis arced more energetically and built more resistance against the deep snow, a slab broke away, about

SCHNEIDER AND RIEFENSTAHL

St. Anton is arguably the birthplace of ski instruction, and the main man behind that was Hannes Schneider, developer of the so-called Arlberg technique. He established the world's first Alpine ski school in 1921, and its fame quickly spread throughout Europe and even to America. If you were to learn how to ski properly, you had to come to St. Anton and spend time under the tutelage of the man known as the Skimeister.

Schneider's celebrity led to movie stardom as well. He collaborated in seminal ski films in the 1920s with such cinematographers as Arnold Franck, the grandfather of mountaineering films.

He also teamed with Leni Riefenstahl, who later became (and remains) a controversial figure in the making of Nazi propaganda movies. Riefenstahl's *Triumph of the Will* is considered a masterpiece both in filmmaking and Nazi proselytizing.

Schneider's career took a very different turn. Unwilling to cast his lot with the Nazi regime, he was tossed in jail for his noncompliant attitude. Eventually he negotiated a release in 1936 and resettled in New Hampshire. But the Nazis were determined to erase every trace of the famous persona of Hannes Schneider. The ski school he had established was stripped of his name and renamed the Arlberg Ski School (Skischule Arlberg), the name it still bears today. The bottom line is this: If you want to go to the source, to the very roots of ski instruction, you must go to St. Anton.

From the summit of Valluga, steep chutes feed into broad, open shoulders of untracked powder.

two feet deep and fifty feet wide. It was not nearly a big enough slide to be called an avalanche, and I remained above it, unscathed. But it sent a clear message about the dangers lurking all over the mountain, of latent avalanches waiting for an unprepared skier or snowboarder to initiate. I had planned on making a grand tour of the Arlberg that afternoon through a kind of hopscotch process of riding lifts and skiing, working northward up the valley from St. Anton to St. Christoph to Zürs and eventually to Lech. But as I watched that slab of snow slide, my wanderlust slid away with it.

Ferdl Nöbl felt the young Scandinavians— "Scandis" as he called them—were particularly guilty of stretching their ambition thin, of taking too many risks, of heading off into potentially

dangerous areas without proper avalanche awareness or gear. I don't know. But I do know that the terrain of the Arlberg, covered with all that snow, is full of temptations that are hard to resist.

WHAT TO EXPECT IN-BOUNDS

St. Anton is just part (the largest part, to be sure) of the Arlberg region, all interconnected by lifts, trails, and the occasional, very short bus ride. The region also includes the towns of Lech, Zürs, St. Christoph, and Stuben. Of the four, St. Anton is certainly the largest, and the sum of its terrain probably the most challenging.

St. Anton's crown jewel is Valluga, its highest peak. A wide variety of terrain is accessible here, from steep powder fields to huge mogul fields to relatively gentle slopes, all above tree line and all surrounded by pyramidlike peaks of granite. The best of Valluga skiing requires a guide, for only guided parties are permitted on the final cable car that goes to the summit. From the summit, steep chutes feed into broad, open shoulders of snow that can remain untracked for days after a storm. The game plan, then, for strong skiers on a clear day after a recent storm is to hire a guide and head straight to the Valluga summit.

If the weather is less than perfect, you'll want to stay lower on the mountain. There is some fine, open tree skiing from the Feldeher-rennügel lift, although to reach the trees requires descending through open, relatively tame terrain. Good tree skiing is also to be had in the Rendl area, across the valley from the main St. Anton complex (Valluga, etc.). Rendl is also an excellent place to go to avoid crowds. Its main drawback is that the runs are relatively short.

There is no shortage of wide-open cruising terrain, particularly in the Kapall and Galzig areas. But if you've got the time and good weather, make a day of it by working your way from St. Anton to Lech and back. Ride the Galzigbahn from St. Anton, ski down into St. Christoph, and continue on (taking a bus to cross the Flexen Pass) into Zürs. Ski a few runs here (the views are among the best in the Arlberg), descend into Lech for lunch, then begin to work your way back to St. Anton. It's a classic, European-style way of skiing, turning a run into a journey rather than just a descent.

OFF-PISTE

Because the Arlberg is so well developed, off-piste runs for the most part are never too far from the beaten track. Valluga, of course, is probably the place to find the best lines. But St. Anton in general attracts a fairly high level of skier, and as a result some of the best lines can get tracked out relatively quickly. Hiring a guide here is sensible not only to be taken to places you wouldn't find yourself, but also to be taken to places where only guided parties are permitted.

Lech and Zürs are known to be frequented by the upper crust—royals and the rich and famous. The long, groomed run with magnificent views is a Lech-and-Zürs staple, and because of that, the good off-piste stuff tends to be overlooked. Guides in Lech and Zürs will insist that they can show you off-piste terrain better than you'll find in St. Anton. That might or might not be true, but the likelihood of finding untracked snow—particularly well after a storm—is probably better.

There are some opportunities, particularly on the Rendl side, to hike and get well away in the high-Alpine country. But to set out without knowing the landscape would not be wise. The familiar, mantric recommendation applies here: Hire a guide.

INSIDE LINE

If you want a taste of the elegance of yesteryear, stay in the St. Antoner Hof or the Alte Post Hotel. But there are also many, many neatly kept guesthouses in St. Anton, where you can get a clean, single room with bath and breakfast for as little as $30 a night.

The Mooserwirt is one of St. Anton's many popular watering holes.

If you want to follow the hard-partying, English-speaking crowd, start après-ski at the Krazy Kanguruh on the lower slopes of St. Anton. Move on from there to the Piccadilly in the heart of town, then end up for dinner at the Underground, a restaurant run by Joan Devey, a transplanted Australian.

St. Anton recently instituted an electronic-scanning ticket system that works beautifully. Just buy a credit card-like ticket, put it in a pocket, and turnstiles scan the ticket before you get on the lift. Very simple, very efficient, very effective.

RESOURCES

General information and snow report: 011-43-05446-2269. Websites: www.skiarlberg.com; www.stantonamarlberg.com. Off-piste guide services: Arrangements can be made through either of the main ski schools—the Skischule Arlberg (011-43-05446-3411) and the Skischule St. Anton (011-43-05446-3563).

THE DISCOVERY ZONE

Crested Butte

Expert boarding with a capital E—steep and gnarly,
tempting and threatening all at once

The spring of 1987. It seems now like a generation ago, and maybe it was. Crested Butte back then was probably best known as a poor man's Aspen, that sin city of the glitterati just to the north, on the far side of the Snowmass–Maroon Bells Wilderness. Crested Butte proudly positioned itself as the anti-Aspen, a place where wealth meant nothing and the average Joe could live as antibourgeois royalty. Archetypal Crested Butters lived in mining era clapboard houses in town, drove rusted, 4x4 pickups with caps, shaved irregularly (certainly the men and possibly the women, too), and rode mountain bikes throughout the winter. They very likely were telemark skiers, because Crested Butte is where telemark skiing experienced a North American renaissance in the late '70s.

One guy who pretty well fit the complete description was Gary Sprung, who was calling me at seven in the morning in my condo at the resort.

Extreme competitor Christian Robertson carves an arc in the backcountry near Irwin Lake Lodge.

Denver ⊛

Rocky Mountains

Grand Junction •

CRESTED BUTTE ⊚

Gunnison •

COLORADO

A 7 A.M. phone call is an intrusion I would normally not abide kindly. But this was different—it had snowed 8 inches overnight, and the day was dawning with a wash of sunlight, beautiful and clear. Sprung, a local photographer, was suggesting we get up to the mountain early and beat the powder-mad crowd.

So shortly after eight, after cajoling the ski patrol into allowing us early lift access, we rode up the mountain and traversed and hiked to the top of the ridge separating the main body of the ski area and the so-called Extreme Limits. When Sprung and I arrived at the ridgetop, not only were we looking at the morning's new blessing of untracked powder but at terrain that presented the illusion of having never been skied before, as if we were the first ever to be there. Just snow, trees, sun, silence, solitude, and the two of us.

We made a couple of dozen turns down the first steep pitch, pausing every once in a while so that Sprung could snap a few photos to capture the magic. The snow had that smoke-light consistency that you typically find in high-altitude Colorado; the base of Crested Butte is above 9,000 feet and the summit near 12,000 feet, and there is simply not enough moisture in the air for

the snow to be anything but light and dry. We cut right into Phoenix Bowl, following a slender line of spruce trees on an even steeper pitch than the first. Launching into each turn felt like jumping from a swimming pool diving board, with the ensuing moment of weightlessness followed by a splash of soft, cold snow.

A POMA lift now does away with the hiking to access the Extreme Limits, and that might or might not be a good development. Many more skiers and snowboarders now go that way—no hiking necessary—and the fresh snow gets tracked up more quickly, and in some places moguls form. But the Extreme Limits terrain remains special and uniquely challenging, part of an overall terrain package that has set Crested Butte in a league of its own.

Alison Gannett, one of a number of talented extreme skiers who has chosen to make Crested Butte her home, says the terrain makes Crested Butte "pretty much the only one of its kind in Colorado." The reason is that the terrain is, in the nomenclature of extreme, *technical,* meaning that a variety of natural elements—an arabesque of trees, rocks, open bowls, variations in fall line and pitch, and so on—comes into play. When a person of Gannett's considerable skill talks of lines that

---

AT A GLANCE

LOCATION South-central Colorado, 25 miles north of Gunnison

SEASON November–March

IN-BOUNDS 1 2 3 ④ 5

BACKCOUNTRY 1 2 ③ 4 5

SNOW 1 ② 3 4 5

TERRAIN ACREAGE 1,160 acres

VERTICAL RISE 2,775 feet

AVERAGE ANNUAL SNOWFALL 280 inches

Top: Skiers and boarders on the top of Scarps Ridge, Irwin Lake Lodge. At over 11,500 feet, it is the highest snowcat-skiing operation in North America. Above: The old town of Crested Butte.

judgmental mistake in choosing your line leads to what Gannett euphemistically calls "mandatory air."

No wonder the U.S. Extreme Skiing Championships have been held in Crested Butte since 1992, and the U.S. Extreme Snowboarding Championships since 1995. Competitors work their way down cleverly, picking a path through razor-sharp rocks and clumps of scrubby, weather-beaten trees, occasionally finding themselves in flight due to mandatory air. Bill Dowell, a safety director for the snowboarding championships, once described the terrain as "expert boarding with a capital E—steep and gnarly, tempting and threatening all at once." Well that's Crested Butte for you.

The 2000 champion, 30-year-old Rex Wehrman from Montezuma, Colorado, won the event in a way that would do Crested Butte's hardcore, antiglamour constitution proud. He showed up with a total of 48 cents left in his bank account, an impoverishment that immediately gained him acceptance into the brotherhood of Crested Butte proletarians. Wehrman then navigated smartly through the maze of rocks and trees decorating a 50-degree slope in Spellbound Bowl, went airborne over a protuberance known as Rabbit Ears Rock, stuck the landing without flinching, and walked away with a winner's check for $5,000. If you can actually make a living skiing radical lines like that—or at least pocket enough money to pay the rent for a couple of months—you attain something close to the status of demigod in the ethos of Crested Butte.

But hold on. . .if you think that's all there is to Crested Butte, this world of gnarliness and mandatory air, you're mistaken, because Crested Butte turns out to have a schizophrenic streak. There is more than one Crested Butte. When you drive up to the resort from town, looping around the hulk of the mountain, you are confronted by a network of oh-so-gentle slopes. Preschool kids can feel comfortable here. I felt comfortable enough to try telemarking for the first time.

It is a mellow pancake of a mountain, full of

can "scare the living crap out of you," you know it can be pretty serious stuff.

But *technical* at Crested Butte is more than just a veiled adjectival reference to confrontations with raw fear. It means you need a variety of skills—the ability to make big, sweeping turns or quick, precise turns; an orienteering ability to assess terrain and choose an appropriate line; an ability to stop on a dime if necessary. Or it might possibly (though not necessarily) mean an ability to jump and land with rock-solid stability, in case a

trails meandering through the mixed aspen-and-spruce forests and over folds and rolls in the landscape. You could spend a week at Crested Butte and remain absolutely oblivious to the presence of all the technical, extreme stuff, almost all of which is shielded from view from the base of the area. The result is that Crested Butte is popular with ordinary folk from such non-snow worlds as Texas and Oklahoma. So what if that contradicts the image of severity that Extreme Limits, the dual extreme championships, and a general aura of extreme that Crested Butte otherwise commands in the collective national consciousness? The Texans and Oklahomans load up the family van, make the overnight drive through Pueblo, Salida, and Gunnison in southern Colorado, and spend a happy week without ever coming close to mandatory air.

There is more than one Crested Butte in a more literal way, too, for there are two towns: Crested Butte (the original) and Mount Crested

THE NOTORIOUS COLORADO SNOWPACK

Among experienced backcountry travelers, the Colorado snowpack has a terrible reputation. It is, says extreme skier Chris Davenport, "one of the worst snowpacks anywhere in the world." Between 1985 and 1999, Colorado was far and away the leading state in the United States in avalanche fatalities, reporting more than the states of California, Montana, Utah, and Wyoming combined. That's why people who venture into the high Colorado backcountry in winter must do so with extra caution.

First, a quick matter of definition: *Snowpack* refers to the accumulated snow on any mountain slope. It typically consists of several layers, a result of storms and wind action over a period of time. The most important thing that makes a snowpack safe—that is, unlikely to avalanche—is bonding between the various layers. Certain types of snow, and certain types of snow crystals, bond together well. But all it takes is one weak layer—or one weak bond between layers—to create a potentially dangerous situation.

Strong bonding is not a feature of the Colorado snowpack. In large part, that's because the snow that falls at high Colorado elevations is typically very dry, light snow. That's the kind of snow that might seem alluring to powder skiers, but without much moisture, it lacks the glue to stick well to the snow beneath it. In addition, the dry snow tends to deteriorate (primarily due to sun exposure and the weight of snow from subsequent storms) in a way that

continued on page 126

continued from page 125

further discourages bonding with new layers.

The last hazardous element in the equation is wind; the Colorado Rockies above tree line are often hit by high winds. The result is a phenomenon called wind loading. This manifests itself most obviously in the formation of cornices, which can break off and trigger avalanches. But more insidiously, wind loading can distribute a deep layer of unstable snow on a slope that might appear relatively benign.

Venturing anywhere into the high, exposed backcountry in winter calls for extreme caution. Unfortunately, the gods of snow tease us dangerously; 90 percent of all avalanches occur on slopes with a steepness of between 30 and 45 degrees, the same steepness that is ideal for powder skiing.

What measures of caution should be taken? First, always have the right safety gear in the backcountry—an avalanche transceiver, a shovel, and a telescoping ski pole to probe with. Second, be keenly observant; if you see evidence of recent slides, for example—particularly on exposures and slope angles where you might expect to be skiing—chances are the snow is unstable. Third, test the snow, by digging pits in the snowpack to check for weak layers and by doing so-called sheer tests, to determine where two snow layers might separate. If you expect to spend a lot of time in the backcountry, learn these techniques by taking an avalanche safety course with an expert. And finally, stay informed. Radio stations in the mountains often broadcast avalanche conditions, typically rated low, moderate, high, and extreme. If conditions are high or extreme, stay away.

The Colorado Avalanche Information Center (CAIC) (303-499-9650; www.caic.state.co.us) is a terrific source of avalanche information and up-to-the-minute conditions throughout the state. The CAIC also conducts avalanche safety seminars. For more general information, the American Avalanche Association (www.avalanche.org) is also a good source. And the Cyberspace Snow and Avalanche Center (www.csac.org) has a worldwide listing of regional phone numbers for avalanche conditions.

Butte (the latter-day resort town). Those citizens of the '70s and '80s who have stuck around— who have matured and started families and who are connected to the place as if it were a physical part of themselves—have tried hard to withstand the corrupting incursions of tourism. In Crested Butte, funkiness is a far nobler concept than convenience or slick modernity.

That's not to say that elements of tourist culture haven't infiltrated, but even those that have fall into the retro-chic category. Preservation efforts—protective ordinances and so on—have gone far to retain the look and feel of an old mining town reinvented as a ski town. So the clapboard homes are still here, but probably with a fresh coat of paint and perhaps housing a restaurant, gift gallery, or ice-cream parlor.

The resort town of Mount Crested Butte, by contrast, is all modern high-rise buildings that look sturdy enough to withstand nuclear holocaust. It is a town almost entirely devoted to supporting the business of skiing and snowboarding—a cluster of hotels, condos, restaurants, bars, and shops. Mount Crested Butte is the American equivalent of a French "purpose-built resort," a place like Courchevel or Tignes where, to my eye, pure function almost entirely supersedes architectural elegance.

Well, so be it, and you know—it works. Bed down up at the resort town, to be close in the morning to any new-fallen snow that might

Arcing a steep turn above the resort town of Mount Crested Butte.

have arrived overnight, and socialize down in the old town. Take advantage of the best that both have to offer.

The official numbers say that there are 1,160 acres of terrain here, a figure that sounds precise enough to be believable. But I don't believe it. "I've lived here for more than 10 years and am still skiing lines I've never skied before," Gannett says, and that sounds more like it. Maybe it's just the intriguing complexity of the place that makes every run at Crested Butte seem altogether different from the one immediately preceding it. Whatever it is, and whatever the true acreage, we ought to take Gannett's word for it: Crested Butte is pretty much the only one of its kind in Colorado.

WHAT TO EXPECT

IN-BOUNDS

Extreme is Crested Butte's claim to everlasting fame. Crested Butte proclaims that it has "more lift-served double-black-diamond adventure terrain than any other ski area in the Rockies." I'm not sure that that's entirely accurate (have these people ever heard of Jackson Hole?), but it's not far off.

Most skiing in Colorado, where the tree line is unusually high (around 11,000 feet), is on trails cut through the trees. Crested Butte's high-end terrain, however, is very different. The bowls on the back (or north-facing) side of the mountain—the North Face, Spellbound Bowl, Phoenix Bowl, and Third Bowl—are characterized by open slopes, widely spaced trees, cliff bands, and rock-line chutes. In other words, you pick your own line rather than follow a designated trail. The same goes for a steep cluster of trails on the front side of the mountain, including Banana, Peel, Forest, and Hot Rocks.

One drawback to this terrain is that the underpinnings are very rocky. A fair amount of

Nightfall on the northwest side of Crested Butte Mountain showing more than 50 percent of the skiable terrain.

snow cover is necessary before the terrain is skiable; early- and late-season skiing can be limited. When the trails are open, extra caution is still called for if the snow cover is thin; a fall under such conditions can be painful or injurious.

If you come to Crested Butte seeking steep, gnarly, technical terrain, you won't be disappointed. Come seeking long, flowing intermediate runs, and you might not be so happy. The lack of pure intermediate stuff is the area's major shortcoming. There are a few decent cruising runs in Paradise Bowl, but the pitch is so mellow that the average intermediate would probably be bored after a day or two.

That said, I wouldn't hesitate to recommend Crested Butte as a place to learn to ski or snowboard. Runs from the Keystone lift are unusually long for novice runs, and they're pretty to boot, winding through spruce and aspen thickets surrounded by terrific views, of mountains both near and far. After a few days of skiing the Keystone runs, most novices should be ready to step up to Paradise Bowl for their first taste of intermediate-level terrain.

One note to snowboarders: There are a couple of flat areas on the mountain, in particular the run-out from Third Bowl and Phoenix Bowl to the base of the East River lift. If you've got one handy, you might want to strap a collapsible pole to your pack, to help maintain momentum when the going gets slow.

BACKCOUNTRY

There is essentially no backcountry immediately beyond the ski area boundaries. For anyone with the means or ambition to venture farther afield, however, opportunities abound, if you happen to have the gear to make it happen. It has become popular among local backcountry skiers to use snowmobiles to shuttle in the backcountry.

The popular place to go is up to Keblar Pass and on from there to the Anthracite Mountains or to Irwin Lake Lodge. In either case, it's mostly wide-open, high-alpine terrain, and you'll have to use climbing skins to get to the really good stuff. But lord, does it snow—Irwin Lake Lodge reports an annual snowfall of 600 inches, making it arguably the snowiest place in all of Colorado. As a result, avalanche safety precautions and savvy are essential here.

Probably the most sensible thing to do is contact Irwin Lake Lodge, which runs a first-rate snowcat-skiing operation. The lodge caters mainly to multiday visitors, but accepts one-day skiers and snowboarders if space is available. The terrain, roughly 2,000 vertical feet worth, is for the most part not exceptionally steep and is doable by anyone with intermediate-level skills. The views alone, of the Maroon Bells–Snowmass Wilderness from the high ridge above the lodge, make the experience worthwhile.

INSIDE LINE

For pure entertainment value, check in at Club Med (www.clubmed.com) at the base of the mountain. It's a "family village," meaning that nightly entertainment involves such stuff as 10-year-olds and Club Med GEs ("gentle employees") dancing the *macarena*. The rooms, however, are spacious and the location, right at the base of the lifts, can't be beat. For less hubbub and more local flavor, check in at the Elk Mountain Lodge B&B (800-374-6521, www.elkmountainlodge.net) in the old town of Crested Butte.

The Mexican food at Donita's (970-349-6674), a popular locals hangout in the old town of Crested Butte, is great, but you might never taste it—the margaritas are huge and powerful. For high-end dining, the place to go is Soupçon (970-349-5448)—haute cuisine served in a rustic, log cabin-like setting.

Check snow conditions before you book your travel arrangements to Crested Butte. Storm pat-

Top: Charging off the top of Spellbound Bowl in an off-piste area on the north face of the mountain. Above: The town of Crested Butte is proud of a certain antiglamour funkiness.

terns are irregular; sometimes it absolutely dumps at Crested Butte, but I've also been there when the snow cover has been so thin that most of the good stuff (such as the Extreme Limits) was closed.

RESOURCES

General information: 970-349-2333. Central reservations: 800-607-0050. Website: www.crestedbutte-ski.com. Backcountry guide service: Call Irwin Lake Lodge (888-GO-IRWIN) for guided snowcat skiing.

The Big Mountain

The mountain is a 3,000-acre treasure chest of first-rate tree skiing

The author, for whom long, high-speed runs are among the Big Mountain's main attractions.

I t was back in the mid-'30s that the first few pioneers, guys like Lyle Rutherford, began skiing at the Big Mountain. Rutherford was a tough-as-nails young railroad man working for the Great Northern Railroad, which passed (and still passes) through nearby Whitefish. He was something of a roughneck in those days, with a penchant for getting into fistfights on his off days in town, and he finally decided he'd had enough of that.

So he joined with a handful of other skiing enthusiasts and built a cabin up on the mountain. They'd drive their Ford Model A's up the road until the plowed surface ran out, hike the rest of the way to the cabin, then climb up to ski down through the tree-freckled snowfields and through the more closely spaced trees covered in rime-encrusted snow. With that, the foundations for something to be called the Hell-Roaring Ski Club were literally laid, and skiing at the Big

Mountain was born.

I spoke with Rutherford in the late '90s, shortly before he passed away, and he was still pretty pleased with what he and his partners had done decades earlier. "We were so damned proud of that cabin," he told me. "Of us regulars, maybe 10 guys would stay there, and we had a lot of women, too. But if anybody began smartin' up with the ladies, he'd get his ass kicked. We went up there to ski, not to fool around."

These many years later, Rutherford might find that he still has plenty of cross-generational soul brothers keeping that original spirit alive. Every winter now, it seems, an itinerant army of 20- and 30-somethings appear at the Big Mountain—alpine skiers, a disproportionate number of telemarkers, and snowboarders, all serious about what they're doing; no fooling around. These winter sport gypsies take up temporary (or perhaps permanent) residence in Whitefish because it is one of the last places in America where you can work at a meager-paying job and still have enough time and pocket change to ski 150 days in a winter. It's the old ski bum formula for satisfaction and success.

The Big Mountain is perfect for the gypsies. It's never crowded; on a big day, maybe a thousand or so skiers show up, and once dispersed across 3,000 acres, they disappear into the immensity of the terrain. Even if a crowd were to assemble, escape is easy into backcountry terrain that begins right at the edge of the ski area boundary and rolls on almost continuously into distant Glacier National Park.

With more than 300 inches of snow a year, there's plenty of snow that barely gets tracked out, and with a 360-degree exposure, there's always some sort of decent snow to ski, no matter what the weather. The mountain forever rewards anyone with an exploratory inclination; it is a 3,000-acre treasure chest of first-rate tree skiing. And it is a mountain that changes in character from one day to the next, reinvented by mood swings in the weather. Never a dull moment at the Big Mountain.

I've skied the Big Mountain on warm, see-forever days in spring, when the jutting peaks of Glacier National Park are pasted to the northeastern horizon and when the green of spring spreads

AT A GLANCE

LOCATION Northwestern Montana, 6 miles northwest of Whitefish, 130 miles north of Missoula

SEASON December–mid-April

IN-BOUNDS 1 2 ③ 4 5

BACKCOUNTRY 1 2 3 ④ 5

SNOW 1 2 ③ 4 5

TERRAIN ACREAGE 3,000 acres

VERTICAL RISE 2,500 feet

AVERAGE ANNUAL SNOWFALL 300 inches

out in the vast, alluvial sweep of the Flathead Valley to the south. A glossy film comes over the surface of the snow, producing a nacreous sheen under the sun on the Big Mountain's south- and east-facing terrain.

But I've also skied at the Big Mountain on days that would have been dreadful and disheartening anywhere else, when fog has shrouded the mountain in a pall of passionless gray. Skiing on days like that at the Big Mountain can be a mystical, comical gas, maybe even more entertaining than skiing on those clear, blue days. Speeding around amidst the Big Mountain's famed snow ghosts—trees thoroughly encased in rime and snow—and running a semiblind steeplechase over the wind-created rolls and lips in the surface of the snow is weird, crazy fun. It can become a bit like a child's game, like a scavenger hunt or musical chairs in motion. You start out with a group and you all head down the mountain with no prescribed route, everyone taking a different line of personal choice through the trees. The preset plan is usually to have the whole group reassemble at the bottom, but that almost never happens. In the fog and the trees and the mesmerizing lure of deep snow, people simply disappear.

Trees, trees, trees. They are the fundamental reason to spend time at the Big Mountain, if you ask me. Dense at the bottom, they thin out gradually and naturally toward the balding summit and become more snow covered and ghostly the higher you go. They provide an essential visual reference on those foggy days, of course, but they also honeycomb the terrain. It is a mountain of thousands of interconnected, tree-lined chambers, and getting from top to bottom can become a labyrinthine journey from one chamber to the next. You start in a glade or small clearing, make a few turns until the open space runs out, slip through gaps in the trees to find new openings and new stashes of untracked snow, and so on. And when you return to the top, intent on skiing approximately the same line again, you end up somewhere entirely different. Such is the varied topography of the mountain, with its interconnected bowls and diverging ridgelines and subtleties in exposure, that choosing a line is usually a happenstance thing, governed by ad hoc, on-the-fly course deviations.

There are a few noteworthy exceptions. On a clear, warm day when the snow is soft, speedballing is the operative concept. I've been a part of that scene—charging down the mountainside with packs of local skiers, telemarkers, and snowboarders in what becomes a madcap chase to the bottom. Three intermediate runs—Inspiration, Toni Matt, or the Big Ravine—make it possible. They are long, wide-open, consistently pitched for the most part, and sparsely populated, and they reach from the summit to the base. There are surprisingly few runs like that in America—runs on which you can throw pedal to the metal for 2,000 or more vertical feet.

In fact, the Big Mountain has a rich history of such high-speed antics. It begins, perhaps, with the likes of Lyle Rutherford, who said to me, "I liked to ski fast. Poking around wasn't for me." Twice the Big Mountain hosted the U.S. national

Opposite: Riding the steep Picture Chutes in Hellroaring Basin, an area with some great tree lines.
Above: The Bier Stube at the Big Mountain embodies the unpretentious character of the Whitefish area.

Skiing into the North Bowl Chute, one of the Big Mountain's few very steep lines.

championships, in 1949 and 1951, and those racers certainly weren't dawdlers, either. Nor was Toni Matt, the man who lent his name to the trail and who came to the Big Mountain in 1948 to head the ski school. Matt was a legend in speed, having schussed the precipitous headwall at Tuckerman Ravine on Mount Washington in New Hampshire in 1939—still one of the most talked-about single runs in American skiing history.

Tommy Moe, the 1994 Olympic Downhill Champion, grew up skiing at the Big Mountain, and although he's since moved on, his stepfather, Cliff Persons, still skis regularly there. His favorite thing, Cliff told me, is to bomb down Inspiration "with my old buddies who don't like to turn too much." If all you want to do is go fast and turn little, the Big Mountain on a clear day is at the center of the universe.

There is nothing gaudy or ostentatious about either the Big Mountain or Whitefish, and thank goodness for that. Whitefish is a railroad town only minimally tinged by the tourism brought in by Glacier National Park, 25 miles to the west, and by the Big Mountain. Even as development on the outskirts of town booms, primarily because of the summer business, Whitefish remains just about as down-to-earth as a ski town can get. If there were ever a town dress code (which of course there never will be) it would have to involve wool and flannel. That telemarking is exceedingly popular on the Big Mountain ought to tell you something; in the culture of North American skiing, telemarkers by and large constitute a wool-and-flannel working class, and proudly so.

Even those few people of wealth, social polish, and pedigree who spend time around Whitefish—a handful of Hollywood types and the like—do so discretely, seeking to be deliberately unfancy or completely unnoticed if they can get away with it. Not all of mountainous

Montana is like that anymore. The rich and famous have conspicuously bought up large tracts of land in Paradise Valley around Livingston—trophy ranches to go with trophy wives, cynics say. And down around Big Sky, a private enclave called the Yellowstone Club has leapt to the head of the class in trying to establish itself as the snootiest ski resort in America. The club opened recently with the requirement that any applying member must provide proof of assets exceeding $3 million before even getting in the door for a tour of the property.

Whitefish and the Big Mountain are a long, long way from that. Whitefish, after all, is the place where for a long time the most talked about show in town was the mouse racing at the Palace, a bar at the borderline of seediness. The mouse races ended when the Palace decided to go a little more upscale and serve food, prompting health officials to declare that the proximity of mice and food was in violation of some code or another. So the races are history, though people in town still talk about them with a deepening nostalgia as the years pass.

The Big Mountain does not inspire awe with soaring peaks or sensational steeps or a powerful mystique. Its appeal is subtler and, yes, more earthy than that. Coming to the Big Mountain is about getting away, about going in-country, about literally getting lost in the woods for a while. Unfortunately, the old cabin that Rutherford and company built is no longer standing. But a few years ago, I embarked on a run with a group of gypsies, wending our way to who-knows-where on the mountain, ending at some small shack in a copse of spruce trees, covered in snow.

We sat in the shack and had a small lunch and shot the breeze for a while, as a snow squall rolled in and encircled the mountain. And then we were off skiing again. But something about that interlude struck me—the company, the trees, the serenity, the burst of snow—as running right into the essence and history of Big Mountain skiing.

Framed by trees on Evan's Heaven.

WHAT TO EXPECT

IN-BOUNDS

Big Mountain can claim some of the best tree skiing in America, with myriad lines set at a perfect pitch, steep but not too steep. The trees provide essential visual guidance on the days when the clouds and fog roll in and visibility is minimal. Local skiers concede that fair-weather types might not be happy coming to the Big Mountain; cold, clouds, and fog are common meteorological phenomena.

Aerial view of Big Mountain and Glacier National Park, some 25 miles east of the resort.

If you come to the Big Mountain looking for long, hero-making steeps, you will be disappointed. There are a few very steep lines, notably North Bowl Chute, a narrow funnel through the rocks. But not many. On the other hand, if you're looking for an astonishing abundance of advanced to expert terrain, set on a variety of exposures through the trees, you will be in pig heaven. Some of the best tree lines are in an area called Connie's Coulee leading into Hellroaring Basin. The pitch is somewhat steeper than on the front face, and the snow, due to a northerly exposure, is usually drier and fresher. In good weather, though, probably the most interesting expert skiing is in the East Rim area on the south side of the mountain. Ridges, tree groves, and open faces come together in a complex package of varying fall lines, and a few rocks and small cliff bands make things interesting. For spring skiing, I'd recommend heading for Hellroaring Basin and catching lines through the steep Picture Chutes just when the snow is turning to corn.

Two main cruisers on the front side of the mountain, Toni Matt and Inspiration, follow long ridgelines that angle all the way from the summit to the base, for over 2,000 vertical feet of high-speed ripping, for those so inclined. Both trails also present the almost constant temptation to dip into the trees—or wide openings through the trees—and search around for any unfound stashes of powder. The Big Ravine, the third of the fast-cruising triumvirate, provides access to Good Medicine, one of the best caches of tree skiing on the mountain.

For lower intermediates, trails on the north side of the mountain, Goat Haunt, Whitetail, and long, winding Gray Wolf are probably the best options. The trails feed gentle, open meadows for the last third of the run.

The Big Mountain might well be snowboarder heaven. The many contours, the wind rolls, the snow ghosts (great for riders who like fly-by hits), tight lines through the trees, and so on, make this a huge, natural-terrain park.

BACKCOUNTRY

The backcountry at the Big Mountain begins at the resort boundaries and doesn't end. There are backcountry possibilities literally as far as the eye can see, which to the northeast is Glacier National Park. The backcountry terrain closer to the resort is similar in pitch and character to the in-bounds, expert terrain—an average pitch of somewhere between 30 and 35 degrees, with lots of trees.

For an introduction to the Big Mountain backcountry, take a run or two with the resort's snowcat-skiing operation, based on Flower Point on the north side of the mountain. If you like that, there's plenty more of that type of terrain on either side of Canyon Creek, the drainage leading away from the north-side base area. A snow road along the creek is popular with snowmobilers, so what local skiers like to do—or try to do—is hitch a ride or tow back to the base once their run is done. Another popular backcountry run close to the ski area is the Big Slide, on the front side of the mountain and beyond the resort's eastern periphery. The name is appropriate—it is an opening in the trees created by an avalanche—so it's probably not the place to go if snow stability is questionable.

Beyond the resort, several backcountry cabins in the mountains along the southern perimeter of Glacier National Park make great base camps for overnight trips. Great Northern, named after the railroad and clearly visible from the Big Mountain summit, and Jewel Basin are local favorites. And within the park all sorts of possibilities, from gentle touring to big-mountain descents, are possible. The big stuff, of course, requires planning, caution, and expertise. But I've done a couple of easy tours in the park (starting where Route 2 summits at Marias Pass), and I can attest that big climbs and descents aren't necessary for the reward of big scenery.

INSIDE LINE

Take Amtrak's Empire Builder (800-USA-RAIL) to Whitefish from Chicago or Seattle. How often do you get a chance to take the train right to a major ski resort?

Stay (or at least have dinner) at the Kandahar Lodge (800-862-6094; www.vtown/Kandahar) up at the mountain. It is worth being there just for the photos on the wall, depicting Big Mountain history and racers (some famous, some not) who have competed there.

Breakfast at the Buffalo Café is all but obligatory at some point during a visit to Whitefish. Fill up on serious pancakes and local gossip, and when you've had more than enough of both, head up to the hill.

RESOURCES

General information, reservations, and snow report: 406-862-1900; 800-858-3930. Website: www.bigmtn.com. Backcountry guide service: The Isaak Walton Lodge (406-888-5700) has its own groomed tracks and backcountry trail network and also guides backcountry tours in Glacier National Park.

Crystal Mountain

Ah yes, the backcountry—Crystal's crown jewel

Pinball. The name won't leave me, conjuring up the image that it does. Pinball and I met each other—or at least we had a passing encounter—on a foggy spring day at Crystal Mountain. I was exploring the mountain with a patrolman named Chet Mowbray and a couple of yahoos who had traveled down from Whistler, British Columbia, about a five-hour drive away. They'd driven down in an old VW bus because they'd heard rumors about Crystal being an unheralded cache of adventurous skiing and because, even if the rumors proved untrue, the beer south of the border was a hell of a lot cheaper.

The four of us hiked south along the main ridgeline from the ski area summit, crossed through the boundary-line gate, and arrived at Silver King, a 7,012-foot highpoint of rock, ice, and snow. It took about 15 minutes of trudging through the deep snow to get there, but there we stood, at the apex of a ghastly looking, doglegged

Crystal, North Back: Lift-serviced backcountry and in-bounds skiing in seamless combination.

sluiceway through the rocks, plastered with wind-blasted, fog-eroded snow and steep as hell. Pinball.

Would we ski it? Enthusiasm within the group was not high, and Chet didn't exactly stoke the flame when he explained the meaning behind the run's name. If you fell skiing Pinball, he said, your head would ricochet from rock to rock like a little steel ball caroming off 100-point posts in an arcade game. Well that was that; just the thought of such pain was a sufficient deterrent. And if we weren't going to ski Pinball we certainly weren't going to venture to its equally daunting neighbor, Brain Damage.

Instead we veered away to the right, heading south down a series of avalanche-created corridors through the trees and onto the flats of Silver Basin. The dense, moisture-rich snow lay on the slope in a uniform, foot-deep stratum—the top of a 5-foot snowpack—and stood in mushroom tufts on the branches of the widely spaced evergreens. Except for the sound of our skis in the snow, it was utterly quiet as the air swirled with lazy wisps of fog—no sound or sight of lifts or other people. Pinball might have been Crystal at its most fearsome, but Silver Basin represented a

more authentic Crystal—trees, deep snow, backcountry, silence.

There was a time, 20 and more years ago, when Crystal Mountain stood at the threshold of American skiing's big time. It was certainly king of the Pacific Northwest, featuring some of the best expert skiing in the country and quite possibly *the* best view. On a clear day looking east from the summit of Crystal, you might feel as if you could almost reach out and touch the enormous, snow-mantled dome of 14,410 foot Mount Rainier, about 10 miles away. Crystal was held in high enough regard to have been chosen as the site for the 1965 U.S. national championships, and many of the world's best, including Jean-Claude Killy, who went on to win three Olympic gold medals in 1968, came to compete. A few years later, Phil and Steve Mahre, native sons of Washington, were winning ski races and Olympic medals and bringing added attention to skiing in the Northwest.

And then along came Whistler (see Chapter 5). Whistler, north of Vancouver, arrived on the scene as a major player in the North American winter-resort scene in the mid-'80s. Whistler

---

AT A GLANCE

LOCATION 75 miles southeast of Seattle, Washington	**TERRAIN ACREAGE** 1,300 acres in-bounds, 1,000 acres backcountry
SEASON Mid-November–mid-April	**VERTICAL RISE** 3,100 feet
IN-BOUNDS 1 2 ③ 4 5	**AVERAGE ANNUAL SNOWFALL** 380 inches
BACKCOUNTRY 1 2 3 ④ 5	
SNOW 1 2 ③ 4 5	

kept growing and amassing accolades from skiers, ski magazines, snowboarders, snowboarding magazines, and just about anyone able to articulate an opinion on such matters. Crystal, on the other hand, remained the same old Crystal, and beset by money woes, it began to look rather small and dowdy compared with flashy new Whistler. Already literally overshadowed by Mount Rainier, by the early '90s Crystal had become financially and psychically overshadowed by Whistler.

As a result, the best ski area in the northwestern United States was relegated to the status of not much more than a Seattle locals' hangout. Maybe that wasn't the worst thing that could have happened, though. Although the base facilities became frayed around the edges, for anyone seeking the simple pleasures of great terrain, good snow, and modest accommodations at a reasonable rate, Crystal could still deliver the goods.

And so, even after an infusion of new capital in the late '90s, it has remained as it has been—a low-key, blue-collar kind of place. How many other ski areas in the world, for example, reserve space in their lots for overnight RV parking? At Crystal, you and your best powder buddies can drive the old camper right to the base of the mountain, pay a nominal charge that's roughly less than a tenth of what you'd pay for a low-end hotel room at Whistler, hook up, and (as far as I can tell) spend the rest of the winter there, almost assured of first tracks every morning. The parking lot, in fact, is where the yahoos from Whistler spent the night, sucking down all that cheap beer in their VW bus and crashing in sleeping bags in the back without worries about who should be the designated driver. If there's a blue-plate special for blue-collar skiers in America, that's got to be it.

New, well-financed owners in the late '90s, armed with a new master plan—encouraged in their investment by the growing affluence of Seattle, less than two hours away—suggest that a fancier Crystal isn't far on the horizon. But for the time being, Crystal remains unadorned and down-to-earth, a throwback to the days when ski areas were ski areas and not resorts.

Put it this way: The absence of resort glitter and amenities leaves the focus at Crystal where it should be—on the mountain itself. Or mountains, to be more correct; the basic configuration of the ski area is composed of series of pyramidlike protrusions along a long ridge. From the ridgeline, the terrain falls away at a pitch ranging from the free-fall steepness of Pinball to the easygoing slope of intermediate Lucky Strike. But for the most part the pitch settles in at about a steady 30-degree angle or slightly steeper—absolutely ideal for powder skiing.

To either side of the ski area proper are the North Back Country and the South Back Country, extending like two wings from the body of a giant bird. Pass through ridgeline gates to the north or south, and you can hike along the ridge

Opposite: The top of the High Campbell Chair, at 7,000 feet. Top: Nightlife is not Crystal's strong suit.
Above: Boarder bivouac, with view of Mount Rainier.

Top: Going big in the Crystal backcountry. Above: Jumping the Hole-in-the-Wall, a famous feature in the heart of Crystal resort.

you've come to Crystal for any other purpose, you've probably made a mistake.

The 14,410-foot hulk of Mount Rainier, rising more than 7,000 feet above the summit of Crystal, might be a sight to behold on a clear day, but it is also its own weather maker. Even on a fine day, a lenticular dish of cloudiness is apt to rest atop Rainier, as if biding its time before becoming a full-fledged storm. The cloudiness around Rainier will then seem to expand gradually and mutate, and pretty soon it's snowing and foggy at Crystal.

I've been at Crystal for three days in a row without the sun ever appearing, with Crystal locals describing for me in detail the searing beauty of seeing the sun shine upon Mount Rainier. When the skies eventually do clear, the presence of Rainier seems that much more immediate and spectacular, the light of the sun on its snow-covered glaciers literally blinding. It quickly makes Crystal seem a small entity—a complete illusion, of course.

What I like about Crystal is not just the uniformly steep pitch of the mountain, but the fact that the steepness is dished out in long, well-meted doses of over 1,000 vertical feet at a time. So what if there is more than 7,000 feet worth of Mount Rainier above the Crystal summit? *Below* the summit is 3,100 vertical feet worth of terrain, and that's only the official figure. Hit the backcountry, and you can add a few hundred feet more vertical if you know where you're going, then hitch a ride back up the access road.

Ah yes, the backcountry—Crystal's crown jewel. It is an unusual concept as defined at Crystal, a different kind of backcountry than pretty much anywhere else I know in North America. It is actually *designated* backcountry, marked as such on the trail map.

Crystal claims (and I quote from Crystal literature) to have "1,300 acres lift serviced, 1,000 acres of backcountry terrain." This is not quite accurate. The 1,000 backcountry acres are really

as far as your legs and desire for untracked snow can carry you. Add it all up, both the in-bounds terrain and the backcountry, and you end up with close to 2,500 acres that sing out with a singular invitation: Ski or snowboard your brains out. If

lift serviced, too; the lifts get you to the top of the main ridge, and once you've gained that elevation, the hiking into the backcountry is pretty easy. And for the most part, once you've completed your backcountry run, you can ski back to the base of the lifts.

What you have then, effectively, is lift-serviced backcountry skiing, a wonderful hybrid if ever there was one. On a sunny spring day some years ago, I skied a long run through the North Back Country with a couple of Crystal locals. The snow beneath the big ever-greens was perfect corn, and we rode that wave as long as we could, skiing both sidewalls of a long gully, until the snow finally ran out. We had to scramble through a boulder field to get back to the road and hike back to the base area, but that was all right. We ate lunch, and then skied in-bounds for the rest of the afternoon.

That's Crystal for you—lift-serviced back-country and in-bounds skiing, in all-but-seamless combination. There's no place quite like it in North America.

WHAT TO EXPECT

IN-BOUNDS

According to Crystal's official statistics, 40 per-cent of the terrain is rated as expert, but I'd say that percentage ought to be higher. I'd say the best steep skiing is in Campbell Basin, with a combi-nation of tree and open-bowl skiing that is classi-cally Crystal. Choose a line, any line—there are hundreds of possible lines in the basin, all of them good. Lower down on the mountain, Exterminator features the same kind of tree/open slope mix.

In both cases, however, the exposure—pre-dominantly east-facing—can cause the snow to deteriorate more quickly than on north-facing slopes. That's particularly true on lower slopes—for example, Exterminator, where temperatures are usually warmer. In fact, if there is a drawback to Crystal, it isn't a lack of snow—between 350

The Goat Shoot, a hidden gem in the North Back Country beyond the designated runs.

and 400 inches a year is plenty—but the variable texture of the snow. On some days it might be powdery, but on other days it can be sloppy and wet. Perhaps the surest bet for crisp, dry snow is north-facing Powder Bowl, Crystal's steepest in-bounds terrain that gets tracked out quickly after a storm.

For experts, however, Crystal is fundamen-tally a mountain to explore, to seek out lines

Boarder heaven in the South Back Country: ideal conditions and perfect form.

between marked runs. Stick to the trails for a while just to get your bearings, but after that you'll be missing much of the best of Crystal if you don't venture off-trail.

The two main intermediate runs are Green Valley and Lucky Shot, which depart from different sides of the Summit House. Even here, you'll find opportunities for exploration—perhaps a shortcut through the trees for a couple of powder turns before returning to the main, groomed trail.

Despite its reputation as primarily an experts' mountain, Crystal actually has some first-rate beginner terrain. There might not be any runs from the summit suitable for novices, but the Quicksilver lift on the lower third of the mountain is almost 1,000 vertical feet totally devoted to novice skiers and snowboarders. And you can also ride the Forest Queen Express to the bottom of Campbell Basin for a 2,000-vertical-foot run—all in all, not a bad amount of terrain coverage if you're just starting out.

BACKCOUNTRY

The backcountry at Crystal is backcountry made easy—lift serviced and avalanche controlled. Although you might want to bring along an avalanche beacon and shovel when entering Crystal's designated backcountry just for the sense of security, they aren't essential. (If avalanche danger is high, the backcountry gates will be closed.) And astute orienteering is not necessarily a prerequisite, either, because the configuration of the terrain is such that pretty much everything funnels back to the base area or the access road. One exception is a beautiful, long avalanche path down the back side of the mountain toward Mount Rainier. Be forewarned if you can't resist the temptation—you've got perhaps a two-hour or more hike to return to civilization once you hit the valley floor.

In my time spent at Crystal, I've found the South Back Country to be more interesting and complex than the North, with more variations in pitch and exposure. That might just have been a matter of dumb luck, and certainly some of the best cold northern snow in the area can be found in the North on Spook Hill. You can also get a longer run in the North by skiing down to the access road and hitchhiking or shuttling back to the base.

There are plenty of backcountry possibilities in Mount Rainier National Park, too. The easiest thing to do is to head up to the Paradise area, one of the snowiest places in North America. The average annual snowfall is over 600 inches, and in the winter of 1971 to 1972, 1,122 inches of snow were recorded. Only go, however, on a fair-weather day; in stormy weather, the road to Paradise is often closed. Although the terrain can be as extreme as you want it to be, particularly the higher you go on the mountain, most of the easily accessible terrain just above the Paradise Inn (closed in winter) is fairly mellow. It might be of particular interest to snowboarders; ripples, seams, and moraine embankments make for a giant natural-terrain park.

INSIDE LINE

Don't expect fancy accommodations at Crystal until the recently conceived master plan begins to be fleshed out. On the positive side: Lodging, especially at the Alpine Inn, (888-754-6400) is relatively cheap.

You definitely want to be up at the base of the mountain on a powder morning; the drive up the access road (if you're staying around Seattle or nearby Enumclaw) is no fun in a snowstorm.

Nightlife is not Crystal's strong suit. The Snorting Elk Cellar in the Alpine Inn is where the hardcore skiers and riders hang out. If you're looking for inside information on where the good snow is—along with a beer or two and occasional live music—the Snorting Elk is the place to go.

RESOURCES

General information: 360-663-2265. Snow report: 888-SKI-6199. Website: www.skicrystal.com. Mount Rainier information: 360-569-2211; www.nps.gov/mora.

Silver King, trophy lift-serviced run in the South Back Country.

Fernie & Beyond

Something this big, this good, and this snowy can't remain a secret forever

Sunrise and moonset over Fernie Snow Valley resort.

Southeastern British Columbia is one of the jeweled secrets of North American skiing, even if the word is leaking out fast and the signs of progress suggest that what's left of the secret might not last long. The region has gained fame as the heartland of heli-skiing, and rightly so, but obscured in fame's wake is much more. Mountain ranges converge—the Rockies, Purcells, Selkirks, Monashees, Kootenays—and in doing so form a microcosm for one of the last, great winter road trips on the continent.

Big mountains, interconnected valleys, a handful of superb ski areas, tons of backcountry terrain, tons of snow. No wonder a whole horde of 20-something wayfarers, bonded by a fast-moving word-of-mouth spread in the subculture of Internet chat rooms, now gad about the byways of southeastern B.C. every winter. They drive around in old cars, living on the road (and on the cheap) to satisfy an unbridled wanderlust, all the while skiing themselves into a collective coma of powder ecstasy. The chat-room word is this: Southeastern B.C. is the epitome of that lifestyle.

It is a region in which civilization, such as it is, remains a protean entity emerging gradually and somewhat haphazardly from a vast mountain wilderness. Mining, logging, hydroelectric development, backcountry adventure, post-hippie radicalism, mainstream tourism, a mountaineering ethos, lift-serviced skiing—all mix and overlap. In the ongoing give-and-take between settlement and wilderness, the wilderness is still way, way out ahead, even if settlement is gaining ground.

Dense forests of spruce, fir, and larch reach up steep mountainsides and then cease abruptly, giving way at higher elevations to rocky cirques, high-alpine basins, and formidable peaks. Glaciers that are all but gone in the continental United States still thrive in these parts; in fact, in a few cases glaciers have been reported to be advancing, in apparent defiance of global warming. These mountains amaze me, not just in their ruggedness and beauty but in their relative anonymity. Immediately to the east, the Rockies—very rocky indeed—draw deserved attention. To the west,

the massively glaciated Coastal Mountains and the resort of Whistler (see Chapter 5) have established their own prominence. But look at a road map of British Columbia, and there's not much in the southeast to suggest a landscape of great distinction. How wrong that impression is.

Travel is not particularly convenient or expedient, a reason to take your time in roaming around these parts. Even today, roads are relatively few, running mostly north and south because that's the way the deeply etched valleys run. A rare exception is the Trans Canada Highway, although an east-west route through notorious Rogers Pass was not something the mountains ceded readily. Between 1885 and 1911, before there was even a road, 200 people—mostly workers for the Canadian Pacific Railroad—were killed in avalanches in the pass. One particularly deadly slide in 1910 killed 62 people. So rugged is the terrain that a highway through the pass wasn't completed until 1962.

In short, this environment is not about to

Overleaf: Snowboarders take in the vast backcountry beyond Fernie before riding down into it.

AT A GLANCE

LOCATION 300 miles southwest of Calgary, Alberta	**TERRAIN ACREAGE** 2,500 acres
SEASON December–mid-April	**VERTICAL RISE** 2,811 feet
IN-BOUNDS 1 2 ③ 4 5	**AVERAGE ANNUAL SNOWFALL** 360 inches
BACKCOUNTRY 1 2 3 4 ⑤	
SNOW 1 2 ③ 4 5	

stoop down and be tamed in a hurry.

That's why human history is a relatively new concept in the region, reaching back not much more than 100 years. A string of communities at the cusp between town and city—among them Cranbrook, Creston, Nelson, Castlegar, and Fernie, with populations between 4,000 and 20,000—were born as railway towns or mining centers in the late 1800s. The memories of that time are still fresh. Drive Route 3 from Nelson to Fernie, and it is easy to visualize that era, when a silver- and gold-mining fever raged, when the trains roared through (as they still do), and when smelters processing raw galena ore churned thick clouds of smoke into the air. I've done so on a dismal day in October, when the ground was muddy and the trees leafless, and the clouds and the mountains merged into a single monochromatic

AN HISTORICAL FOOTNOTE

A few years ago, while driving through the beautiful Slocan Valley west of Fernie, I stopped at a store in the tiny hamlet of New Denver for gas. A couple of teenage girls were buying sodas in the store where I stopped, and my first thought, as I looked at them, was that they were Japanese tourists. Yet they were dressed in a very North American way, and they spoke perfect English.

It was a riddle that found its answer in a curious footnote in Canadian history. During World War II, New Denver was the site of a Japanese-Canadian internment camp. Shortly after the Pearl Harbor bombing in 1941, men of Japanese heritage between the ages of 18 and 45 were sent to labor camps in eastern Canada. But women, children, and older men were relocated in New Denver, in an area known as "the Orchard."

If you wanted to keep a group of people in check, there were few places in Canada better suited for the task than the Slocan Valley. Mountains rise sharply on both sides of the valley, in what is now Valhalla Provincial Park to the west and Kokanee Glacier Provincial Park to the east. The abruptness of the mountains shut off almost all reasonable routes of escape.

Living in shacks with little heat, water, or food, the Japanese-Canadians managed to tough it out and survive the war. And many discovered that what began as an internment ironically might have become a form of salvation. For if you were going to live in western Canada, could there possibly be a more beautiful place than the Slocan Valley? Apparently not, at least in the minds of those interned Japanese-Canadians who chose to stay after the war ended and raise their families in the area.

mass. It was a scene somehow infused with the aura of a different time, as if I were driving into a sepia-toned photo of yesteryear.

But October gives way to November, when winter gradually descends from the mountaintops to the valley floor to reinvent—and to recolor—the landscape. Winter comes early and stays a while. Storms roll in from the west, crashing first into the Monashees before moving east through the Selkirks and Purcells, eventually reaching Fernie, near the western slope of the Rockies. The Monashees get pounded with as much as 800 inches or more every winter, while the mountains around Fernie, the last link in the snow chain, are relegated to the leftovers. But you know what? The leftovers add up to 360 inches per year, no petty sum. And when the storms take a slightly different tack, Fernie bears the brunt, getting pummeled in a way that has become the stuff of local legend. As former Canadian Olympian and downhiller Rob Boyd puts it, "When it comes, wow!"

I single out Fernie among southern B.C. communities not only because it has a 2,500-acre ski area right on the outskirts of town, but also because it's got everything you'd ever expect to find in the region—a condensed version of the region's greatest hits, if you will. Fernie has the complete package: the terrain, the snow, the scenery, the accessible and wildly beautiful backcountry, the funky town. It could very well be the be-all and end-all of any road trip; there is enough in Fernie alone to satisfy all winter sport needs.

I visited Fernie for the first time in the summer several years back, driving down a main street lined by squared-off brick buildings, with the granite ramparts of the Lizard Range a commanding presence high in the near distance. There was an absence of pretension in town so heartening it almost made me want to weep with nostalgia; it wasn't so long ago (in the '60s and even '70s) that ski towns in Colorado such as Steamboat Springs and Breckenridge looked and felt like this. Above the town and descending from the crest of the

Top: View of 2nd Avenue. Although change is afoot, Fernie remains a quiet Western town. Above: Skiing down Polar Peak, Fernie.

Lizards, the ski resort—officially Fernie Snow Valley—was a series of steep bowls feeding trails that hung like tentacles through verdant forests.

When I drove up to the base, just to get a sense of what kind of ski area it might be, I was most impressed by what little was there: a couple of small lodges, a few lifts, stark and empty, not much else. Most ski areas are a bit desolate between seasons, but this had an almost eerie emptiness to it. When I talked with a few local folk back in town, they told me that, in the heart of winter, it wasn't much different. Fernie was still by and large a deserted place, and as such it was pretty much their private stash. Who, after all, in the big, wide world of winter sport, had ever heard of Fernie, other than people who lived in Fernie?

That's changed in the last few years, both in Fernie itself and in the surrounding area. Lodges have been built; new, faster lifts have been added; 130 miles to the north near Golden, a whole new ski area (Kicking Horse Resort) has come into being, promising more than 4,000 acres and 4,000 vertical feet. Meanwhile, a slew of cat-skiing and heli-skiing operators have been guiding more and more people into the southeastern-B.C. back-country. Something this big, this good, and this snowy can't remain a secret forever.

Locals have responded with predictable con-tradiction—proud for the acclaim that this beau-tiful thing of theirs has earned, disenchanted that the powder that once was theirs alone is now get-ting tracked out in a hurry. This is a familiar lament, a chorus intoned in mountain towns wherever ,you go. Too many people, not like it used to be. A once pristine world ravaged. In other parts of the world—in the central Rockies of Colorado, perhaps—there might be some validity in that. But don't worry yet about Fernie in particular and southeastern B.C. in general. There is plenty of space in the mountains here to get away from everyone else for a while and find your own fresh tracks.

So here's the plan. You get in the car and drive to Fernie, because Fernie is your logical starting point. The Columbia River Valley, sepa-rating the Columbia mountain ranges (the Purcells, et al.) to the west and the Rockies to the

east, cuts a long, wide swath in a northerly direc-tion. Route 3 winds west from Fernie through the mountains to ski areas such as Red Mountain and Whitewater, relatively small places with big repu-tations for deep-powder tree skiing. Thus does Fernie make sense as a starting point, lying at the meeting of road-tripping axes.

And what a place to start. You look up at the mountain, with its half-moon bowls of white making for a tempting, beautiful sight. The weather might not immediately be perfect—clouds collide with those granite ramparts and sometimes get stuck for a spell of inclemency—and the snow might not be fresh. But give it time. The snow will come, and when it does, wow.

Your first run at Fernie will go something like this: You roam around the mountain, because reconnaissance is at the pith of Fernie skiing. Steep chutes drop through the trees and rocks from the ridges separating one bowl from another, so per-haps you begin by slipping through a harrowing narrows known as Corner Pocket and find your-self jettisoned into the belly of Lizard Bowl. Or turn the other way, into the Concussion Chutes, set through the trees on an entirely different expo-sure, ending up in Currie Bowl. And continue on down the mountain, through the thickening trees and meadows of sometimes nettlesome alder brush, riding on through gullies that form natural halfpipes. It is a sequence of interconnected moments as much as a single, fluid run, on a mountain that is vascular in its intricacy.

By the time you reach the bottom, you've taken on every kind of terrain and snow imagina-ble, and you haven't even begun to plumb the depths of the area's potential. Siberia Bowl, Timber Bowl, Cedar Bowl, out-of-bounds Fish Bowl, and all sorts of stuff to hike to—all remain to be considered. Then it will snow, one of those epic dumps famed in Fernie, and it's a whole new mountain. The town basically closes down as the local horde heads up to the mountain to pig out.

That's Fernie Snow Valley for you, and

maybe that alone will be sufficient. It's a big area, after all, roughly equivalent in acreage to Jackson Hole. But it is also like a foyer at the forefront of a multichambered mansion of backcountry possibility. I wouldn't even begin to try to quantify the terrain, but here's one way at least to begin to get a grasp of it: There are snowcat operators in the region with permit areas covering more than 50 square miles, and at last count something like ten snowcat operators were in business. The heli-ski operators can claim even larger permit areas, each perhaps ten times as large. Yet with the backcountry divvied up into these not-so-small fiefdoms, that still leaves enormous tracts like wild Kokanee Glacier Provincial Park and even wilder Valhalla Provincial Park, both to the west of Fernie, for those who want to venture out on their own by hiking up and skiing down. Kokanee Glacier's 12-person Slocan Chief cabin, which dates back to the end of the 19th century, lies at 6,600 feet and at the foot of some of the best north-facing powder slopes in the entire region.

Does it all add up to the best backcountry skiing in the world? I don't know. There is probably somewhere out there that is wilder, or bigger, or snowier, or more accessible. Perhaps even more beautiful, though that's doubtful. But when all elements are factored in, and when you have in Fernie a 2,500-acre giant of a ski area to serve as your lift-serviced base camp, it's hard to imagine that it gets much better than this. Travel around, give it some time, and stay for a while.

WHAT TO EXPECT

IN-BOUNDS

First an overview of the regional layout. Fernie is located in the far, southeastern corner of British Columbia. Golden, where Kicking Horse Resort is located, is about 110 miles to the north. Rossland, where Red Mountain is located, is about 150 miles to the west. Golden, Fernie, and Rossland, then, form three points of an almost equilateral triangle, within

In southeastern B.C., the backcountry is measured not in acres but in hundreds of square miles.

which all that great backcountry terrain lies.

Someday, Fernie Snow Valley (the ski resort) might be overshadowed by emerging Kicking Horse Resort. But for the time being, when the terrain, snow, scenery, and town are all considered, Fernie is still the star of southern B.C. One thing I like about Fernie is the balance of the terrain, in more ways than one. Not only is there plenty for skiers and riders of all abilities, but the mountain also breaks down into approximately

Into the mystic: Cloudy day in the valley, sun-drenched paradise at higher elevations.

equal parts: open-bowl skiing, widely spaced trees, and tree-lined runs. In an average Fernie run, you'll probably encounter all three.

Recently installed high-speed quad chairs now make for a relatively quick ride to the top, a development that can be considered both good and bad. The good, of course, is the shorter lift ride. The bad is the fact that more people get to the fresh snow more quickly, meaning that the powder can get tracked up in a hurry. That, at any rate, is the worry among locals.

Yet if you're willing to keep traversing high under the granite escarpments leading up to the Lizard Range summits, you can usually find untracked snow well after a storm. The longer it has been since a storm, the farther you traverse— simple as that. Also, Fernie's five main bowls are often opened sequentially after a big dump, so that if the fresh snow has been tracked up in one bowl, just wait—another bowl might soon open,

with a whole new blanket of powder for the taking. Thereafter, if you enjoy the pleasures of skiing crud—snow chopped up by previous skiers and riders but still plenty soft—Fernie is dreamland.

After a few days at Fernie, head over to Red Mountain, with a stop along the way at Whitewater if you have the time and motivation. Rossland has a similar character to Fernie—a ski town that seems to have sidestepped modern pretensions. The same can be said for the ski area itself, with lots of steep—sometimes very steep—tree skiing. The area reports something like 300 inches of snow a year, a figure that seems ridiculous. It has to be more than that.

BACKCOUNTRY

There is plenty of room to explore at Fernie— boundary openings permitting—in Fish Bowl, on the far side of in-bounds Cedar Bowl. But if you really want backcountry in southeastern B.C., you'll want to venture farther afield.

I'd suggest starting at Island Lake Lodge, just outside Fernie, if you can afford the price tag of snowcat skiing. The terrain is similar to the terrain within the ski area, with a notable exception: untracked powder is all but guaranteed. Among Island Lake's original investors were snowboarding legend Craig Kelly and Scot Schmidt, the godfather of extreme skiing. If these guys think that this is prime powder country, you know it has got to be good.

Fernie at night.

Given the healthy population of hardcore backcountry enthusiasts, here is no shortage of local knowledge—in Fernie, Rossland, or Golden—about where to find great do-it-yourself backcountry skiing. Certainly Kokanee Glacier must rank high on the list, primarily because the Slocan Chief cabin can serve as an ideally located, high-alpine base camp. But because the cabin is small (sleeping just 12) and popular, you need to reserve space (through a lottery) well in advance. You can also join up with a guided group based out of the cabin.

Rogers Pass, west of Golden, is also a great place to establish a backcountry base camp; there's plenty of fine terrain within a relatively short distance from the highway. The drawing card of Rogers Pass—snow, and lots of it—can also be its curse. Avalanche danger here can be extreme.

INSIDE LINE

Fly into Calgary and drive to Fernie, if you've got the time. You can get connecting flights into smaller regional airports in Cranbrook and Castlegar, or you could fly to and drive from Spokane, Washington. But the scenery on the drive from Calgary, through Banff and Kootenay National Parks and the Rockies, is something special.

For comfortable accommodations at a reasonable price, try the Little Witch Log Inn (888-423-9772).

Check in at the Mean Bean for your morning coffee and muffin.

If you want to hang with the ski bums, hit the Park Place Pub for après-ski pool and foosball.

If you plan to stick around for a while, get Fernie's one-month pass. It begins paying for itself after ten days of skiing.

RESOURCES

General information: 250-423-4655. Snow report: 250-423-3555. Website: www.skifernie. com. Backcountry guide service: For cat skiing at Island Lake Lodge, call 888-422-8754 (www.islandlakelodge.com). For Kokanee Glacier skiing contact Kokanee Glacier Mountaineering (250-505-2155; www.kokanee-glacier.com). Reservations for the Slocan Chief cabin are chosen by lottery. Lottery applications must be in by early October.

La Grave

As far as a mountaineering ski area goes,
you can't find any better

I'd like to think that I discovered the place before it was discovered. It was not by my own design, certainly; a guide led me there without my knowing where we were going. In April of 1991, I was visiting Les Deux Alpes, the largest ski resort in the Dauphine region of the French Alps. One afternoon, I joined a French couple and the aforementioned guide, who enticed us with the grand idea of skiing from the top of the resort over the Dome de la Lauze, a sort of humpbacked glacier, and continuing on down to the valley on the other side. We would end up in a small village, far from the madding resort crowds, where we could refresh ourselves with a small meal and wine before returning to Les Deux Alpes. The name of the village was La Grave.

It was a great run, very wild, over glaciers and through larch forests for close to 7,000 vertical feet, with the 13,068-foot la Meije, a pyramid of granite resembling Wyoming's Grand Teton, as

Dave Gauley ski mountaineering to an unnamed peak for a descent, La Grave, France.

our backdrop. The powder was really something else— surprisingly dry and tractable for so late in the season—and the sun shone, reflecting off patches of exposed glacial ice on the flanks of la Meije. When we reached the village, the wine, served in a clear, unlabeled bottle, was cold and cheap, and our *déjeuner*—consisting of nothing more than cheese slices, mustard, and fresh baguettes—was just right.

Apparently I didn't know the treasure that I had happened upon that day. Not long thereafter, the popular ski filmmaker Greg Stump produced a movie called *P-Tex, Lies & Videotape*, in which a mysterious Vallée X was prominently featured. That was followed by a story in *Powder* magazine about the very same Vallée X, extolling its virtues as a wild, steep, dangerously exciting place, with the best off-piste skiing in France.

Vallée X, of course, was La Grave. And once the good word started circulating, both cinematically and journalistically, La Grave became a discovered place, with so many Americans, Australians, Canadians, and Brits circulating that

English, in this tiny enclave of France, seemed virtually to become the primary language.

Ironically, what attracted all the foreigners to La Grave was—and is—that there wasn't much there at all. La Grave might well be Europe's ultimate expression in lift-serviced minimalism. The trail map shows four lifts and three runs, and even that's an exaggeration. There is essentially just one lift—a rickety, rust-bucket cable car originally built to provide summer hikers access to the high glaciers. And there are essentially no runs, just a couple of vaguely marked routes that might change from time to time with the change in snow conditions or glacial movements. There is no grooming and essentially no ski patrol or marking of such life-threatening hazards as 300-foot crevasses and cliffs. In the town itself, there are no night clubs, no resort cluster of boutiques and restaurants, and only one or two inns of any substance.

But the terrain. . .now that's another story. There is well over than 6,000 vertical feet worth of it and five glaciers. La Grave is a jumble of couloirs and long, long powder runs, of steep tree skiing and wide-open glacial routes, of rock faces

---

AT A GLANCE

LOCATION 45 miles east of Grenoble in the French Alps	**TERRAIN ACREAGE** Unknown
SEASON Late December–April	**VERTICAL RISE** Roughly 7,000 feet
IN-BOUNDS 1 ② 3 4 5	**AVERAGE ANNUAL SNOWFALL** 300 inches
OFF-PISTE 1 2 3 ④ 5	
SNOW 1 2 ③ 4 5	

Preparing to descend the 55-degree-plus Pan Rideaux Couloir.

barely covered by a thin patina of snow and ice and on the whole a place where falling can have serious, painful consequences. Not all of La Grave is big-risk, big-mountain stuff, but much of it is, and that is the heart of the matter from which the place derives its newfound fame.

I asked Alison Gannett, an extreme skier who has been featured in a number of ski films, what she thought of La Grave after her first visit a few years ago. "At first, I was surprised how small it was," she said. That's the kind of comment you might expect about a place with basically one lift and two runs. But after her first impression, she began looking and exploring around, and from that point on it was as if she had stepped right through the looking glass. La Grave—the real La Grave—revealed itself.

Armed with ropes, ice axes, and crampons, Gannett and her partners found themselves in the kind of places they'd have a hard time imagining, let alone skiing. And getting to those places— scrambling over exposed rocks, traversing across bulletproof glacial ice, rappelling over cliffs—was itself no piece of cake. She remembers at one point standing at the mouth of a couloir she estimates to have been 6,000 feet long—give or take a thousand feet or two. That's a good deal longer than your average run-of-the-mill couloir at a place like Chamonix, or at least it was in Gannett's well-traveled eye. And of course Gannett and friends had to try it, because backing away from something like that would have been a very bad form of freeskiing behavior. They ended up in a tiny mountain village, miles down the road

Opposite: Dave Gauley and Rick Armstrong prepare to rappel into the Pan Rideaux Couloir.

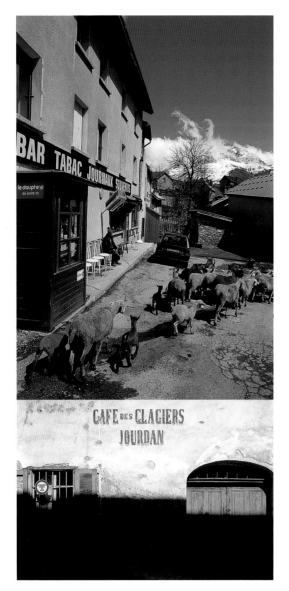

Top: A local herder moves his flock of goats and sheep to pasture. Above: Cafe des Glaciers Jourdan. Skiers relax here after touring from La Grave to La Cassette.

more technical than anywhere else in Europe," she says, and that's saying a lot. *Technical* in this case is a mountaineering code word for hard as hell, requiring mountaineering skills, equipment, savvy, and guts. Says Gannett: "As far as a mountaineering ski area goes, you can't get any better."

Guides' descriptions of various La Grave routes typically don't allow much wiggle room for the timid. For example: "Very exposed. . .a 52-degree cliff face. . .high risk of slipping on hard-packed snow. . .overhanging glaciers and long couloirs of avalanches [sic]", ". . .some skiers have gone down and the outcome has not been lucky. . . ," and so on. The great mantra of La Grave, repeated repeatedly by guides in leading clients down the couloir- and crevasse-riddled terrain, is this: "Don't fall."

As a result of all of this, La Grave has grown into something of a mystical, mythic Valhalla in the collective mind-set of American extremism, where all the great freeriding *übermensches* come to escape the mundane world of ordinary mountains. In the gospel of freeriding, La Grave is the last station of the cross, where the devout must come to prove their worthiness and gain immortal benediction.

Or at least that's the stuff you might be led to believe in hearing the apostles of La Grave's considerable virtues talk about the place. La Grave's legend has been able to keep growing in large part because, despite having been discovered, it still remains relatively undiscovered. Six-thousand-foot couloirs, 55-degree slopes, 300-foot crevasses, 100-foot rappels over rocks and icefalls, and basically scare-your-pants-off terrain—along with spare accommodations and no nightlife—aren't exactly mass-market drawing cards.

And so as the legend grows, bolstered by all the ancillary stories and statistics, I can't be sure where the fact ends and the fiction begins. I have heard, for example, that more than two dozen people have died in the notorious Trifide Couloirs alone.

from La Grave; and isn't that the off-piste way of the Alps—to ride lifts from one village and end up skiing into another village far away, and then riding the bus back with local schoolchildren and grocery-shopping grandmothers.

Gannett was sold on the place. "It's a lot

The late Alex Lowe climbing the Couloir Divine for a late-spring powder run, La Cassette, France.

Every year, an event called the Derby de la Meije is held at La Grave, one of the most hairball races imaginable. The derby is a 7,000-vertical-foot race down la Meije, without control gates or any of the safety fencing used in something as blasé as, say, a downhill race.

The event attracts more than 500 competitors on alpine skis, telemark skis, monoskis, and snowboards, and to call it dangerous is a ridiculous understatement. I've heard reports that in one year, five competitors died; in another year, two competitors died. Again those numbers probably mix fact and fiction, although I wouldn't discount them altogether. In a race like this, death seems a reasonably possible outcome. But I'm not sure what to make of the popular rumor that La Grave's lifts will be shut down if more than seven

skiers die in a single winter. Apparently that fatal border has never been crossed, although in some years only because—again according to legend—snowboarders don't count as skiers.

All right then—that's La Grave, the mythic killing fields of France. Fortunately, it isn't all so dire and dangerous. There is still plenty of terrain that doesn't belong in the don't-fall category, particularly in the larch trees on the lower third of the mountain. And the snow quality is exceptional, primarily because, as Gannett says, "It's the most north-facing place I've ever been." With the north slopes being protected from direct solar radiation, the snow remains dry well into spring, and I can vouch for that. Furthermore, there are two terrific resorts close by—Serre Chevalier and Les Deux Alpes—that offer up plenty of mainstream skiing

Telemarker descends the first crux of the Trefide Couloirs.

WHAT TO EXPECT

IN-BOUNDS

The main lift, a rather antiquated cable car, reaches in three stages from the village of La Grave (4,620 feet in elevation) to the base of the Dome de la Lauze at 10,560 feet. From here, T-bars extend another 1,000 feet higher.

The main routes down the mountain are relatively easy, although the pitch steepens for the last 1,500 vertical feet through larch forests. Although the pitch for the most part is relatively gentle, what can give trouble to intermediate skiers is the condition of the snow. No grooming means no certainty; powder, breakable crust, warm slop, ice—you must take whatever hand you're dealt.

The main runs are long enough and the scenery exquisite enough to keep you happy for a day or two. But to come to La Grave for any period longer than that, you ought to be ready to ski terrain that will probably scare you.

Couloirs and glaciers are what have made La Grave famous, fingering down off the mountainside at pitches ranging between 40 and 60 degrees. It isn't essential to ski this terrain with a guide—one of the things that attracts people to La Grave is the libertarian, no-rules nature of the place—but hiring a guide is strongly recommended. Not only do the guides know where to go, but they also can keep you from getting in over your head too quickly. In other words, they'll start you on 35-degree slopes and gradually work up to the tougher stuff.

Traversing, hiking, and semitechnical scrambling over highly exposed rock and ice might be necessary to reach some of La Grave's most notorious lines. Guides can generally provide whatever gear (harnesses, ropes) might be needed. But if you're someone who gets vertiginously uneasy climbing or rappelling on exposed faces, you might want to reconsider heading for La Grave. You can always ride the lifts and head over the mountain to enormous Les Deux Alpes or head down the road to the resort of Serre Chevalier.

to complement wilder La Grave.

Actually, I think the main reason to spend any amount of time in La Grave is to appreciate its beauty and unvarnished simplicity. I remember well the dry snow and the steep pitches in my visit to La Grave, in the time before discovery. But more lasting is a memory of sitting in red plastic chairs on a concrete sidewalk, drinking wine in the warm April sun with the dark hulk of la Meije and its apron of glaciers looming above us. It was the classic coda to punctuate a fine long run, unadulterated by resort hype and tourist schlock, and I'd return to La Grave just for that.

Sunset on La Meige, where each year the Derby de la Meije is held, a 7,000-vertical-foot race without control gates or any of the safety fencing used in a conventional downhill race.

Both are fully rounded resorts, with plenty of terrain for all abilities.

Not all of La Grave requires a high skill and confidence level. But the stronger and more confident you are, the more you'll like the place.

OFF-PISTE

All of La Grave is essentially lift-serviced off-piste (or backcountry) terrain.

INSIDE LINE

The cool place to stay in La Grave is La Chaumine (011-33-5044-7397; U.S. phone: 888-756-6537; www.skierslodge.com), an all-service inn that provides guide service in addition to lodging and all meals. It's about 1½ miles outside La Grave, but because there isn't much in La Grave itself, that doesn't matter much. La Chaumine caters to an English-speaking clientele, but be forewarned—the testosterone level among so many strong skiers and riders (or those who want to think they're strong) can be pretty high.

If you're looking for full resort amenities, you're best bet is probably to stay in Les Deux Alpes (www.2alpservices.com) and ski to La Grave across the Dome de la Lauze. Of course it isn't as convenient as staying in La Grave, and you'll have to quit your day relatively early in order to leave time to make the trip back to the other side.

RESOURCES

General information: 011-33-04-7679-9005. Central reservations: 011-33-04-7679-9246. Website: www.la-grave.com. Backcountry guide service: Bureau des Guides is 011-33-04-7679-9021. Former World Extreme Skiing Champion Doug Coombs leads a weeklong steep-skiing camp at La Grave (www.dougcombs.com/lagrave).

Las Lenas

*Skiing in the midst of a landscape extraterrestrial
in its treeless, desolate beauty*

Imagine being a 21-year-old downhiller on the U.S. Ski Team, entering the prime of your competitive life. You'd already been lucky enough to ski the big mountains of North America and Europe, with a license to go 80 miles an hour or faster on the scariest downhill courses in the world. You had reason to think that you'd pretty much seen it all—that you'd taken it to the limit. Then you came to Las Lenas and the Andes.

The year was 1985, sometime in August.

Doug Lewis had won a bronze medal in downhill a few months earlier at the World Championships in Bormio, Italy. The U.S. Ski Team was on its way to Las Lenas for summer training and racing. No big deal, Lewis figured. Same routine, new location, right?

Not quite. The trip became like a sequential journey through a carnival funhouse of mirrors, with each new stage becoming, as Alice might have said, curiouser and curiouser.

". . .endless, untracked powder all the way down—so much powder that it was truly epic."

First the hyperkinetic bustle of Buenos Aires, and an initial immersion into the foreign sounds and smells of South America. Then by plane to the small city of Malargue in the Argentine heartland, on an arid, windswept plain from which the hulking Andes to the west burst with an absolute conviction of vertical upthrust. (Malargue has received a bit of international notice recently as the site selected for a giant cosmic ray observatory. The observatory will, according to one local official, "unveil the mystery of the highest-known energies in nature.")

Next, the xerophytic landscape of the plateau ramping up and into the mountains, with the wobbling bus carrying the team in relentless front-range winds. And finally, high in the mountains, Las Lenas itself, a small, self-contained resort in the midst of a landscape extraterrestrial in its treeless, desolate beauty. The hypermodern cluster of buildings on the white apron of the high Andes could have passed for a fleet of spacecraft, just settled upon a planet far, far away.

Now you might think that this phased transition, from familiar America through Buenos Aires to Space Station Las Lenas in the Andean moonscape, might have dazzled the young American.

And maybe it did. But in the end, literally above and beyond all that, what really opened his eyes was the skiing itself. "It was the most outrageous, out-of-bounds skiing I'd ever seen," Lewis recalls. "A run would usually begin with a steep chute. Then that would be followed by a long, constant pitch, with endless, untracked powder all the way down—so much powder that it was truly epic."

You hear this kind of story all the time from anyone who has spent any time in Las Lenas. Experienced skiers—extreme skiers and snowboarders, world-class racers in training, alpine guides who live the life of endless winter, and just regular folk—travel to Las Lenas and invariably return amazed. Perhaps that's because the whole idea of skiing in summer—of discovering that in summer (at least south of the equator) there can be winter—is itself counterintuitively amazing. But there's more to it than that. All tales of Las Lenas seem to find their focus in the same attributes—the lunar landscape, the steepness, the long runs, the snow. Consider each:

The lunar landscape. The Andes of Las Lenas have what Lewis describes as an "edginess" to them—sharp, rocky ridges and hard knuckles,

---

AT A GLANCE

LOCATION 660 miles west of Buenos Aires, Argentina	**TERRAIN ACREAGE** between 10,000 and 15,000 acres
SEASON Mid-June–mid-October	**VERTICAL RISE** 4,034 feet
IN-BOUNDS 1 2 ③ 4 5	**AVERAGE ANNUAL SNOWFALL** 250 inches
OFF-PISTE 1 2 3 4 ⑤	
SNOW 1 2 ③ 4 5	

LAS LENAS | 165

The Andes of Las Lenas are as barren as any mountains in the world.

with an austerity that is almost frightening in its beauty. These mountains are as magnificently barren as any mountains in the world, without even the rumor of a tree for miles around and (at least in winter) with little vegetation. The naked ground is due to a conspiracy of natural factors: elevation, the semiarid environment, the ferocious winds that sometimes blow. But whatever the reasons might be, these mountains don't look as if they belong on this planet. And when the moon itself shines upon Las Lenas at night, with its light refracted in the white of the snow with barely a shadow, the luminescence is indeed unearthly.

Add to that an even eerier, or at least less expected, paleontological phenomenon. If you begin poking around the rocks as you hike beyond boundaries for off-piste skiing, you stand a good chance of finding fossils. High in the mountains, above 11,000 feet, in the heart of the continent and far from the sea, you can come upon the fossilized remnants of marine creatures. They are a testament to the power of tectonics, which somewhere between 45 and 100 million years ago raised the Andes from the bed of an ancient sea. In fact, the tectonic work hasn't been completed yet; in places the Andes are still rising.

The steepness. Las Lenas' steepness finds its most brazen expression in the Marte chair, which ought to be included, along with the likes of the Aiguille du Midi cable car in Chamonix, France, and the Snowbird, Utah, tram, as one of the world's great lifts for adventurous skiing. Chris

Opposite: Explore beyond the boundaries, and you find many couloirs and chutes, some as steep as 60 degrees.

Davenport, the 1996 World Extreme Skiing Champion, says simply: "In terms of steepness and the terrain it accesses, the Marte chair is the best double chair in the world."

It must certainly qualify as one of the most improbable lifts, given its location. It has no business being where it is, rising above a near-vertical wall of rock marbled with snow, seemingly accessing no useful terrain. In the middle of the night in 1987, the lift was taken out by an avalanche, as if the gods of snow were saying: That lift has no right to exist. But there it is.

You get to the top of the Marte lift, and skiing still might seem an unlikely proposition. But gradually routes reveal themselves, fingering through the rocks, and steep as all get-out. Davenport isn't the only guy who thinks this is very good stuff. The word-of-mouth comes from almost every expert skier I know who has been to Las Lenas: If there is a single compelling reason to come to the place—one single reason above all

others to ski in South America—it is all the free-fall skiing from the Marte lift.

Although the Marte skiing is up-front, in-your-face steepness, it is really only a beginning, the hub in the axle of Las Lenas possibility. Hike and traverse a bit, explore beyond the loosely defined boundaries, and you come across all sorts of couloirs and chutes, some as steep as 60 degrees. And when you add to that steepness the lunar eeriness, you might find that in standing above a precipitous chute, defined by nothing but rock and snow and with no apparent safe harbor, your innards swell with a raw, distilled terror.

The long runs. A good friend of mine remembers scrambling beyond the top of the resort to an off-piste couloir that, in the warmth of the September sun, was covered with an even layer of corn snow, like the surface of a perfectly iced cake. He scoped out the couloir and confidently figured he'd be able to ski it top to bottom. The line was straight and uncomplicated, and the pitch

FOSSILS

The whole business of fossils fascinates me—the whole idea of finding evidence of the sea more than two miles above sea level. In this respect, I am not alone. Charles Darwin discovered seashell fossils in the Andes of Chile, documented at least in part in his book, *Voyage of the Beagle*. Darwin got lucky—he arrived after an earthquake, which helped to expose paleontological evidence that would otherwise have been buried. Present-day paleontologists continue to be drawn to the Andes, which are considered a relatively untapped treasure trove of prehistoric finds.

Fossils discovered in the Andes have encouraged paleontologists to make several intriguing hypotheses. A relatively recent discovery in the Andes, for example, has led scientists

to surmise that the *Tyrannosaurus rex* was not the largest meat-eating dinosaur, as was previously believed, but rather another razor-toothed, needle-nosed giant.

But I find more interesting the discovery in the Andes of a fossilized monkey skull. This led some researchers to hypothesize that monkeys "rafted" to South America from Africa on floating vegetation 30 million years ago. What a picture that makes—monkeys on the high seas.

I can't say with absolute assurance that you will find fossils when visiting Las Lenas. But I can say that the top of the resort is called Cerro Los Fossiles—the mountain of fossils. At least in name, you have come to the right place.

There is loads of lift-accessed backcountry terrain, from steep couloirs to wide-open bowl skiing.

even, and what was to stop him?

But big mountains like the Andes have a way of deceiving the eye, of telescoping large dimensions into something that appears manageable. About 100 turns into the couloir, spent of oxygen in the high altitude, the unstoppable skier stopped. And looking below, he realized that he was barely halfway to the bottom.

Las Lenas has a way of engendering stories like that. Lewis describes the terrain as "bigger than your vision"—an affirmation, I suppose, of the dimensional illusion that deceived my couloir-skiing friend. But to say that the runs at Las Lenas are long might itself be a deception. The total lift-serviced vertical, after all, is about 4,000 feet—not small, certainly, but smaller than at major resorts in the Alps. What makes Las Lenas long is

the continuity of the pitch. A run of 2,000 or 3,000 vertical feet without letup—no flat spots, no crossing roads, no commercial interruptions—is a hard find anywhere in the world, north or south of the equator.

The snow. The snow might come irregularly to Las Lenas, but when it does, it can blow in with a biblically diluvian intensity. At some point every winter, an epic, all-consuming storm will arrive; 9- to 10-foot dumps are not uncommon, and it has been known to snow as much as 20 feet in one continuous surge over the course of several days. This display of meteorological muscle is what locals refer to as the Santa Anna, the annual mother of all storms.

The Santa Anna usually arrives somewhere between late July and late August, and if you

September at Las Lenas when the austral spring sun warms things up.

bunker mentality fellowship among resort guests, cloistered tightly together like shipwreck victims in the high, snowbound Andes.

But if you come later in the season, when the warmth of September begins to recompose all that snow and turn it into corn, and if the elements—the sun, the melt-freeze cycle of spring days, the snow itself—cooperate, you might find yourself in the midst of something close to corn snow perfection. "The most awesome corn you could ever imagine," one friend of mine enthused after a run down a sun-drenched, off-piste face at Las Lenas. Well maybe so. Las Lenas is famous for the stuff, although your timing needs to be right. You need to be there at the moment of transformation, after the ice melts and before slush sets in. That's usually late in the morning. Take a few runs and after that, do what Argentines at Las Lenas do: Pull a chaise into the high-Andean sun, roll up your sleeves and put your dark glasses on, and enjoy a glass of the fine local wine.

Las Lenas is still a relative youth as ski resorts go, having come into being in 1983. Perhaps because of its youth, and no doubt because of its location in the Southern Hemisphere, it remains in relative obscurity. But allow time for the word to spread, for people like Doug Lewis and Chris Davenport, both fervent votaries for adventurous skiing, to return with stories filled with superlatives—the best, the most outrageous, the steepest, whatever. Let word-of-mouth confirm that Las Lenas represents the best lift-serviced skiing in South America.

WHAT TO EXPECT

IN-BOUNDS

According to official Las Lenas statistics, 5 percent of the terrain is suitable for novices, whereas 65 percent is suitable for advanced skiers. These numbers are either a) incorrect or b) indicative of a very large ski resort. Or perhaps both. Fact is, the novice terrain at Las Lenas is by no means insignificant. On the lower quarter of the mountain, two

happen to arrive in its midst, you could be very lucky or completely shafted. You might have the best powder day of your life; there is nothing in the world more satisfying than very deep snow and very deep terrain, if you can dispel from your mind any avalanche trepidation. On the other hand, you might find yourself restricted to the village for days with almost all the lifts closed. At such times, Las Lenas has been known to breed a

The whole idea of skiing or boarding during the Northern Hemisphere's summer is itself amazing.

lifts (Venus and Eros) are entirely devoted to novice skiing.

That said, let's be realistic: Las Lenas isn't about novice skiing. At Bariloche, Argentina's other major resort, 70 percent of the terrain is rated novice or intermediate. If gentle skiing is your priority, Bariloche is the place you ought to go in Argentina. The main reason to come to Las Lenas is to be challenged.

The skiing from the Marte lift, supplemented by what is accessible from the short Iris POMA that rises above it, is the main reason for Las Lenas' in-bounds notoriety. The terrain here is indeed steep, usually involving a chute that feeds a more open face, and long. *Finding* runs here, however, can be almost as challenging as skiing them. From the plateau at the top of the resort, there is little

indication where chutes descend between the rocks. Proceed prudently—if you err in choosing your line, you might find yourself trapped in a cul-de-sac of rock.

The Marte skiing, however, by no means represents all of the advanced skiing at Las Lenas. Lower down on the mountain, there is excellent advanced terrain from the Vulcano and Caris chairs. And you don't necessarily need to face the super-steeps of Marte to enjoy a run from the top. Jupiter 1, a beautiful, long run that descends over terrain rolls created by glacial deposition, is one of the more popular runs at the resort.

You could come to Las Lenas and do what the considerable majority of Argentine tourists do—stick to the groomed intermediate trails. You would no doubt enjoy yourself in doing so. But to

fully appreciate what makes Las Lenas special, you ought to be willing, snow conditions permitting, to take on an extra challenge, to scare yourself at least a little bit.

OFF-PISTE

From the top of the resort, you can head in three directions: up, right, or left. Almost immediately above the resort is the giant bowl of Cerro Entre Rios, which Chris Davenport calls "one of the best lift-accessed ski tours at any ski area in the world—2,000 feet of world-class, big-mountain skiing." Perhaps so, although Davenport's definition of "lift-accessed" is a liberal one. Skiing Cerro Entre Rios requires a strenuous climb at high elevation (above 11,000 feet). Cerro Entre Rios is just one of four major peaks above the resort that can be hiked and skied, the highest of which is 12,372 foot Cerro Torrecillas. All of this, as Davenport suggests, represents world-class, big-mountain skiing, meaning that no outing here should be undertaken lightly, or without a guide.

Easier to access is the terrain of Juno Bowl and Cerro El Collar, to the right of the main area. The access here involves traversing and moderate hiking—no long, steep, laborious ascents. There is an enormous amount of varied terrain here, from steep couloirs to wide-open bowl skiing. You could probably spend a full week in this area without skiing the same line twice.

Wherever you go off-piste in Las Lenas, you need to exercise pronounced caution in assessing snow stability. Avalanche warnings and closures at Las Lenas are loosely applied, at least by litigious American standards.

INSIDE LINE

The fanciest (and priciest) hotel in Las Lenas is the Piscis. It is also the biggest and most active in terms of nightlife. For a more modest price and a little less commotion, try the smaller Gemini. Note: You'll get the best lodging deals in all-inclusive packages (see Resources for tour operators).

Make sure to leave time in your travels for a couple of days in Buenos Aires.

Be prepared to stay up late. Argentines like to eat late (10 P.M.) and party later (till who knows when).

Because South Americans like to party late, they tend to sleep late. If you want the mountain pretty much to yourself (especially on a powder day), start at 9 A.M., when the lifts open.

Innstruck Pub is the popular hangout, but the insiders' spot might be Bash. But don't worry—Las Lenas is relatively small, and it won't take you more than a day or two to figure out the party scene.

Take some time off after skiing to check out the hot springs—*termas*, in local parlance—located about 6 miles down the road from the resort.

RESOURCES

General information: 011-54-627-71100. Website: www.laslenas.com. Reliable tour operators: Ski Vacation Planners (800-822-6754; www.skivacationplanners.com) and Moguls Ski and Snowboard Tours (800-666-4857; www.ski-moguls.com). Some packages include visits to other South American resorts as well, particularly Portillo in Chile and Bariloche.

Opposite: The Santa Anna, the annual mother of all storms, usually arrives between late July and late August; 9- to 10-foot dumps are common, and it has been known to snow as much as 20 feet in one storm.

BEYOND BOUNDARIES

Chugach Mountains

"...the mother lode of heli-skiing possibility."

It was absolutely nuts, a case of seat-of-the-pants free enterprise and backcountry adventure joining forces to spin recklessly toward potential catastrophe. For a mere $40 or so, you or anybody could have a go at it. Get yourself flown to the top of a remote Alaskan summit and from there, may luck be with you, you had to figure out how in the hell you were going to get out of there alive.

It worked like this: Helicopters would park at the base of the mighty Chugach Mountains along the Richardson Highway north of Valdez. Then they'd wait for business to show up—groups of seven or eight skiers or snowboarders who'd chip in five bucks apiece for the chance to throw caution out the window. The pilot would then drop the group on a searingly beautiful mountaintop, from which there might or might not be a safely skiable route back to the bottom. The pilot, after all, was interested mainly in a safe

Hiking on a ridge in The Library, one of countless heli-skiing and -boarding opportunities.

ALASKA

Anchorage • Valdez • Chugach Mountains
• Girdwood • Cordova

GULF OF ALASKA

landing area; getting down was the skiers' problem.

No rules or regulations, no supervision, no previous big-mountain experience necessary. No guides—you were on your own. No signs of civilization, no marked routes, no help should you get into trouble. No avalanche beacons, shovels, or emergency equipment required. Basically no nothing.

"Those first few years were a joke," says Dean Cummings, who now runs H2O Guides, a heli-skiing service based in Valdez. "If you had 40 bucks, you were in. It was very loose." The one heli-ski operation that did exist was equally loose, run by a guy who, among other things, was reportedly operating without insurance. "It was inevitably going to crash on him," says Cummings. "He lost his shirt for not paying bills and left town."

Ah yes, the good old days—the formative years of Alaskan heli-skiing, when the World Extreme Skiing Championships, first held in 1991, began bringing attention to one of the most spectacular patches of skiable turf on the planet. It was a paint-by-numbers, heli-skiing dreamland: 6,000-vertical-foot descents, as much as 80 feet of snow a year, 50-degree slopes on which the snow stuck and held, thousands of square miles of mountains that for the most part had not only not been skied, they also hadn't even been named.

The World Extremes opened eyes. Cummings, the 1995 champion who competed in the inaugural event in 1991, and Doug Coombs, champion in 1991 and 1993, were particularly noteworthy converts. Both went on to establish their own heli-skiing companies, recognizing the pressing need for guided skiing rather than the ad hoc insanity of the early '90s. They were like provisioners preparing for a gold rush—or perhaps more appropriately in this case, a white rush. The Chugach Mountains north of Valdez represented the mother lode of heli-skiing possibility, and Cummings and Coombs knew that when the word spread, the rush would be on.

Geology and meteorology come together here in a perfect, synergistic partnership. Moisture-laden storms track in from the Pacific, first colliding with islands that form the outer barrier around Prince William Sound and losing some of their gale-force ferocity. Passing over the relatively warm waters of the Sound—surprisingly, Valdez is the northernmost ice-free harbor in the United States—the storms pick up additional moisture before slamming into the mountains.

The snow has enough moisture in it to paste itself to steep slopes, and because the Chugach are particularly jagged and rough edged, there is a

AT A GLANCE

LOCATION Valdez is 50 miles east of Anchorage, Alaska

SEASON Mid-February–mid-May; late March is prime time

TERRAIN SUMMARY 7,000-foot summits, with descents to sea level possible; more than 1,500 square miles

VERTICAL RISE Runs of 2,000 to 6,000 vertical feet

AVERAGE ANNUAL SNOWFALL 400 inches in Valdez; as much as 1,000 inches at higher elevations

natural anchoring system to help prevent the snow from sliding. Subsequently, after the first frontal storm surge, cold air pushes in from the north and the snow lightens up. An initial foot or two of wet snow, bonding safely to preexisting snow layers, might be followed by another foot or two—or more—of light snow ideal for powder skiing. Finally, the climate is generally warmer than might be expected of Alaska. It might be 40 below zero 100 miles inland, but sub-zero days in Valdez are relatively rare, occurring only a handful of times in an average winter.

Great, stable snow, relatively warm weather by Alaska standards, wild mountains—so what more could you ask for? I remember speaking to Eric DesLauriers, a well-traveled extreme skier who lives in the Tahoe area, talking rapturously about his first trip to Alaska. This was a guy who had skied big stuff all over the world, but the Chugach, he said, were special. Slopes too steep to ski anywhere else in the world were skiable in the Chugach. The snow wasn't prone to sliding and sluffing off as it might be in, say, Colorado or the Alps. You could be ripping through powder in places that would be unskiable cliffs and icefalls in some other mountain range of the world. He spoke like a white-rusher who'd hit pay dirt, and his eyes shone with the look of a man in a state of bliss—like someone holding his first-born child in his arms.

Well I'm not sure that report was the kind of thing to set me to packing my bags; 50 degrees is still 50 degrees, which is pretty damned steep. Each time you come to the apogee of a powder-turning sequence on a slope like that—each time your skis rise to the surface of the snow in the transition between turns—there's a hairy moment of free falling involved. I wasn't sure I was ready to stomach that moment repeatedly, perhaps 100 or more times, in a single run down a 2,500-vertical-foot face.

Valdez has a boom-town quality to it in March and April, when all the hot-shit ski bums from the continental United States—"the core skiers and riders," as Cummings calls them—show up. It is a scene that has been compared (and rightfully so) to the surf scene on the North Shore of Oahu in early winter, when all the world's great big-wave riders, many living on a five-and-dime budget, show up and hang around waiting for a storm set with 15-foot swells to roll in. So it is with skiers and snowboarders in Valdez; they hang out and fish or ice climb to bide their time until the conditions are just right, when the skies clear and the snow's safe. They're willing to wait for days, because they've saved up their hard-earned money just for this. When the Chugach goes off, it's like nowhere else in the world.

But the core big-wave crew now have company; Chugach heli-skiing is transitioning toward a more broad-based realm in which those without extreme-level skills and chutzpah are welcome. This is a big, vast mountain range, after all, and the possibilities are essentially infinite. There are relatively low-angle glaciers and plenty of slopes no steeper than your average black-diamond run in mainstream resort land.

Chugach skiing isn't all about terrain like famous Meteorite Mountain, where sometime a long, long while ago a meteorite crashed into the

Above: Ski bums at the backcountry heli-pad, Thompson Pass. Opposite: Arcing a turn in the deep Chugach powder. Overleaf: Hans Johnstone on the glacier in The Library, Chugach Mountains.

mountainside and gouged out a 2,600-vertical-foot face at a sustained 50-degree pitch. It isn't all about skiing the Tusk, an equally precipitous pinnacle of rock protruding above a series of granite folds known as the Books, so named because they appear like a collapsing row of books on a shelf. That's the kind of Chugach terrain that splashes spectacularly into the ski world consciousness through photographs and movies, as well it should. But it speaks to me less of the athleticism of those captured on film than it does of the spectacle of the mountains themselves, still so wild and untamed, draped so completely with ghostlike sheets of snow, so full of possibility. It's steep, all right, but it's a whole lot more than that.

I came to Alaska in the winter of 1993 to ski in the area around Girdwood, to the west of Valdez. I was impressed foremost by the immediate wildness of the country—the quick transition from relative civilization to complete wilderness. I was impressed, too, by the convergence of mountains and sea, by the sight of the white-cloaked Chugach Mountains rising abruptly from the waters of Turnagain Arm.

On maps, the Chugach appear to be not much of a range at all, dwarfed by Mount McKinley and the Alaska Range to the northwest and by the Wrangell and St. Elias Mountains to the northeast. But as I looked out on this uniform procession of peaks serrating the horizon, it was clear that no map could do the Chugach Mountains justice, because no map can do justice to the immensity of Alaska.

Cummings's permit area alone covers 1,500 square miles, and he and his guides and pilots have established well over 400 landing zones, from which a countless number of runs descend. And of course Cummings is not alone; by 2000, at least six heli-ski operators were in business between Girdwood (to the west) and Cordova, to the east of Valdez. Furthermore, the mountains are still being charted, because the heli-skiing business, a child of the '90s, is still relatively young.

Thousands of runs have yet to be skied; in fact, many of the mountains haven't even been climbed yet. Spend a week heli-skiing in the Chugach, and it is all but a certainty that you will be able to claim a precious first descent, be part of a group laying down the first-ever tracks on one run or another. And it probably won't be on a sick-steep slope, because most of those have already been bagged by the core bums, whose main purpose is to do just that (go as steep as possible), and by professionals skiing and riding for film crews that are a regular presence in the Chugach in late spring.

That said, you might find yourself descending a run in the Chugach you would never consider elsewhere, a run so steep it would ordinarily register a quivering fear in your knees. That's because the relationship in the Chugach between mountains and snow is indeed a rare and special phenomenon, just as DesLauriers describes it. As a result, it removes—or at least lessens—the

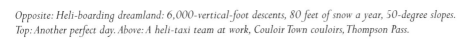

Opposite: Heli-boarding dreamland: 6,000-vertical-foot descents, 80 feet of snow a year, 50-degree slopes.
Top: Another perfect day. Above: A heli-taxi team at work, Couloir Town couloirs, Thompson Pass.

greatest risk of steep-slope skiing, which is the long, accelerating slide for life. "You can open up the envelope here, because if you tumble, the soft snow will stop you," says Cummings. "You're not going to tomahawk off the mountain."

Well thank goodness for that.

WHAT TO EXPECT

It snows heavily in the Chugach Mountains. In the winter of 1999 to 2000, 17 feet of snow had fallen by December in Valdez, where at sea level the snowfall is relatively modest. At higher elevations, the estimate was between 30 and 50 feet of snow by December 1.

Such abundance can be both a good and a bad thing. Lots of snow obviously contributes to a quality powder experience, but it can also mean that there are many days when the visibility or the stability of the snow makes skiing and snow-boarding either impossible or unsafe. *Down time* is

RECOVERY: PRINCE WILLIAM SOUND

On March 24, 1989, Captain Joe Hazelwood of the *Exxon Valdez* radioed from Bligh Reef in Prince William Sound that he had "fetched up hard aground" and that he was "evidently leaking some oil." That might have been one of the great understatements in ecological history; in all, about 11 million gallons of oil were released into the Sound.

At least 28 damaged species and resources were identified, including sea otters, bird species, and nesting beds for salmon eggs. The case against Exxon made its way to the courts, eventually resulting in a jury award of $5 billion against the oil giant. The money (most of which had not been paid by Exxon ten years after the spill) was supposed to finance the cleanup and to pay restitution to, among others, fishermen whose livelihood was affected by the spill.

oil is gone, and many affected species are thought to be in reasonably good shape. This has encouraged Frank Sprow, Exxon vice president for environment and safety, to proclaim, "We see the Sound as essentially recovered. There is a growing consensus in the scientific community that the Sound has returned to a thriving, robust and productive state."

But others aren't so sure. "There is still some oil out there," says an official for the National Marine Fishery. "It's less than 1 percent of the original beach coverage, but it's not hard to find. . . . Exxon says you can't find *Exxon Valdez* oil out there. Well that's crap. Of course you can." In addition, only 2 of the 28 affected species and resources (bald eagles and sea otters) were, on the tenth anniversary, deemed to have recovered fully.

More than a decade later, what is the ecological status of the Sound? It depends on whom you ask. Scientists generally agree that life in the spill zone has made a significant rebound. Most of the

Nevertheless, Prince William Sound, recreationally speaking, is thriving. Ten years after the spill, sea kayak and recreational boat traffic in the Sound had more than doubled.

an embedded idiom in the language of Valdez heli-skiing, and anyone planning a six-day excursion to the Chugach should count on at least one or two down days.

The snow is typically denser than the snow in continental ranges in places like Colorado and Utah. This is why it adheres to steep faces and bonds well, creating unusually stable conditions. But special gear is also required to make the most of it. If you're a skier, don't even think of heading for the Chugach without bringing—or making arrangements to use—a pair of extra-wide skis. They are typically available for rental from heli-ski operators.

Despite rumors to the contrary, Alaskan winters are not 23 hours of darkness interrupted by an hour of dim daylight. In December and January—in the days bracketing the winter solstice—days are indeed very short. But daylight returns quickly, at the rate of seven to eight minutes a day at times. That might not sound like much, but it adds up quickly. And by March in the Valdez, daylight accounts for 16 or more hours of every day.

In a typical Alaska heli-skiing experience—and I use *heli-skiing* to cover both skiing and snowboarding—groups are divided according to ability, and terrain is selected according to the ability of the least accomplished member of the group. Most runs cover between 2,000 and 5,000 vertical feet, although in February, when there is usually a reliable snowpack down to sea level, some runs can exceed 6,000 vertical feet. On average, about 20,000 vertical feet are covered in a day. But if the weather, daylight, and fitness of a group permit it, 40,000 vertical feet in a day are certainly possible.

The Chugach Mountains form one of the world's great snowbelts, but conditions are not always perfect. Wind, sun, and warm, moist air later in the season can wreak havoc on the snow surface. Put it this way: Go heli-skiing in the Chugach and you will ski deep powder, but don't expect every turn to be in deep powder. Wind-packed snow, sunbaked crust, glacial ice, and other less-than-ideal conditions are possible.

All in all, given the possibility of extended down time and imperfect snow, you might find that the total hours you end up powder skiing on a Chugach trip are relatively small. But hey—it's all about quality, not quantity. Poll any number of people after their first trip to Valdez, and almost all will respond like Eric DesLauriers—as if they had discovered the fount of perfection, the best skiing of their lives.

INSIDE LINE

The Totem Inn (907-835-4443) is heli-skiing headquarters in Valdez, both for lodging and for hanging out when the weather is uncooperative. But there are plenty of other places to stay in Valdez, including a dirt-cheap hostel (907-835-2155).

Bring all the toys in the closet when you come to the Chugach. Kayaking, fishing, ice fishing, ice climbing can all be part of the scene, especially if the weather high in the mountains doesn't permit skiing.

One advantage to basing your operations in Girdwood is that a very good ski area, Alyeska, is there. You can mix in lift-serviced skiing with heli-skiing. The downside: The snowfall is not quite as abundant as it is around Valdez.

RESOURCES

H2O Guides (800-578-HELI or 907-835-8418; www.h2oguides.com) operates out of Valdez, in the eastern mountains of the Chugach range. Chugach Powder Guides (907-783-4355) operates out of Girdwood in the west. A decent website for general tourist information (lodging, activities, history, etc.) for southeast Alaska is www.alaskagold.com.

Columbia Mountain Backcountry

The heart of one of the world's most exquisite, unspoiled mountain environments

I f you were to ask Hans Gmoser, he'd probably tell you that the thing that changed heli-skiing forever was the flush toilet.

Gmoser, a crusty Austrian mountain guide who moved to the mountains of eastern British Columbia in the '50s, was the man who invented heli-skiing in the '60s. He was a guide's guide, a man with a love affair with rock, ice, fierce weather, and backcountry deprivation. Eastern British Columbia was the perfect world for some-

one like Gmoser. The multiple ranges of the Columbia Mountains—the Purcells, the Selkirks, the Monashees, and the Cariboos—were like the Alps before civilization. Raw, steep, and glaciated, with 6,000 or more feet of vertical relief, they showed hardly a hint of human intervention other than a few logging roads and old mining camps. Gmoser was particularly inspired by a subrange known as the Bugaboos, where 1,500-foot granite obelisks rose out of a pool of glacial ice.

Backcountry traverse on Crescent Glacier in the Bugaboo Mountains.

When he first came up with the idea of ferrying skiers to high-mountain ridges as a way of avoiding the drudgery of hours of trekking and climbing in deep snow, he did so with a pang of guilt. Mountains weren't supposed to be easy.

He and the first few heli-skiers stayed in an abandoned mining camp, and even that struck Gmoser as an indulgence. To a hardcore mountain man like Gmoser, in order to respect the mountains—and for the mountains to yield back cosmic respect of their own—you had to suffer. If you sought something from the mountains—let's say a clean and perfect run through 3,000 vertical feet of untouched powder snow—then the mountains had the right to demand something in return. Mountaineering was supposed to be a quid pro quo deal, in which the human payback came in the form of frostbite or hours of waiting out a storm, of the exertion of a 3-mile hike through snow 2 feet deep or the discomfort of overnighting in a tent at 15 below zero.

But the early mining camps of Gmoser's heli-skiing operation, Canadian Mountain Holidays (CMH), were soon replaced by remote lodges, accessible only by helicopter, that were decadently luxurious by back-country standards. There would be gourmet food, plush comforters on every bed, electric lighting—and, of course, flush toilets. The makings of what would become a small heli-skiing empire were in place.

CMH now comprises 11 distinct areas with a total of more than 7,000 square miles of terrain, larger than the states of Connecticut and Rhode Island combined. It was Gmoser's own doing, this softening of the rugged mountain life. But he wasn't necessarily happy about it.

"You could say that a lot of these people don't really deserve to be brought into such a pristine environment if they are not willing to do it on their own and pay the real price," Gmoser told me a few years back. "Nowadays, if you can't give people a private room with a private bath, they tell you, 'well in that case, I just can't come.' You wonder if they are coming to ski or to go to the bathroom." Not long thereafter, he retired as president of CMH.

I admire Gmoser as a mountain man of principle, who probably felt he had betrayed his principles and made irrevocable, recreant compromises. Maybe he felt he was trivializing the mountains he

---

AT A GLANCE

LOCATION Several locations, southeastern British Columbia

SEASON December–early May

TERRAIN SUMMARY Summits top out above 10,000 feet; more than 7,000 square miles of terrain, about half high-alpine skiing, half lower-elevation tree skiing

VERTICAL RISE Runs of between 1,200 and 6,000 vertical feet

AVERAGE ANNUAL SNOWFALL 400–700 inches

Skiing in an unnamed backcountry bowl near Kicking Horse Resort north of Golden, B.C.

loved, making access as painless and easy as going to an amusement park. I'm sure he felt that people didn't fully appreciate the rare splendor of the remote backcountry in which they were skiing. But there's no doubt that in doing what he did, in inventing the heli-skiing business, he threw open the doors to a brave new world for a large population. To be away in the mountains, to ski or snowboard down a remote glacier surrounded by rocky peaks and deep blue sky, no longer had to be a private party to which only skilled mountaineers were invited.

I first went on a heli-skiing trip in the mid-'80s, to CMH's Bobbie Burns Lodge. The lodge was just a few miles as the helicopter flies from the Bugaboo lodge where the whole heli-skiing

thing began. With the other clients for the week, I rode in a bus from Calgary through Banff and Lake Louise, through the spectacular Canadian Rockies. We continued west and south through a broad, low-elevation valley known as the Columbia River Trench, with the Rockies to the east and the Columbias to the west. We were ultimately delivered to a wholly ignoble site—a brown, dusty field with a wooden outhouse and not much else, where the helicopter would pick us up and carry us to the lodge. In such surroundings, the powder skiing prospects seemed unpromising.

But enter the glory of helicopter transport in the mountains. Within minutes, flying over deep green forests and winding mountain streams and even a bear doing some spring foraging, we reached the snow level and soon thereafter the lodge. A good day's hike and maybe more if you had to trudge through deep snow, from barren land to the snowy threshold of high-alpine British Columbia, had been dispensed with a 20-minute helicopter ride.

It was an extraordinary week of skiing, maybe still the best week of skiing I've ever experienced. For six straight days the weather was sunny and windless. On north-facing slopes, the late-April snow was still dry, light powder; on south-facing slopes the corn snow, released from its overnight freeze by the warming midmorning sun, would set up perfectly. The terrain was a perfect mix: open bowls framed by buttresses of granite; long, easy glacier runs; steep, avalanche-created corridors through the trees—the whole ball of wax. Every ridgeline yielded a panorama of jumbled peaks and glaciers to take your breath away, for more perfect mountain architecture can hardly be imagined. It was true wilderness—no signs of highways, power lines, or even (as far as I could tell) logging cuts.

We would lunch in the sun on a frozen lake beneath the silent mountains and a dome of blue sky, and there was something very satisfying in

A Canadian Mountain Holidays (CMH) helicopter picks up skiers. CMH invented heli-skiing in B.C.

knowing that the nearest human settlement was at least 30 miles away. We skied from eight in the morning until six in the evening, wearing just windbreaking shells over T-shirts because the fine weather allowed it. In six days we easily amassed over 150,00 vertical feet worth of skiing. It was something else, even if it might have given a mountain purist like Hans Gmoser reason to question his invention.

Heli-skiing isn't always like that, of course. The Monashees, the most westerly of the Columbia mountain ranges, are particularly notorious for heavy snowfall, being blasted in some areas by more than 700 inches of snow a year. The weather is often gray and unruly, hanging over the mountain summits for days on end. For the sake of both visibility and safety, much of the skiing is at lower elevations, among the giant evergreen trees.

At higher, more exposed elevations above tree line, the wind can blow so hard, it virtually polishes the snow. I've seen an avalanche in the Cariboos rip so much snow off the mountainside that only the underlying glacial ice was left. A midwinter thaw-freeze pattern can create an ice crust on the snow surface that is essentially unskiable and highly avalanche prone should new snow fall.

As Gmoser said to me with some relish, "Every day the mountains are different, with different moods. Some days you feel angry at them because the wind is blowing and the snow isn't any good. Some days you just feel like it is the start of a honeymoon and everything is just perfect."

Heli-telemarking near Roger's Pass, one of the snowiest areas of the Columbia Mountains.

But all in all, perfection or something close to it, is more likely than not. Over the course of a winter, the guides develop an intimate relationship with the terrain and the weather. They know where to find the best snow, and given all the available terrain out there, they have many options to choose from. They confer in the morning, select appropriate locations, and then begin shuttling four groups of 11 skiers to the mountaintops. If the snow or weather proves to be terrible, there is always—always—another ridge or basin or forest to explore. That's the beauty of so many square miles of terrain.

Canadian Mountain Holidays is now a multi-million-dollar enterprise, the world's largest heli-ski operator. But the mountains of eastern British Columbia are vast, a larger chunk of turf than most people might imagine, angling to the northwest from the U.S.-Canadian border for roughly 500 miles. It is, unquestionably, the center of the heli-skiing universe, or at least it is until Alaska's full potential is tapped. There's plenty of room for other operators to enter into the heli-skiing business, and enter they have. Mike Wiegele (see box, opposite), a transplanted Austrian like Gmoser, created a magnificent compound outside the middle-of-nowhere crossroads of Blue River. Selkirk Tangiers operates out of Revelstoke; Purcell Helicopter Skiing operates out of Golden.

Several lodges accessible only by helicopter—including Purcell Lodge, Selkirk Mountain Experience on Durrand Glacier, Mistaya Lodge, and Battle Abbey (which is operated by CMH)—are devoted to randonnée (aka alpine touring) and telemark skiing. The helicopter deposits you at the remote lodge, departs, and then it's gone, reappearing several days later to return you to civilization. Using climbing skins, you hike for your downhill fun rather than ride the helicopter, contouring up open slopes in zigzagging patterns.

Needless to say, you spend a lot more time going uphill than downhill, on average maybe an hour of climbing for every five minutes of skiing. But you come to appreciate it, and I can attest to that, having spent a week at Battle Abbey with none other than Gmoser himself and a few friends. We'd climb and ski runs of as much as 3,000 vertical feet, registering a total of as much as 10,000 feet at day's end—a long and hard day's work, believe me. But I found myself enjoying the uphill climbing more than the descents. It was almost as if my mind escaped inside itself, because

the slow movement—one step in front of the other, each making a soft, crunching sound in the fresh snow—was hypnotic. These moments make you think of things you would never have imagined thinking about—an old girlfriend, the art of baking bread, the deeper mysteries of the cosmos. The mental part of climbing becomes like a dream. After that, making the mental transition to the speed of going downhill is like being awoken by an alarm clock.

Randonnée skiing is not as frenzied as heli-skiing can sometimes be. There isn't the urgency to embark and disembark swiftly from the chopper so that it can keep its appointed rounds with other

GETTING FAT

When Mike Wiegele, Canadian Mountain Holidays' principal rival in the heli-skiing business in British Columbia, began encouraging clients to use extrawide skis in the early '90s, many cynics scoffed. The skis were dubbed "fat boys"—appreciatively by some, with derision by others. But the skis revolutionized deep-powder skiing.

Skis of conventional width, generally 60 millimeters wide or narrower at the waist, would dive deep into the snow and require skill and strength to prevent hopeless submersion. Traditional powder technique required a down-weighting of the ski to effectively springload it, giving it the energy necessary to lift back above the surface of the snow between turns. The trampoline effect was thrilling, but if the timing was wrong, or the down-weighting too pronounced, or the balance of the skier not quite right, the chances of getting tripped up or losing control in deep powder were excellent.

The extra-wide skis—fat skis as wide as 90 millimeters at the waist—enabled a skier to stay within a few inches of the snow surface. You could, in essence, surf the top layer of the snow, as if on a snowboard, and simply tilt the skis one way or the other to turn. You didn't have to be an expert skier anymore; if you were a decent intermediate, you could jump on a pair of fat skis and be a competent heli-skier.

At first, expert skiers suggested that using fat skis wasn't real skiing, that it made skiing so easy that it amounted to cheating. But by the end of the millennium, every big-mountain backcountry skier in Alaska and British Columbia was using some form of fat skis. Although the skis opened the door to heli-skiing for intermediates, they also raised the bar of possibility for experts. Fat skis made it possible to carve wide-arcing turns in powder at speeds exceeding 50 mph and of soaring over cliffs with the confidence that the wide skis would provide an extra-stable platform to land on.

Blue sky powder day at Roger's Pass, Glacier National Park, Columbia Mountains.

groups of skiers and snowboarders. But you know, the whole reason to come to these mountains, whether your means of going uphill is a helicopter or skins on your skis, is simply to be in the heart of one of the world's most exquisite, unspoiled mountain environments. At least that's the reason to come if you happen to have the heart of a true mountain man like Hans Gmoser.

WHAT TO EXPECT

During its formative years in the '70s and even '80s, helicopter skiing was considered a sport for which only the brave and the talented need apply. No longer. Any skier with at least intermediate skills on groomed snow (anyone who can make a decent parallel turn) can now have at it.

There is no "typical" heli-ski run in British Columbia. I've skied runs of less than 1,000 ver-

tical feet through the trees, and I've skied runs of over 5,000 vertical feet on open glaciers. Super-steep runs (over 50 degrees) are rare, although not because such terrain doesn't exist. For a group with the appropriate skills, a guide might consider taking on something that challenging, but for the most part the pitch of the terrain falls in the 20- to 40-degree range. In large heli-ski operations (e.g., CMH and Mike Wiegele's), groups are usually divided according to ability and are guided to terrain that is appropriate.

Perhaps the most challenging skiing in the region is in the Monashees, known for steep tree skiing through deep snow. But wherever you go, weather and snow stability dictate what terrain is skiable. In an average heli-skiing week, you'll probably spend about 60 percent of your time in open high-alpine terrain, the rest in the trees at lower elevations.

Most operators usually offer a guarantee of between 15,000 and 20,000 vertical feet per day, or about 100,000 vertical feet a week. If weather conditions or mechanical problems prevent you from reaching the guaranteed number, the operator refunds your money proportionally. But no operator likes parting with money, so you can be certain that everything will be done within the bounds of reason and safety to reach the target number. Refunds are exceedingly rare. On the other hand, you're charged for any extra skiing you do. In my first heli-skiing week in the Bobbie Burns, for example, I skied about 150,000 vertical feet, so I had to pay for the 50,000 extra vertical not included in my original package. It can be an expensive add-on, but if the snow is good it's well worth whatever you can afford.

The snow quality is probably at its peak in February and early March, but don't rule out April. The weather warms, the days are longer, and the snow on north-facing slopes, particularly at higher elevations, remains cold and dry. Conversely, January at this latitude can be bitterly cold.

INSIDE LINE

In most cases, don't bother to lug along your own skis. Most operators can set you up with rental skis or boards that are ideally suited to the snow and terrain you'll be skiing.

Bring an extra pair of gloves and goggles. Gloves can get very wet, mostly from the handling of skis when getting in and out of the helicopter. And there is probably no more essential piece of equipment for powder skiing than good goggles, so a backup pair is psychological reinforcement.

For a pre-heli warm-up day, consider trying one of several snowcat-skiing operators in eastern B.C. The cost is typically about half of what a day of heli-skiing costs, and you should still be able to get in at least 12,000 vertical feet.

Skinning up to a favorite run near Snowpatch Spire, Bugaboo Mountains.

RESOURCES

CMH Heli-Skiing (800-661-0252; 403-762-7100; www.cmhski.com) and Mike Wiegele Helicopter Skiing (800-661-9170; 250-673-8381; www.wiegele.com) are the two largest operators.

Southern Alps

"The heli landed me on the steepest,
most humbling terrain I've ever encountered."

I came to the South Island of New Zealand in May, a month representing an antipodal hiatus between seasons. Fall had more or less ended, but winter had not quite begun. It was too early to ski, but it wasn't too early to fly up onto the flanks of Mount Cook and inspect the possibilities, to get a feel for what skiing might be like in the Southern Alps.

The Mount Cook Airport was a forlorn-looking outpost at the hardscrabble end of the mountain's glacial zone, where a fan of silt had completed its muddy sprawl and the grasses of a broad, flat plain begin. I boarded a small plane, and only when we were airborne, with the plane's engine thrumming loudly as we made our way up above the giant trench carved out by the Tasman Glacier, did it become evident how big a mountain complex this was.

From the airport, Mount Cook was clearly visible at what appeared to be relatively close

Jason Onley drops into snowboard heaven in the Southern Alps near Mount Cook.

range. But as we proceeded above the glacier, it became obvious that the mountain hadn't been particularly close at all. The Tasman measures 18 miles long, from its source high on Mount Cook to its alluvial terminus. It is a half mile wide. And once we arrived and landed at the approximate headwaters of the glacier, where the Tasman and Franz Josef Glaciers diverge (the former flowing east, the latter west), my goodness, what a world.

All around us, as we stood on the level expanse of ice that had provided us a safe landing area, crevasse-riddled ice and snow lay in crumpled and swirled patterns—a work in geological progress, very unsettled. A month or so later, we could have skied right from that spot, down either the Tasman or the Franz Josef, on a long, gentle, classically glacial run.

In the business of mountain making, the Southern Alps, of which Mount Cook at 12,349 feet is the highest, are relatively new to the process. They aren't much more than 20 million years old, barely beyond infancy in geological terms. Glaciers—something like 360 in all, with the Tasman being the largest—are still hard at work eroding and smoothing the hard edges and toothy spikes that tectonic upthrust created millions of years ago. The result, if you can appreciate the sculptural art of mountains, is a work of raw and beautiful incompletion. It will take a few more million years of glacial and meteorological activity to temper the jagged red-gray peaks that protrude insistently, like giant shards of rock, from the glacial jumble of seracs and crevasses.

Perhaps because of their youth, the glaciers of the Southern Alps can be unusually frisky. This was something that Dick Durrance, America's first great Olympic racer, discovered upon coming to New Zealand in 1937 for summer training on Mount Cook's Ball Glacier, a spur of the larger Tasman. (In those days, the only way to get to New Zealand was by steamship, a trip that took three weeks from San Francisco, by way of the Fiji Islands.) The American party encamped in a hut at the edge of the glacier, and all around them, the glacier churned away under the inexorable pull of gravity. Durrance, a man not easily disconcerted when in the mountains, was disconcerted.

He is quoted in John Jerome's biography, *The Man on the Medal,* as saying: "It was a very fast-moving glacier. Every day, we would cross over from the moraine at the edge of the glacier, and

---

AT A GLANCE

LOCATION The Southern Alps rise near the west coast of New Zealand's South Island

SEASON June–September

TERRAIN SUMMARY Runs of between 2,000 and 4,000 vertical feet, almost entirely above treeline. At least 8 heli-ski companies operating in the 450-mile Southern Alp range.

VERTICAL RISE Runs of 1,000 to 7,000 vertical feet

AVERAGE ANNUAL SNOWFALL 400 inches

Crossing the Sheila Glacier, Mount Cook. Glacier skiing in New Zealand has been compared to skiing the Vallée Blanche in Chamonix, France (see Chapter 6).

our tracks would've moved down a foot and a half during the nights. . . . When you were walking up, you could hear the crevasses cracking and opening, and there were all kinds of avalanches breaking off the face of Mt. Cook and thundering down the very precipitous face. . .". A foot and a half a day might not sound like much, but in glacial terms, it is the speed of a runaway train. At night in the hut, Durrance was haunted by nightmares of being consumed in the rictus of some yawning breach in the ice.

Rising up suddenly with their brash youthfulness, the Southern Alps are broadly exposed to every winter storm that comes roiling in from the Tasman Sea to the west. The result is a surprising amount of snow, particularly in the midst of a climate that is otherwise generally mild.

Fly into Christchurch (on the east coast of

the South Island) in August, and you'd be hard pressed to believe that there could be any snow at all. The Canterbury Plains around Christchurch are still green. Even in Queenstown, in the heart of the mountains and a principal center for all things adventurous on the South Island, midwinter temperatures are typically in the mid-40s (F). By any normal ski town standards, that is balmy. But move into the nearby mountains and things change in a hurry. The Southern Alps, in their sudden elevation gain, rush through climate zones as quickly as any mountains in the world that I know of. You might be surrounded by lush greenery at lower elevations, but on the peaks of the relatively slender Main Divide—New Zealand's version of the North American Continental Divide—as much as 400 inches of snow fall in a year.

As a result, the Southern Alps now rival

Hiking along the lake at the bottom of the Sheila Glacier in Hooker Valley, with Mount Cook in the background.

Alaska as a world center for heli-skiing and rival perhaps the Alps themselves—those in Europe, that is—for alpine touring. At least ten heli-skiing operators are in business within a couple of hours drive of Queenstown, and that count doesn't include a good number of fixed-wing pilots willing to fly you into the backcountry.

Queenstown is sometimes referred to as the Chamonix of the Southern Hemisphere, and not without justification; it seems that about one of every three people you meet in town is an Alpine guide. That's understandable. The mountains closest to town are the Remarkables, earning the name because of their remarkable angularity, which makes them handsome in the way a face with high cheekbones and a pronounced jawline is handsome. Look up at those mountains from town, and whatever Alpinist genes might be simmering in your system must certainly start to burn.

But the truth is, you don't really have to be an Alpinist at all—at least from a skiing perspective—to feel the burn or to get in on the action. Despite their hard-edged, coltish nature, the Southern Alps willingly cede a truly wild ride to just about anyone capable of not much more than being able to stand up on skis or a snowboard. I'm not sure there is anywhere else in the world where you can become so completely immersed in a glacial wilderness without even the skills to make it down an intermediate run at your home hill.

The Tasman Glacier, to wit, is by no means a difficult run, assuming you have a competent guide to lead you around those frisky crevasses. The main route descends roughly 4,000 vertical feet in 7 miles, averaging out to a little over 10 degrees in pitch. Sometimes there is no pitch at all, where the Tasman flattens completely. There might be 10,000-foot peaks that line the glacier,

Top: The Empress Hut at the base of the Hooker Face on Mount Cook. Above: Looking for a route through the seracs on Sheila Glacier.

for those seeking to climb and ski much more precipitous descents. But as my friend, the writer and ski instructor Lito Tejada-Flores wrote about skiing the Tasman: "Remarkable is the fact that such dramatic skiing can be so technically easy, so forgiving, so accessible to skiers of literally any level."

That might be the Southern Alps' everlasting gift to adventure-minded humanity: It is glacial adventure for everyman. Glacier skiing in New Zealand has been compared to skiing the Vallée Blanche in—where else—Chamonix, France (see Chapter 6). But because it is so out there at the edge of civilization, so wild, so removed from crowds (with no lifts, after all), it might possibly be even better than that.

All that said, the Southern Alps also have terrain to allow you to go as big as you want, as big as anywhere else in the world. In the fall of 2000, I spoke with Charlotte Moats, a 19-year-old American extreme skier, after she had returned from participating in a spirited event called the World Heli Challenge, held in Mount Aspiring National Park northwest of Queenstown. The idea was to bring together many of the world's best extreme skiers and snowboarders for a series of events to put their extreme skills to a wide-ranging test. For anyone of a mind to push their limits on 50-degree slopes or do backflips off cliffs, the Southern Alps stood ready and able to deliver.

Among the Challenge events was a Chinese downhill, in which all the competitors started simultaneously in a race through a 5-inch layer of new snow down the Tindle Glacier. It was a mad dash in the wilderness, through powder snow at speeds of close to 60 mph, with the first person to the finish being declared the winner. That person was Moats.

After that, she and her fellow competitors went freeskiing, and what amazing skiing it was. "I've seen Alaska, Europe, North America, and South America, and the Alps of New Zealand are among the very most impressive," Moats said.

Snowboarder Jason Onley looks very small against the icefalls and seracs below Mount Cook.

"The heli landed me on the steepest, most humbling terrain I've ever encountered." The impressiveness was both physical and visual, for many heli-skiing runs in New Zealand feature a rare, two-toned beauty. The snow line usually ends high and abruptly, cutting the mountains in half horizontally, and as you descend through the white of snow, you can see, far below, the green of the valley floor.

A message should be seen in that: No one ought to come to New Zealand just to ski. Moats figured that out. Skiing for her was just one piece that fit seamlessly into a gorgeously complicated, natural puzzle, all seasons included at once. "It's simply paradise on earth," Moats said, and went on in explanation: ". . .stunning and diverse geography . . . lush rain forests. . .ferns twice your size . . .the longest waterfalls in the world. . ." And so on, with no reference to skiing or snow at all. "It blows my mind that the whole world hasn't moved

there yet," was her summary.

I know what she means. New Zealanders seem to take an odd pride in reporting the fact that there are something like twenty sheep for every human being, a statistic that suggests not only that the country's population is overwhelmingly ovine but also that humans are remarkably few. The lack of humanity is hard to figure. Sure—New Zealand might be isolated islands on the far side of the world, but where else in the world do winter and summer come together so seductively in such a drop-dead-gorgeous mountain world?

I have two photos of New Zealand, taken during a visit in 1984, that continue to remind me of what a mind-blowing place it is. One is of Lake Wakitipu, near Queenstown; the other is of the New Zealand countryside in a location I can no longer recall. Both photos seem at first to be about a quality of light, of the sun knifing through

Carving turns below Mount Cook.

clouds, highlighting the washboard contours of mountain ridges and the green of valley pastures. Yet I'd like to think the photos project a quality deeper and more suggestive than mere light: an aura of fecund, prelapsarian Elysium. In its balance of land and sky, of white-topped mountains and verdant valleys, of rich, settled flatlands and ever-restless glaciers, New Zealand is close to a modern paradigm of Edenic perfection. Paradise on Earth? Maybe.

WHAT TO EXPECT

There are several, commercial, lift-serviced ski areas in New Zealand, perhaps the best of which are Treble Cone, Coronet Peak, and Mount Hutt. But they are all modest in size, with vertical rises measuring 2,000 feet or less. They are perfectly satisfactory for a warm-up day or two, to rid yourself of the effects of jet lag. But in and of themselves, they aren't enough to justify travel halfway around the world.

In fact, probably the best lift-serviced skiing in New Zealand is at club-run ski areas, where the lifts are usually nothing more than rope tows. Typically, the areas will rent you a device called a nutcracker that attaches to the tow. The name derives from the pain it can inflict if not properly employed. Glen Plake, the extreme skier known for his spiked Mohawk hair, has told me that one of his favorite places in the world to ski is Craigieburn Valley, a club-run area west of Christchurch. The lifts might be rudimentary and old-fashioned, but the terrain is first rate. (Craigieburn bills itself as "steep, deep, and cheap.") If there is fresh snow and a full moon, the club members might even start up the lift for a little night skiing. Another popular club area is Temple Basin in Arthur's Pass National Park.

Still, the reason to come to New Zealand is to go deep into the mountains, for heli-skiing or touring. The Southern Alps extend in a fairly narrow band for about 250 miles near the South Island's west coast, from Arthur's Park in the north to Mount Aspiring National Park in the south, with Mount Cook in the approximate middle. A number of subranges are involved here— among them the Arrowsmith, Palmer, Ragged, Humboldt, and Richardson Mountains—providing natural subdivisions for the helicopter operators to divvy up the landscape.

The quality of the snow is probably less of a sure thing than it is in other heli-skiing kingdoms such as Alaska and British Columbia. There is no shortage of snow, of course, but the radical variations in climate exacted by the mountains' vertical upthrust mean that a descent can lead from dry powder to corn to crust to no snow at all. Or

Skiing powder on the back side of Mount Hutt with green farmland below.

it might be powder from top to bottom. You never know. But given the versatility of the helicopter to range far and wide, the chances of finding good snow are very, very good.

Although skiing might be the main theme of your trip, you should also be ready to fish, golf, mountain bike, surf, hike, windsurf, etc., etc. It might be a bit chilly at times in winter for these activities, but sunny days in the 60s (F) in Queenstown in August aren't uncommon.

INSIDE LINE

Queenstown caters to mainstream tourism, meaning that as a hub of activity—restaurants, shops, touristy activities, and so forth—it's the place to set up base camp. But if you're looking for a little more youthful, laid-back atmosphere, head 50 miles north to Wanaka.

How good a deal are club fields? For something in the neighborhood of 30 to 40 bucks a day, you can get lodging, food, lift tickets, and plenty of company. Just don't be surprised if you find you have to pitch in washing the dishes.

Take the time to drive to Milford Sound on the west coast. Photographs of the Sound have been published in many magazines, but no photograph can do these waters and the surrounding rain forest justice.

RESOURCES

General information: Tourism New Zealand: 011-64-4-917-5431; www.purenz.com. Website on New Zealand skiing: www.snow.co.nz. Heli-skiing operators: Among the reliable operators are Harris Mountains Heli Ski: 011-64-3-442-6722; www.heliski.co.nz, which is based in Queenstown, and Backcountry Helicopters (011-64-3-443-1054; www.heliski.net.nz), which is based in Wanaka. Ski-touring guide service: Alpine Guides (011-64-3-435-1834; www.alpineguides. co.nz) leads ski-touring trips on the Tasman Glacier, and also offers heli-skiing.

The West Coast

You can ski 3,000-foot runs through a tapestry of Arctic color

O n the west coast of Greenland, where two fjords meet, sits what is left of an old Danish settlement. A lone building still stands above rocks smoothed by the combined forces of glacial activity and the sea. A person might easily perceive this to be a sacred stepping-off point to the world hereafter, a place where terrestrial life, both literally and symbolically, comes to an end.

On this spot, a cairn is built in memory of the late extreme skier Trevor Petersen, killed in an avalanche in Chamonix, France, in 1996. His ashes are here. And various small items—hats, sunglasses, gloves, and so on—have been left here, too. These items were gifts Petersen had given to the local Inuits, with whom he had struck up a powerful friendship after visits (with other extreme skiers and entrepreneurs) to inspect the possibilities of establishing a commercial heli-skiing operation in Greenland. Upon his death, in deference the Inuits felt it proper to return those

Extreme skier Jeremy Nobis loads helicopter, Hamborgerland, Greenland, spring 2000.

GREENLAND

Sisimiut

HAMBORGERLAND

Arctic Circle

Maniitsoq

gifts to Petersen in memoriam.

Petersen considered Greenland a special place, and not just because it was one of the last truly wild places on earth where an extreme skier could live his dreams to their fullest. Stretching for hundreds of miles along the west coast, on both sides of the Arctic Circle, was a chain of snow-covered mountains almost entirely unskied and barely explored. Yet in addition to that, Petersen and his extreme-skiing brethren held Greenland in special regard because of the bond they managed to strike up with the Inuits.

No doubt the two sides were drawn to one another by a mutual fascination, by a curiosity in the realization that each saw Greenland in a light entirely different from the other. If you were a skier, the mountains were your focus, because that's obviously where the action was. But if you were Inuit, you looked instead to the sea. Greenland life to the Inuits was about fishing, whaling, and hunting seals and walruses. The Inuits had such little interest in the mountains that so inspired Petersen and company, that they didn't bother to give most of them names.

Presumably if you must make a go of surviving year-round in Greenland, it makes little sense to look inland for inspiration or sustenance. After all, 80 percent of the land is entombed in ice. In the heart of the island, the ice is more than 10,000 feet thick, a mass so heavy that the ground literally sags below sea level under its weight. Yet in the outlying sea waters, warmed by the nearby Gulf Stream, life flourishes. Hence, 95 percent of Greenland's export economy is based on fishing.

The skiers admired the Inuits for their indomitable adaptability, the hibernal stamina that enabled them to make a go of it in a world in which winter lasts ten months. Historically, white people haven't been nearly as tough. The first settlers arrived in 982 A.D., led by Erik the Red, a belligerent fellow chased out of both Norway and Iceland for murder and other mayhem. Erik, according to legend, conned would-be settlers into joining him by talking up "the green land" he had discovered to the northeast of Iceland. (In Erik's defense, Greenland's climate was milder then than it is today. But to call the land green still seems an ambitious case of marketing chutzpah.) Of the 25 ships Erik led, 11 never even made it to Greenland, and those settlers who survived might have wished they hadn't. The original settlements lasted for about 500 years, without great distinction and never with a total population of more than 3,000, before eventually dying out altogether.

AT A GLANCE

LOCATION West coast of Greenland, just north and south of the Arctic Circle

SEASON April-May

TERRAIN SUMMARY Too vast to quantify

VERTICAL RISE Runs of between 1,500 and 4,000 vertical feet

AVERAGE ANNUAL SNOWFALL 400 inches

Top: *Appusuit Ski Center.* Above: *Henrik, a local fisherman and master boatman, on The North Face/Warren Miller Films expedition.*

In short, although Greenland might be a place you'd want to visit, you probably wouldn't, unless you were Inuit, ever want to live there. It is a place, however, in which an adventure-minded skier could, for a brief few months, find something close to nirvana.

In the cusp of the seasons, in April and May, the weather warms and days begin to stretch for 18 hours or more of crystal-clear Arctic light. Jagged 6,000- to 8,000-foot mountains rise right out of the sea, their flanks scoured and carved into steep faces and chutes by glaciers moving to the sea as fast as 100 feet a day. The snow that has fallen during the course of the long winter—an average of 400 inches in all—stays around well into spring, piling up deeply and incapable of melting in the persistently frigid air of incessant winter. That snow, says extreme skier John Egan, who was there in Greenland with Petersen, is "the lightest, fluffiest, most glorious powder in the world."

You can ski 3,000-foot runs through a tapestry of Arctic color—the white of snow, the blue of pristine glacial ice, the slate gray of rocks, and the black green of a sea mottled with icebergs. But even the skiers weren't going to venture too far from the sea. Roughly 20 miles inland, the mountains became engulfed in ice. Vertical possibilities for alpine skiing ended there, in a world quickly transformed into a flat, glacial plateau. You had to agree with the Inuits on this—the heart of Greenland was an inhospitable, terra incognita, more than 700,000 square miles of ice that swallowed up entire mountain ranges.

In fact, as Petersen and Egan and others helicoptered around and skied run after run that had never been skied, they found some of the best terrain—and the most agreeable climate—wasn't even on the coast at all. It was on Hamborgerland, an island just off the coast, near the community of Maniitsoq. Late in the season at lower elevations, just before you might ski right into the sea, the temperature could be relatively balmy, well above freezing, with the melting snow turning to the texture of mashed potatoes. You could put on your fat skis, says Egan, and bomb down the mountain through the soft mush, ending right at the ocean's edge—sun-drenched spring skiing, Greenland style. And if you were lucky, you might stand atop a run on such a day, as Egan once did, and see whales breaching far below. Where else on Earth could a skier do something like that?

Yet if Greenland skiing is capable of being that kind of warm, relatively effortless romp in the park, it can also turn its back and be far less accommodating. Such wilderness, in such an Arctic climate, does not bow down submissively, predictably, or on a regular basis. Extreme skier Jeremy Nobis came to Greenland in the spring of 2000 with snowboarders Jay Nelson and Megan Pischke, guide Peter Mattson, and film crew, in a trip sponsored by The North Face and Warren Miller Films. The team had planned a ski-mountaineering expedition that would include the first descents—by both skis and snowboard—of Assassat, a 7,021-foot mountain.

They figured that 18 days, for the Assassat expedition as well as heli-skiing in Hamborgerland, was a sufficient window of opportunity. But Greenland had other ideas. Camping in the ice-clad outback at the foot of Assassat, the team spent days waiting out stormy weather that smashed against tent walls, and ended up aborting the plans to climb and descend the mountain. Lesson learned: Greenland weather, like a domineering wilderness matron, can be stern and sparing in its generosity. The heli-skiing in Hamborgerland came off as planned; that was the team's reward.

It all left a deep impression on Nobis. "I've freeskied in the Himalayas, New Zealand, Europe, and Alaska, and Greenland is every bit as challenging—every bit as crazy and gnarly—as any of them," he told me after returning. "You've got glaciers all the way to the top of the mountains, and mountains that fall 8,000 feet straight into the sea. Being there was a challenge all the time." He then added, with true stiff-upper-lip mountaineering spirit, "Part of the high of what we do is in the struggle."

Paul Fremont Smith, an instrumental figure in the Egan-Petersen journeys, says of Greenland, "It is the ultimate wilderness, of a huge scale that people of adventure love. No photo can fairly transport that scale to you." In other words, there is more of everything—from perilously steep couloirs to relatively mellow glacier runs—than even the greediest adventure skier could possibly imagine. If there is a shortcoming, says Smith, it is

ARCTIC CIRCLE RACE

It has been billed by its organizers as "the hardest race in the world" and "the world's toughest skiing," and maybe it is. Beginning and ending in Sisimiut, the 100-mile Arctic Circle Race is to cross-country skiing what the Ironman is to triathlon, or the Iditarod to dogsledding. The route covered is classically Greenlandic—glaciers, frozen fjords, wind-scoured snow, ice, and exposed rock. In its official welcome, the race committee includes this disconcerting line: "It is essential that you are in good condition, with a stable mentality. . ."

Given the inherent hardship of the event, and given the relative remoteness of Greenland, it is somewhat astonishing that more than 150 competitors considered themselves physically fit and mentally stable enough to line up for the 2000 race. Perhaps more astonishing is that the winner, a lanky Swede with immortal lungs named Staffan Larsen, managed to complete the circuit in 8 hours, 22 minutes, and 50 seconds. After all, it took Fridtjof Nansen 40 days to travel 300 miles in his 1888 Greenland crossing. Of course Nansen didn't benefit from the well-placed support of 200 race volunteers and a groomed track. But still, 100 miles over rugged Arctic terrain in 8-plus hours. . .

If for some reason this sort of aerobic punishment appeals to you, you can register for the race at the Arctic Circle Race website: www.acr.gl.

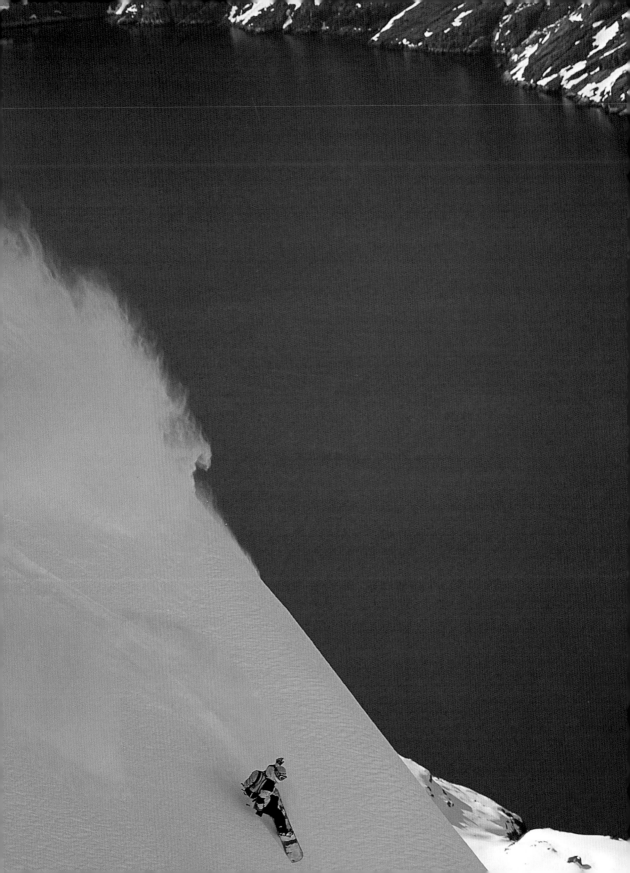

that the skiing culture is "all so fresh, so new," having been introduced to communities along the west coast only in the early '80s. To ski Greenland still requires some expeditionary initiative— arranging for guides, for mountain transportation, for other logistical requirements—from anyone considering a trip there. As small Greenland communities try to come to grips with the enormous skiing wealth that their surrounding mountains represent (with little support from the Danish government, according to Smith), they have yet to put all the necessary pieces in place.

Despite what Smith says, however, adventure skiing in Greenland does have an important history that predates the 1980s. In 1888, Norwegian Fridtjof Nansen led a 40-day, 300-mile skiing expedition across the ice cap, a story told in his book, *The First Crossing of Greenland*. It was such a compelling tale that it might well have inspired the modern age of skiing. No less an authority than Sir Arnold Lunn, the famous Englishman credited with the invention of modern ski racing in the 1920s, said of Nansen's account: "No book has had a greater influence on the development of skiing." (One of Norway's great heroes, Nansen would go on to a distinguished career as a diplomat and scientist and was awarded the Nobel Peace Prize in 1922 for his work on behalf of refugees and prisoners of war.)

Although Nansen's book might indeed have romanticized skiing and spurred modern interest in the sport in Europe, it also went far in spreading the word about Greenland as a cradle of Arctic deprivation. Who, except for the hardiest of explorers, would want to put up with a frigid, unforgiving place like that?

But that perception of Greenland is changing now in small increments, perhaps because there seem to be fewer and fewer such pristine places left in the world. Adventure tourism is beginning to trickle in; during the precious few days of summer, when the coast sheds its mantle of snow, sea kayakers, climbers, trekkers, mountain bikers, and wildlife viewers are coming in small but increasing numbers.

So why not skiers as well? The weather can still be brutal even in April and May; the quick-hitting ferocity of storms in Greenland is the stuff of local legend. Yet typically storms pass more rapidly than in places like Alaska or British Columbia, according to Smith. After the storms pass, the night sky clears brilliantly with the whirls and spirals of the aurora borealis. And all that glorious powder waits to be skied.

Even on down days, when the weather won't permit backcountry travel, Greenland delivers a bonus. As Smith points out, "There is a culture there." There are lessons to be learned about Arctic living in general and the life of the Inuits in particular—their economy, their art, their good nature, their powers of survival. Apparently Trevor Petersen took the time to learn those lessons, to make the connection, and there is a monument on the west coast of Greenland that stands as a testament to that.

WHAT TO EXPECT

Unfortunately, no major commercial outfitters were running alpine skiing trips to Greenland at the writing of this book. That might well change, but for the time being you'll be obliged to organize most trip logistics on your own.

Opposite: Megan Pischke makes turns, with the Sermilinn Fjord far below. Above: Skiing down to the ocean near Maniitsoq.

First descent of Hamburgler Couloir, Hamborgerland Island, just off the coast near Maniitsoq.

There are two ways to get to Greenland's west coast. One is to fly either to Copenhagen or Reykjavik, and transfer to a flight to the international airport in Kangerlussuaq, at the end of a 110-mile-long fjord of the same name. From there, it's a short flight to the communities of Maniitsoq or Sisimiut. It is also possible to fly from Ottawa to Iqaluit, on Baffin Island, and charter a plane from there for the flight to Maniitsoq or Sisimiut.

Although skiing might be possible in many locations along the west coast, Maniitsoq, just south of the Arctic Circle, and Sisimiut, just north of the Arctic Circle, are the areas of primary focus. These are small but by no means bare-bones communities; both have fine, comfortable hotels,

with all modern amenities, from which visiting skiers can base operations.

There are, in fact, ski lifts in Greenland, but they are short, primarily for the amusement of local skiers, and certainly inadequate for full exploration of the terrain. And let's face it: The point of going to Greenland is for big-mountain adventure skiing, not for very modest lift-serviced skiing. Snowmobiles, snowcats, and helicopters—and motorboats and kayaks in traveling up fjords—provide transportation to the really good stuff.

Local tourist offices can help with arrangements for uphill transportation as well as local guides. But it is all but mandatory that you hire an experienced alpine guide to come with you. Local guides might have local knowledge of the terrain, but you'll also need the expertise of an experienced alpine guide on snow stability, glacial travel, etc.

What's the skiing like? The coastal landscape is defined by three features: mountains, glaciers, and deeply cut fjords. In country this big, the only thing lacking is tree skiing. You can experience long, gentle runs on the Apussuit Glacier near Maniitsoq or steep couloirs on Hamborgerland, as well as pretty much everything in between. A typical Greenland run, if there is such a thing, covers between 2,000 and 4,000 vertical feet.

Almost anyone who has skied in Greenland returns saying that they've barely tapped the potential. So if you're looking for a place in the world to record a first descent or two, Greenland is probably as good as it gets. Be prepared for storms, when skiing in this treeless environment is not possible. But also be prepared, when the weather cooperates, to take advantage of the extended daylight and ski long, long days.

It is possible to ski year-round in Greenland, but for the best combination of snow, weather, and light, April and May are the most agreeable months. Before that, the weather can be very cold; in summer, when most of the coastal snow has melted, the skiing is restricted primarily to relatively flat glaciers, with their year-round cover of snow.

INSIDE LINE

There are excellent hotels in both Maniitsoq (Hotel Maniitsoq; 011-299-81-30-35) and Sisimiut (Hotel Sisimiut; 001-299-86-48-40; www.hotelsisimiut.gl).

Be careful about craftwork you might want to bring home with you. Some items—such as carvings made of walrus ivory or articles made of polar bear fur—cannot be brought into the United States.

Greenland, says John Egan, "is definitely fat-ski country." In deep powder or deep mush, the wide boards will make a big difference.

RESOURCES

General information: Greenland Tourism (011-45-33-69-32-00; www.greenland-guide.dk). Airlines to Greenland: First Air (800-267-1247) and SAS (800-221-2350; www.flysas.com). Air travel within Greenland: Greenland Air (011-299-34-34-34). Tourism organizations: Maniitsoq Tourist Service (Maniitsoq Turismeselskab; 011-299-81-38-99) and Sisimiut Tourist Information (011-299-86-48-48; www.sisimiut.gl).

For guide service, consult with the tourist offices in Maniitsoq or Sisimiut for recommendations.

Top: Carving a turn above Hamborger Sound. Above: The town of Maniitsoq.

The Vinson Massif & the Antarctic Peninsula

"The last great, true wilderness on Earth. . ."

I have never been there, nor is a trip on my agenda anytime soon. In fact, few people have been there, and even fewer have skied there. At the bottom of the world, Antarctica is, both literally and conceptually, the most remote continent on earth. It is an icebox representing almost 90 percent of the world's ice, which in turn represents 75 percent of the world's supply of fresh water.

All but 2 percent of the continent itself is under a permanent sheet of ice that on average is well over a mile thick. It is, without question, the world's coldest continent, where, at Russia's Vostok Station in July of 1983, the world's coldest temperature, -128°F, was recorded. Even at the height of summer in December, temperatures can plummet to 40 degrees below zero.

Antarctica is also the windiest continent. Katabatic winds—cold, dense surface flows that sweep down from the highlands and can exceed 100 mph—can turn even a clear day into a

Snowboarder Steven Koch, with Vinson Massif beyond, 1999.

blizzard of blowing snow. And surprisingly, given all that ice and snow, Antarctica is the driest continent. On 3.7 million square miles of the continent's interior (mostly in East Antarctica), less than 5 centimeters of precipitation fall in a year, an aridity that compares to the driest parts of the Sahara.

There are no roads, no native human inhabitants, no native foodstuffs (unless you can survive on foraging for hard-to-find moss), and only a handful of scientists and adventurers. Anyone who comes to Antarctica must be genetically resistant to cabin fever; because of the harshness of the weather, much time is spent indoors, in huts or tents. You must be prepared for the possibility of being confined indoors for days on end, when storms rage with such wind-chilling intensity that just a few minutes outside could mean severe frostbite or even death by exposure. It can be so sensationally cold that planes may not be able to fly. At such extreme temperatures, the metal of a plane can become brittle, potentially losing its structural integrity. In some places, small communities have been built underground as shelter from the severe elements.

In this odd and isolated world, people occupy themselves in unusual ways, largely in the name of science. (In fact, the 1959 Antarctic Treaty essentially established Antarctica as an international open-air laboratory for scientific study.) So it is that there are people down there examining such esoterica as cosmic microwave background radiation—the leftover glow in space from the Big Bang—and meteorites locked in the Antarctic ice.

On the face of it, Antarctica is not a place you'd want to visit—unless, perhaps, your passion is investigating the birth or decay of the cosmos. And yet. . .

If you are someone who loves snow and mountains, if you are fascinated with the loneliest place on the planet, you cannot help but be fascinated with Antarctica. Gordon Wiltsie, an adventurer and photojournalist who has been to Antarctica ten times, calls it "the last great, true wilderness on Earth, a place of indescribable loneliness and vulnerability." Wiltsie spoke with me about Antarctica with some reluctance: "I'm against what you're doing," he said, not unkindly but without great enthusiasm about the idea of a book encouraging interest in travel to Antarctica. Antarctica is, in its own way, still unspoiled—a pristine polar paradise that Wiltsie fears might be threatened by increased human visitation.

I respect and appreciate his sentiment, but I don't see Antarctica becoming a Disneyland or a Las Vegas or any kind of tourist trap anytime soon.

AT A GLANCE

LOCATION South of everywhere
SEASON November–January

TERRAIN ACREAGE Unknown
VERTICAL RISE About 3,000 feet on the Antarctic Peninsula; up to 8,000 feet on the Mount Vinson Massif
AVERAGE ANNUAL SNOWFALL Widely variable

The severe climate aside, the cost of an Antarctic trip—$15,000 per person minimum and possibly more than $50,000, depending on the itinerary and logistics—is likely to deter most potential visitors. Roughly 3,000 tourists visit in a year, and many remain ship-bound, observing the continent from afar and never setting foot on land. Due primarily to international agreements —Antarctica is also one of the last frontiers of global cooperation— severe restrictions are imposed on all human activity and behavior.

VINSON MASSIF

So that leaves Antarctica to the hearty few, those with plenty of disposable income (or generous sponsors) and an expeditionary zeal that allows them to see extraordinary beauty beyond the potential hardships. If one area in particular attracts mountain adventurers, it is the Vinson Massif, the prominent feature of the Ellsworth Mountains in West Antarctica. At 16,067 feet, Mount Vinson is the high point of Antarctica, and as such it is an obvious destination for people like snowboarder Steven Koch, who climbed and descended the mountain in December of 1999 in an effort to become the first person to snowboard the highest peaks of all seven continents.

Unless you are someone on a mission— someone like Koch—skiing Mount Vinson itself might not be a particularly inviting enterprise. As Wiltsie says, "the conditions can be horrendous. There are huge crevasses and seracs, and you might encounter ripply blue-water ice, in which case you're in for a ride." But in the smaller, rounded hills surrounding Mount Vinson, says Wiltsie, "there are plenty of opportunities to make wonderful turns in heavenly snow."

Those opportunities alone might be enough to commend the Ellsworth Mountains. But it is the scenery, says Wiltsie, that is unrivaled: in one direction, massive peaks with 8,000 feet of relief, rising out of a bed of ice more than a mile deep; to the south, the vast polar plateau, reaching toward the South Pole; the air filled with parhelions, so-called *sun dogs,* in which ice crystals prismatically separate the sunlight into its chromatic constituents. The intensity of the summer light and the clarity of the air bring such magnificent scenery into brilliant focus, a clarity that exists nowhere else on Earth. (No wonder cosmologists come here to stare into the deep reaches of space.)

It is an eerily sterile world, to be sure. There is no life in inland Antarctica, save for the rare bird that is "very, very lost," as Wiltsie puts it. The wind can rise suddenly and unpredictably and temperatures can plummet, and just as suddenly the plane that was supposed to pick you up at the base of Vinson and return you to the relative comfort of a community near the coast cannot fly. "You can be isolated for days," says Wiltsie, "and the wind can howl against your tent and drive you crazy." If there is a characteristic that Antarctica demands, other than a tolerance of cold, it is patience.

Yet if you are someone like Wiltsie, with an abiding love for true wilderness, the absence of any timetable or script—and a complete submission to the iron-fisted authority of natural

Above: Katabatic winds can turn a clear day into a blizzard of blowing snow. Opposite: About 80 miles from Mount Vinson, the Patriot Hills are a jumping-off point for trips to the Ellsworth Mountains.

forces—is a part of the appeal. And when the weather is right, with the summer sun of December or January circling above the horizon for 24 hours a day, any mountain adventurer able to do without sleep can absolutely pig out. At 80 degrees south latitude, the time of day at the height of summer is all but meaningless, lost in a continuum of never-ending noon.

ANTARCTIC PENINSULA

That is one Antarctica. But if you think you've got Antarctica figured as nothing but a frigid, barren Eden, think again. The continent reveals a new self in the Antarctic Peninsula, which extends like a giant tusk toward South America's Cape Horn. The peninsula is, in relative terms, tropical Antarctica, where temperatures in the summer months reach above freezing and where rain is not uncommon.

In November of 1999, ski mountaineer Rick Armstrong traveled to the west coast of the Antarctic Peninsula with a seven-man team to explore the skiing possibilities on 3,000- to 4,000-foot mountains that rise right out of the sea. The team traveled from Argentina across the notoriously stormy Drake Passage aboard a 240-foot icebreaker, the *Akademik Shuleykin.*

The Russian ship, originally outfitted and commissioned for scientific study, had been leased to a commercial ecotourism company, and Armstrong and companions were along for the ride. The ship would moor in bays filled with icebergs calved from glaciers where the mountains meet the sea. The aroma of penguin guano, wafting more than a mile offshore, was a declaration of the presence of Antarctica's most recognizable living beings. While most of the boat's passengers spent their time in observation—of the habits of penguins and seals and the scenery in general—Armstrong's team ventured ashore aboard a motorized inflatable raft. Just finding a landing spot along a shoreline featuring 100-foot icefalls was not easy.

But once on solid ground, the team would climb and ski mountains that had never been climbed, skied, or in some cases even named before.

"The most incredible trip I've ever been on . . . the trip of a lifetime," Armstrong kept repeating when I spoke to him after his return. That was really saying something; Armstrong has climbed and skied mountains from Alaska to India. The mountains of the Antarctic Peninsula, surrounded by glaciers and riddled with couloirs, reminded Armstrong of Alaska. He was impressed in particular by a mountain that "formed its own peninsula, with the sea on both sides," featuring four couloirs as much as 3,000-feet long. The team managed to ski three of the couloirs, encountering all sorts of snow conditions—"from sludge to powder," as Armstrong described it—and pitches as steep as 60 degrees. The team bestowed upon the mountain the ultimate encomium, naming it Lowe Peak in honor of the late and legendary Alpinist, Alex Lowe, who probably would have been on the trip had he been alive.

And after a ski like that, they'd return to the ship and look out, in the long-lingering daylight of November, at the spectacle of Antarctica—the massive glaciers, the gray black walls of granite draped in snow and blue ice, the penguins indulging in their comic behavior. Armstrong would lounge on deck "just checking out the wildlife and the scenery in the middle of the night."

THE WHOLE IDEA OF ANTARCTICA must mesmerize anyone with any interest in adventure, for to go to Antarctica is a means, at least in part, to establish kinship with the greatest expeditionary efforts of the 20th century. I must assume that it is impossible to travel to Antarctica without some thoughts of Scott, Amundsen, Shackleton, and the like. In the three-day crossing of the Drake Passage, Armstrong immersed himself in the reading of Caroline Alexander's *The Endurance: Shackleton's*

You must be prepared for the possibility of being confined indoors for days on end when storms rage.

Legendary Antarctic Expedition (Knopf, 1998). The survival of Ernest Shackleton's 27-man party for two years (1914 to 1916) in an icebound Antarctic world without a single loss of life was, as Alexander described it, "one of the greatest epics of survival in the annals of exploration." (Shackleton himself wrote: "We had seen God in His splendours, heard the text that Nature renders. We had reached the naked soul of man.")

Modern means of transportation and communication, of course, might now make a journey to Antarctica seem a bit tame by comparison. Commercial cross-country skiing expeditions to the South Pole—supported by planes or helicopters, radio communications, and so on—are now possible. If you have two months and $45,000 to spare, you can join Adventure Network International on the 600-mile trip.

But the conveniences of this new era by no means make Antarctica easy to endure. It is essentially the same extravagantly untamed place it was early in the 20th century. It is still Earth's final frontier, the king of terrestrial superlatives—the coldest, wildest, windiest, driest, loneliest place on the planet. That it can also claim a magnificent skiing potential that has barely been tapped seems almost beside the point. It is the enduring wilderness that really matters.

WHAT TO EXPECT

If the idea of a trip to Antarctica moves you, you will almost certainly have to deal with Adventure Network International (ANI) (see Resources) in making your plans. ANI is the only commercial outfitter and trip organizer currently operating in Antarctica. ANI offers several preset trips, includ-

Base camp, Vinson Massif Ski and Snowboard Expedition, December 1999.

Antarctica. Because ANI's efforts are focused on West Antarctica, that's likely where your focus will be, too.

You're faced with two choices—visiting the interior or visiting the Antarctic Peninsula. ANI's main encampment in the interior is in the Patriot Hills, about 80 miles from Mount Vinson, and that's where a trip in that region is likely to begin. Although there reportedly is decent skiing in the Patriot Hills, the really good snow is in the Ellsworth Mountains nearby, accessible by a short flight.

If you instead choose the Antarctic Peninsula, the principal route there is by boat from Argentina. It is a three-day trip, and it can be a rough ride; 50-foot waves in the Drake Passage, where waters of differing temperatures from the Atlantic and Pacific Oceans meet, are not out of the question. Yet once within the relatively sheltered waters close to the peninsula, a ship like the *Akademik Shuleykin,* the ANI-chartered boat on which Rick Armstrong traveled, provides a pretty comfortable base camp as it travels from one bay to the next. Dining room, bar, comfortable bed— it certainly offers creature comforts usually not encountered in expeditionary travel.

Antarctica isn't perpetually frigid; Gordon Wiltsie reports that on a good day in January in the Ellsworth Mountains, the temperature can climb to 20°F. And temperatures rise above freezing on the Antarctic Peninsula. Still, anyone who ventures to Antarctica should be prepared for extreme cold. That means bringing not just the right clothing and equipment but the right mindset to cope with the limitations (not being able to go outside) that cold can impose.

What's the skiing like? The possibilities are all over the map, both in terms of terrain and snow. The above-ice vertical relief of Mount Vinson rises to 8,000 feet, and that represents the maximum vertical descent possible. However, 2,000- to 3,000-foot descents are more the norm, particularly on the Antarctic Peninsula. As

ing a guided cross-country ski to the South Pole, but no trip specifically includes downhill skiing (or snowboarding). Hence, if you want to go skiing, you'll probably have to work with ANI to create a customized itinerary.

Keep in mind that Antarctica is a much bigger place than many people imagine. Covering almost 6 million square miles, it is twice the size of Australia. So don't think that in visiting Antarctica, you're going to experience all of

much as anything, the length of any run is dictated by the fact that anything you ski down you must climb up, sometimes in difficult snow conditions. A 2,000-vertical-foot descent might require more than three hours of climbing. Your physical fitness as much as the size of the mountains will determine the length of your runs.

Visitors to Antarctica have told me about powder, corn snow, wet slop, and absolutely bulletproof ice. The ice in particular can be rough and, if the wind has been blowing, entirely stripped of snow. In short, sharply tuned equipment is highly recommended. At the same time on this coldest and driest of continents, the powder can be corresponding light, dry, and fabulous for skiing.

Going to Antarctica, even on an organized trip, is still a trip deep into the wild. That means that there are considerable hazards and inconveniences—cold and deep crevasses in particular come to mind—but they aren't insurmountable for those who take appropriate precautions. Mountaineering skills aren't essential, but a certain mountain savvy—an ability to make an impromptu read of mountainous, glaciated terrain—can be invaluable. So too, given all the climbing involved, is physical stamina.

Finally, Antarctica doesn't necessarily run on schedule. Storms can come out of nowhere, stranding planes or ships for days. Allow plenty of extra time in your travel plans—say three or more weeks for a two-week trip.

INSIDE LINE

Antarctica is the iceberg capital of the world. In August of 1992, an iceberg 41 miles long and 13 miles wide broke from a glacier and drifted into the Bellinghausen Sea (near the Antarctic Peninsula), creating a significant shipping lane hazard.

In a two-week Antarctic trip, Rick Armstrong shot 60 rolls of film. Take that as a lesson: Bring plenty of film. Don't expect to come across

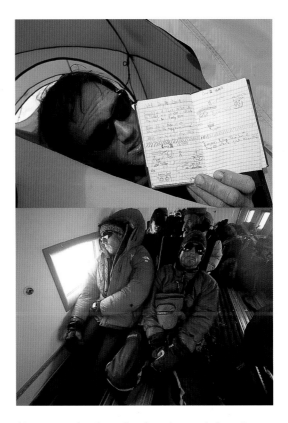

Top: Extreme skier Doug Coombs with journal. Above: Return flight of the 1999 American team.

an Antarctic camera store where you can replenish a dwindling supply.

In December and January, daylight lasts around the clock in most of Antarctica. An eye mask, particularly if you will be overnighting in a tent, can be useful for blocking out light and promoting sleep.

Walk among the penguins, who have no fear of humans; in Antarctica there are no land-based predators.

RESOURCES

General travel information and outfitter: Adventure Network International (ANI), 15a The Broadway, Penn Road, Beaconsfield, Buckinghamshire HP9 2PD United Kingdom (011-44-1494-671-808; www.adventurenetwork.com).

PHOTO CREDITS

INDEX